Praise for Mark Feinsand's
The Franchise: New York Yankees

"Mark Feinsand has expertly chronicled the greatest franchise in sports history, covering the Yankees from Y to S in this book. It is an essential primer for Yankee fans of any vintage and for all sports fans who want to spy the secret sauce of greatness from 1903 to today." —Michael Kay, YES Network play-by-play broadcaster

"The Yankees are defined by their generations, from Babe Ruth to Aaron Judge. Mark Feinsand connects the dots of these generations and shows how this *Franchise* is the stuff of legends. A must-read for any baseball fan." —David Cone, five-time World Series champion; YES Network/ESPN analyst

"For more than two decades, Mark Feinsand's coverage of the Yankees has imbued in him an encyclopedic knowledge of baseball's most storied team. *The Franchise: New York Yankees* is his gift to fans—a deep-dive into the lore, the tales, the moments that make this book just like the team it's about: unforgettable." — Jeff Passan, ESPN senior MLB insider; *New York Times* best-selling author of *The Arm*

"The history of the New York Yankees is so vast, it would seem almost impossible to produce a complete account of the team's journey. In *The Franchise: New York Yankees*, Mark Feinsand has accomplished that Ruthian task, bringing new life to pinstripe lore. Yankees fans will relish reading about Ruth and Gehrig, Mantle and Maris, Jeter and Rivera, the rivalries, the acquisitions, the titles. But *The Franchise* is a necessary document for all baseball fans, explaining in vivid detail why the Yankees are the most successful, compelling team in the sport." —Ken Rosenthal, Fox Sports reporter; senior baseball writer, The Athletic

"No reporter has covered the Yankees more extensively for the last two decades than Mark Feinsand, and this book draws on the relationships and trust he's built with dozens of pivotal pinstriped figures. Feinsand is the ideal tour guide to tell the history of sports' most storied franchise, taking readers behind the scenes for fresh, revealing stories that every diehard fan will want to know." —Tyler Kepner, *New York Times* national baseball columnist; author of the best-selling *K: A History of Baseball in Ten Pitches*

"Yankees fans will love digging into *The Franchise: New York Yankees*. From legendary players to fierce rivals, the rich history of the Yankees comes alive page after page." —Tom Verducci, *Sports Illustrated* senior writer; Fox Sports and MLB Network analyst; *New York Times* best-selling author of *The Cubs Way* and *The Yankee Years*

"The Yankees have the most successful history in baseball, a history that is filled with memorable players and unforgettable teams. Mark Feinsand does a superb job navigating through that history in *The Franchise: New York Yankees*. From the owners to the executives to the managers to the players, Mark deftly spotlights all of the iconic names who helped make the Yankees the Yankees." — Jack Curry, YES Network studio analyst and three-time *New York Times* best-selling author

NEW YORK YANKEES

A Curated History of the Bronx Bombers

MARK FEINSAND

TRIUMPH
BOOKS

THE FRANCHISE

The Library of Congress has catalogued the previous edition as follows:

Names: Feinsand, Mark, author.
Title: New York Yankees : a curated history of the Bronx Bombers / Mark Feinsand.
Description: Chicago : Triumph Books, [2022] | Series: The franchise | Includes bibliographical references. |
Identifiers: LCCN 2022010716 | ISBN 9781629379944 (hardcover) | ISBN 9781637270394 (epub)
Subjects: LCSH: New York Yankees (Baseball team)—History. | New York Yankees (Baseball team)—Humor. | New York Yankees (Baseball team)—Miscellanea. | Baseball—New York (State)—History.
Classification: LCC GV875.N4 F445 2022 | DDC 796.357/64097471—dc23/eng/20220201
LC record available at https://lccn.loc.gov/2022010716

This book is available in quantity at special discounts for your group or organization. For further information, contact:

Triumph Books LLC
814 North Franklin Street
Chicago, Illinois 60610
(312) 337-0747
www.triumphbooks.com

Printed in U.S.A.
ISBN: 978-1-63727-286-2
Design by Preston Pisellini
Page production by Patricia Frey

For Dena, Ryan, and Zack, the three most important people in my franchise.

In memory of George Gero, one of the biggest cheerleaders I've ever had. Miss you and love you, Georgie.

CONTENTS

PART 3 The Captains

PART 4 The Game-Winners

PART 5 The Acquisitions

Foreword

WHEN I WAS FIRED BY THE ST. LOUIS CARDINALS IN JUNE 1995, I figured my days as a big-league manager were behind me.

I had managed for—and been fired by—all three teams I played with during my career: the New York Mets, the Atlanta Braves, and St. Louis. My record was under .500, and although I knew I could succeed in that role if given the right opportunity, it's rare for a manager to have a fourth chance. It's part of the game.

When that opportunity presented itself less than five months later, it was a no-brainer.

It was impossible to know at the time, but accepting the managerial job with the Yankees was the best decision I had made in my baseball career.

The publicity wasn't very favorable when George Steinbrenner hired me, which I understood. You can't have a record 100 games under .500 and expect people to be jumping up and down. But I was excited to find out if I could do it. New York didn't scare me and neither did George.

My brother Frank cautioned me, saying, "Are you crazy? You know how many managers George has had?" I told him I was going into this with my eyes wide open, but I just wanted to find out if I could do it. I was pretty confident in what I did, but it really didn't show in my win-loss record. I think I needed to find out for sure if what I was doing was basically traveling the right path.

What happened over the next 12 years was remarkable. We went to the postseason every year, winning six American League pennants and four World Series championships. I had the chance to manage some of the most talented players in the world, two of whom—Derek Jeter and Mariano Rivera—now have plaques in the Baseball Hall of Fame in Cooperstown. The fact that I have one in that hallowed hall is humbling for me, and I owe it all to my time with the Yankees.

I knew what I was getting into when I accepted the job and I never looked back once. Being a Yankee was always a proud thing for me. The last couple of years were difficult because I think that, probably on both sides, neither one of us knew how to say goodbye, but it was always exciting being with my hometown team and to have the success we did. It made New York a very small town for me, and it was great.

It was a magical run, no question.

Joe Torre

PART 1

THE ARCHITECTS

1

The Original Boss

IF NOT FOR JACOB RUPPERT, THE NEW YORK YANKEES WOULD not be the New York Yankees.

The club had already changed its name from the Highlanders to the Yankees in 1913, two years before Ruppert and his partner, Tillinghast L. Huston, purchased the team.

But Ruppert, the son of a brewer who had already served as a United States congressman and been a colonel in the National Guard, was determined to make the Yankees more than second-class citizens in the New York baseball world.

The Yankees had been playing their games at the Polo Grounds, the home of the Giants, who at the time were the class of the National League. The Yankees were a perennial also-ran in the American League, posting losing records in each of the three years prior to Ruppert's purchase.

"For $450,000, we got an orphan ball club," Ruppert later said, as quoted in the *New York Times*. "Without a home of its own, without players of outstanding ability, without prestige."

The Yankees finished no higher than fourth place during Ruppert's first three years as owner, prompting him to make a change in the manager's office. Bill Donovan was out and Miller Huggins was in, and while Huggins' arrival certainly made an impact, it was Ruppert's purchase of Babe Ruth from Boston Red Sox owner Harry Frazee for $100,000 prior to the 1920 season that turned things around for the franchise.

Ruppert also made another move that year that would help change the franchise's fortunes, hiring Ed Barrow to become the team's primary executive—what we now call a general manager—a position that did not exist within most baseball organizations at the time. Barrow, who had followed Ruth to New York, would help the Yankees purchase more players from the Red Sox in subsequent years, including Waite Hoyt and Carl Mays.

"Back in the day, nobody gave owners credit for making ball clubs successful," baseball historian John Thorn told the *New York Times* in 2010. "With the Yankees, Ed Barrow got the credit."

Ruth swatted 54 home runs in his first season with the Yankees, then hit 59 in 1921, leading the club to its first-ever World Series appearance. The Yankees lost to the Giants, but Ruth's presence had given the club relevance, even as it continued to play its home games on the Giants' turf.

The decision to purchase Ruth turned out to be a franchise-altering move for the Yankees, but there were critics who believed the Babe was little more than a sideshow. He was the strongman at the circus; the guy hanging around the golf range challenging people to see who could hit the longest drive.

"There were still a lot of people who thought that's not how you play the game; they felt that baseball was meant to be played moving base by base, using hit-and-runs and sacrifices and all of that," said Marty Appel, author of *Pinstripe Empire*. "They thought Babe was destroying a pure scientific game with his brute strength. Even in Boston, a lot of people were happy with the deal, because they felt, 'Good, we don't want his kind here.' It obviously turned out that Ruth became the greatest drawing card of his time, but people weren't universally in love with that acquisition."

Dissatisfied with his team's status as tenants at the Polo Grounds, Ruppert proposed a plan to Giants owner Horace Stoneham to jointly construct a new stadium, but Stoneham declined.

Ruppert and Huston closed their own deal in late 1921 for land in the Bronx, later breaking ground on construction for their own ballpark.

"The Yankee Stadium is a mistake," Ruppert said, according to the *New York Times*. "Not mine, but the Giants."

The relationship between Ruppert and Huston grew complicated that year, leading to Huston's sale of his share in the team to Ruppert, who became the club's sole owner in May 1922.

Yankee Stadium opened in 1923.

"[The Giants] didn't want to share the Polo Grounds with the Yankees anymore, which sort of forced Ruppert's hand to find his own place and build his own stadium," Appel said. "It was the first ballpark to legitimately be called a stadium when it opened in 1923. In Washington, they tried to call Griffith Park 'Griffith Stadium,' but it was kind of a joke; it really didn't have that grandeur at all. John Brush with the Giants briefly tried to call the Polo Grounds 'Brush Stadium,' but that didn't take.

The magnificence of Yankee Stadium merited it being called a stadium and even that was precedent-setting."

The 1923 season not only saw the Yankees open their new home, but the club christened it with its first World Series championship, finally overcoming the Giants for the title.

"It all came together in 1923," Appel said. "It was the culmination of his work."

Ruppert's fingerprints were all over the club, and not just from his decisions to hire Huggins and acquire Ruth. He paid attention to details that many of baseball's other owners did not, carrying through on his vow to make the Yankees a first-class operation in every possible sense.

"He goes out and buys Babe Ruth and builds Yankee Stadium, and immediately it was the first-class operation in all of baseball," Appel said. "Even little things were indicative of his determination that the Yankees be first class. He was the first owner to make sure that they had two sets of uniforms for every game, so that on doubleheaders—which were frequent—they would always take the field in fresh uniforms for Game 2. As trite as that might sound, that was unheard of back then."

The Yankees returned to the World Series in 1926, falling to the St. Louis Cardinals, but New York won the championship in 1927 and 1928, the final two titles prior to Huggins' death in September 1929.

Ruth badly wanted to replace Huggins, but Barrow was not interested in his slugger assuming managerial duties. In an effort to assuage his star's ego, Ruppert gave Ruth a two-year contract extension worth $80,000 per season, an extraordinary sum at the time.

Pitcher Bob Shawkey took over as manager for one year, but Ruppert and Barrow hired a minor league skipper named Joe McCarthy in 1931. That year, Ruppert also played a key role in the creation of a minor league farm system, an issue that had been bubbling within the game for two years. In 1932, Rupert hired George Weiss to lead the farm system, launching another Hall of Fame executive career.

Though Ruppert certainly flexed his financial muscle to bring in players, including Ruth, he mostly relied on Barrow to target the right talent.

"What defined George Steinbrenner was being an activist owner who spent big money and saw free agency as a way to give him an advantage over everybody else, then moved in for the kill," Appel said. "Ruppert would famously say, 'I just like to sit back, see us score seven runs in the first inning, and then slowly pull away.' His influence over Barrow's ability to spend and to go get who he wanted was great, so he was very much an activist owner in that sense."

During Ruppert's time owning the Yankees, the club acquired more than a dozen players who would eventually be enshrined into the Hall of Fame, including Ruth, Hoyt, Lou Gehrig, Joe DiMaggio, Lefty Gomez, Bill Dickey, Tony Lazzeri, and Red Ruffing.

The Yankees won seven more AL pennants and six more World Series titles before Ruppert died in January 1939. According to the *New York Times*, Ruth was the final non-family member to visit Ruppert before he passed, telling him, "Colonel, you are going to snap out of this, and you and I are going to the opening game of the season."

But Ruppert, who had been in ill health since the previous April, died the following day.

"It was the only time in his life he ever called me 'Babe' to my face," Ruth told the *Times*. "I couldn't help crying when I went out."

In April 1940, the Yankees dedicated a plaque in honor of Ruppert, which now hangs in the Stadium's Monument Park.

GENTLEMAN • AMERICAN • SPORTSMAN
THROUGH WHOSE VISION AND COURAGE THIS
IMPOSING EDIFICE, DESTINED TO BECOME THE HOME
OF CHAMPIONS, WAS ERECTED AND DEDICATED
TO THE AMERICAN GAME OF BASEBALL.

Ruppert's decision to purchase Ruth not only led to the first successful seasons in Yankees history, but some would argue that the move set the stage for a century of players wanting to don the pinstripes.

"Even 100 years later, free agents now still think, 'I'd love to wear that same uniform that Babe Ruth wore,'" Appel said. "It still has its impact and its influence even a century later."

Ruppert was elected to the Baseball Hall of Fame by the Pre-Integration Era Committee in December 2012, receiving 15 of a possible 16 votes. He became the seventh owner to earn induction in Cooperstown.

"Ruppert turned a sad-sack franchise into a dynasty," Peter Morris, a baseball historian who was on the committee that elected Ruppert, told the *New York Times*. "He's one of the few owners about whom you could say if he had not lived, baseball would have been different."

Ruppert's legacy on the Yankees can never be underestimated; from the 10 AL pennants and seven World Series titles to the acquisition of Ruth to the erection of Yankee Stadium, his impact on the franchise was as large as anybody in team history.

"It took him forever to get in the Hall of Fame; he really should have been in there long before he was selected," Appel said. "A lot of people today don't even know the name at all. Steinbrenner surpassed him in the number of years of owning the team, but Ruppert just laid the foundation which is still there today."

Shaping the Dynasty

IN MODERN-DAY BASEBALL, THERE MAY BE NO MORE IMPORTANT person in a baseball organization than the general manager.

That wasn't always the case.

Prior to the 1920s, teams generally operated without somebody in that role, as owners and field managers would often be responsible for the scouting and signing of players. That changed with the hiring of Ed Barrow by the New York Yankees and later Branch Rickey by the St. Louis Cardinals, setting the course for executive careers over the next century.

"It was a much simpler business back then, of course," said Marty Appel, author of *Pinstripe Empire*. "There were no broadcasting rights to assign, everything was local, and there weren't that many streams of income."

Barrow was hired by Yankees owner Jacob Ruppert in October 1920, leaving his position as manager of the Boston Red Sox to become New York's business manager and secretary.

"The acquisition of Barrow gives the Yankees another practical baseball man who knows every angle of the game," the *New York Times* wrote after his hire.

Barrow's baseball expertise was not in question. As the owner of the Paterson Silk Sox in the Atlantic League, Barrow signed Honus Wagner to his first professional baseball contract in 1896. Barrow was later appointed president of that league, then, after buying an Eastern League club in Toronto, he was named manager for the Detroit Tigers in 1903, his first official role with a big-league club.

In 1911, Barrow became president of the International League, but he returned to the American League in 1918, accepting the managerial job with the Red Sox. Boston won the World Series that year, thanks in part to Barrow's decision to use pitcher Babe Ruth in the outfield 59 times. Ruth tied for the league lead with 11 home runs, emerging as such an offensive threat that Barrow saw his future as a hitter, not a pitcher.

"At an exhibition game against the Giants at Tampa, Babe caught hold of a pitch and nudged the longest drive I have ever seen," Barrow told the *Saturday Evening Post*. "That strengthened my belief that my moundsman could do my Red Sox more good taking his cut at the plate daily."

"He seemed to have a gift for recognizing talent," Appel said. "He recognized that converting Ruth to an everyday player was going to be in the long run a much better thing for the Red Sox."

Yankees manager Miller Huggins had endured frequent run-ins with co-owner Tillinghast Huston, but once Barrow was installed in his position, he told Huggins to worry about his own duties and not concern himself with the outside noise.

"You're the manager, and you'll not be second-guessed by me," Barrow told Huggins, according to the Society for

American Baseball Research. "Your job is to win; mine is to get you the players you need to win."

The Yankees won their first-ever AL pennant during Barrow's first season, then another in 1922. New York finally broke through for its first World Series title in 1923, the same year the club opened Yankee Stadium.

Barrow's club won the World Series again in 1927 and 1928, the final championships prior to Huggins' death in late 1929. Barrow brought on former Yankees pitcher Bob Shawkey to manage the club, but following a disappointing third-place finish in 1930, Barrow made another change, hiring Joe McCarthy to take over as manager.

Unlike modern-day general managers, Barrow's actions were covered by the press, but he was not subject to the second-guessing that can engulf those in such positions today.

"If you look at the 2021 season versus when Barrow was there, there was no social media demanding that Barrow get fired every time the team went into a losing streak," Appel said. "He had the confidence of his boss, Ruppert, and the self-confidence of 'I know what I'm doing here.' He didn't have everybody screaming for his ouster as soon as they had a bad week."

The Yankees won the World Series again in 1932, and although Ruth departed after the 1934 season, the Yankees—led by Lou Gehrig and a young outfielder named Joe DiMaggio—won four consecutive titles from 1936 to '39.

Even after the Yankees' four-year championship run was halted by a third-place finish in 1940, Barrow—who had been named team president following Ruppert's death—confidently predicted that his team would return to glory the following season.

"I know of no reason why we shouldn't come right back and finish on top again," Barrow told the *New York Times* in December 1940. "Some of our key men fell below par last Summer. Maybe they just had an off season.

"But even if it develops that they have permanently slowed up, and even if we fail to swing one important deal, we are confident our influx of young players will sufficiently bolster the Yankees so that they'll be every bit as strong as they were up to 1940."

Barrow was correct. The Yankees returned to the World Series in each of the next three seasons, winning the championship in 1941 and 1943.

The Yankees were the greatest dynasty the sport had ever seen, and Barrow was the architect responsible for assembling the club's star-studded roster. Other baseball executives had experienced success, but Barrow's track record made him the first legendary figure in that role.

"Certainly today, 100 years later by reputation, we don't look at anybody before Barrow and say, 'This guy built the Cubs empire or the Pirates empire or anything like that,'" Appel said. "He was the first one who really put his fingerprints on acquisition and development of players—and frequent World Series appearances."

Barrow was promoted to chairman of the board of directors by the team's new ownership in early 1945, though that position held little power within the team's new hierarchy. Barrow retired at the end of 1946, having guided the Yankees to 14 AL pennants and 10 World Series titles.

Following Barrow's retirement, Arthur Daley of the *New York Times* wrote, "The New York Yankees lost their most valuable possession just before the start of the New Year. No. It wasn't the Yankee Stadium. Nor was it Joe DiMaggio. It was

Edward Grant Barrow, the man who made the Yankees what they are today."

Barrow was elected to the Baseball Hall of Fame in September 1953, dying at the age of 85 just three months later. On April 15, 1954, the Yankees dedicated a plaque at Yankee Stadium in honor of Barrow, which would later be moved into Monument Park after its creation in the mid-1970s. It read:

MOULDER OF A TRADITION OF VICTORY
UNDER WHOSE GUIDANCE THE YANKEES WON
FOURTEEN AMERICAN LEAGUE PENNANTS AND
TEN WORLD CHAMPIONSHIPS AND BROUGHT
TO THIS FIELD SOME OF THE GREATEST
BASEBALL STARS OF ALL TIME
THIS MEMORIAL IS A TRIBUTE FROM THOSE
WHO SEEK TO CARRY ON HIS GREAT WORKS

When Barrow was promoted to team president in 1939, it opened the door for another promotion within the club. George Weiss, who had run the Yankees' farm system since 1932, was named the team's secretary, filling a role previously held by Barrow.

Their roles didn't change much; Weiss continued to run the Yankees' farm system, an operation that allowed young players to develop until they were ready to contribute to the major league club. His system had helped feed the roster with one talented player after another throughout the club's dynastic run, making him as integral to the Yankees' success as Ruppert or Barrow.

"Weiss and Rickey were head and shoulders above everybody else when it came to figuring out how to run a farm system," Appel said. "They were setting the blueprint for how you run an organization."

Three Hall of Famers were developed through Weiss' system—Yogi Berra, Joe Gordon, and Phil Rizzuto—while longtime Yankees contributors including Hank Bauer, Spud Chandler, Jerry Coleman, Charlie Keller, Vic Raschi, and Red Rolfe all came through the minor leagues on their way to the Bronx.

When Larry MacPhail, Dan Topping, and Del Webb purchased the Yankees in 1945, Barrow had been pushed out of his role running the club. MacPhail had taken over decision-making responsibilities, and while Weiss was given the title of vice president, his influence on the Yankees had waned under the new ownership.

The Yankees won the 1947 World Series, which proved to be another turning point for the franchise. Fueled by alcohol, MacPhail had a meltdown of sorts at the team's victory dinner, yelling at a number of people, including Weiss, whom he fired during his fit of rage.

Within one day, Topping and Webb had purchased MacPhail's share of the team, rehiring Weiss as the Yankees' general manager.

"That kind of established Weiss' power on through the late '40s and through the '50s," Appel said. "He didn't want to know the players, because he didn't want any personal likes or dislikes to influence his roster decisions."

Having been trained by Barrow, Weiss took an efficient, business-like approach to his job. According to Appel, Weiss was known for being "cold, humorless, and devoid of personality or sense of humor," disinterested in any part of the business other than the product on the field.

When a team employee once approached Weiss with a proposal to market the Yankees to fans, the GM famously banged his fist on his desk and replied, "You expect me to allow every kid in this city to walk around in a Yankee cap?"

Weiss' first significant move came in late 1948, when he hired Casey Stengel to replace Bucky Harris, a MacPhail hire who had guided the Yankees to a third-place finish in 1948 after winning the World Series in 1947.

Prior to the 1949 season, Weiss expressed confidence that the Yankees would return to prominence—much the same way his former boss, Barrow, had done nearly a decade earlier.

"From all the comments one hears and reads, one would think the Yankees finished somewhere in the second division last October instead of a mere two games from the top," Weiss told reporters. "I think much of our so-called plight has been greatly exaggerated."

Like Barrow in 1940, Weiss' assessment proved to be prophetic. The Yankees won the World Series in 1949, the first of five consecutive championships for New York. No team before or since has ever won five straight World Series titles, as the Yankees saw DiMaggio hand the center-field baton over to Mickey Mantle in the middle of that run. Berra and Whitey Ford were also promoted to the Yankees early in that run as Weiss' farm system continued to produce.

Despite finishing second in 1954 and losing the World Series the following year, Weiss received a contract extension after the 1955 season, ensuring he would remain general manager through the end of the decade.

The Yankees won the World Series in 1956, then again in 1958, winning four straight AL pennants between 1955 and '58. After the Yankees wrapped up the 1956 championship, Weiss was already thinking about areas of need on the roster for the following season.

"There's always something that could stand improving," Weiss told the *New York Times*.

New York finished third in 1959, then lost a seven-game World Series to the Pittsburgh Pirates in 1960, their 10th pennant in Weiss' 13 seasons as general manager.

Rumors swirled in the aftermath of the World Series loss that Weiss and Stengel would not be back with the Yankees, though it took three weeks for that news to become official. Weiss moved into an advisory role with the club, while Stengel was let go, part of an apparent youth movement within the organization.

Weiss went on to become the first team president for the New York Mets, bringing Stengel along to manage the expansion team. The first-year club lost 120 games, and although the Mets lost no fewer than 95 games in each of Weiss' five seasons at the helm—he retired after the 1966 season—he helped assemble the roster that would shock the world just three years later when the Miracle Mets won the 1969 World Series.

Weiss has never been honored by the Yankees in Monument Park, but he was elected to the Baseball Hall of Fame by the Veterans Committee in 1971, one year before his death at age 78.

Steinbrenner Stories

GEORGE STEINBRENNER WAS ONE OF A KIND.

There had been plenty of overbearing owners in professional sports prior to Steinbrenner's purchase of the Yankees in 1973, and while several have tried to follow in his footsteps in the years since his heyday, none have matched the gregarious, provocative nature that The Boss brought to the Bronx during his 37-year reign.

An entire book could be written on Steinbrenner's impact on the Yankees, Major League Baseball, the entire sports world, and all of pop culture. In fact, Hall of Fame baseball writer Bill Madden did just that with his terrific *Steinbrenner: The Last Lion of Baseball*, the best work on The Boss to date.

In the interest of space, let's allow some of the myriad people impacted by Steinbrenner to tell his story in their own words.

Marty Appel, who worked in the Yankees' public relations department from 1968 to 1977, was in the middle of the action during the early years of Steinbrenner's regime. Steinbrenner's influence on the Yankees and the entire sport was immense, but for those in his employ, life was often complicated.

> Everybody has their stories and mostly they're true. Media generally loved him, because he was a great New York character and he was always good copy. Opposing teams loved him because he filled their ballparks when the Yankees came to town. It was only the 40 or 50 of us who worked in the front office who found him very difficult to work for, but in the end, who cares about the 40 or 50 of us? He was really changing baseball and winning over players who wanted to go to the Yankees because he had such an open pocketbook. He was the perfect guy to come along for the New York Yankees.

Steinbrenner's biggest impact on the sport came in the mid-70s, when free agency changed the structure of how rosters were built. Bill Madden—the aforementioned Steinbrenner biographer—believes The Boss' approach to free agency separated him from the rest of baseball's owners.

> Most of the owners thought it was going to be the end of baseball; George saw it as a vehicle to quickly return the Yankees to a championship-caliber franchise. Free agency was the thing—and he was right. If he had tried to return the Yankees to greatness the old-fashioned way, just by making trades, developing a farm system, and making good draft picks, it would have taken a long time and maybe it would have never succeeded. Who knows? But he went right into

it, starting with Catfish [Hunter], Reggie [Jackson], and Goose [Gossage]. They were the cornerstones.

George was a visionary when it came to free agency, and he was a visionary when it came to television—and those are the two reasons he should be in the Hall of Fame. George was a one-of-a-kind owner, even in his day. There weren't any owners like George and there will never be another one.

Bucky Dent was traded to the Yankees in 1977, playing shortstop during the back-to-back title seasons of 1977 and 1978. He played five and a half years with the Yankees, then managed the club for the final 40 games of 1989 and the first 49 games of 1990 before being fired by Steinbrenner.

You knew the ground rules; the bottom line was to win. He wanted you to look like a Yankee, wear the uniform right, have your hair cut. Image was important to him. He didn't want any excuses; you just had to win. I really enjoyed playing there; you knew you were going to win because he was going to do something to make the team better every year, whatever it took. Everybody knew he was just very impatient with losing; he didn't think he was supposed to lose. He took care of his players. That Yankees uniform meant a lot to him.

From time to time, Steinbrenner's players would have a little fun with him, as Dent recalled with this 1978 incident.

Goose [Gossage] and I were in the training room in '78; I had fouled a ball off my leg, so I was in there at 7:00 AM. I'm sitting there reading the paper and all of a sudden, I felt the paper move; I looked up and it was George. He said to Gene Monahan, "I need a Vitamin B12 shot." Gene said, "OK, just go over there and drop your pants." Gene gets the needle and is about to give him the shot when Lou Piniella comes around the corner and says, "Hey, Geno, just close your eyes and throw it; you can't miss!" Gossage and I almost fell off the table laughing. George looked at Lou and said, "You're going to get your fat ass on that scale every day, and every day you're overweight, I'm fining you." Piniella was that way; he could say things to George.

The back pages of the New York tabloids were Steinbrenner's personal real estate during his reign, especially in the days before social media. Michael Kay, who wrote for both the *New York Post* and the *New York Daily News* before embarking on a career as a Yankees broadcaster, admired the way Steinbrenner used the newspapers to get his message across.

He knew how to manipulate them. He knew which writers were important in terms of the back page and which people he wanted to reach. I think he probably would have been a master at Twitter. He probably would have been able to cut out all the writers, because he would have gotten his messages out there.

I've been told by a lot of people that knew George Steinbrenner very well that Donald Trump used to sit in the owner's box and just watch George intently; the way George dealt with people and just the way George acted. I've heard people say that Trump idolized George, so the way Donald Trump was able to utilize Twitter, I'm sure that George Steinbrenner would have utilized it, as well— just not in a political way, but to run his team.

Brian Cashman's tenure with the Yankees began in 1986 as an intern, and by 1989, he was a full-time member of the team's baseball operations department. Cashman watched Steinbrenner torment one general manager after another, though other employees were not immune from The Boss' wrath.

That's why they created human resource departments. He was impossible to work for because he was so demanding; I always joked that he was an equal opportunity killer. If you were an employee, it didn't matter who you were, how high or how low. We were all hired at various points to work for him and try to support him in every way, shape, or form. We collectively kind of bonded together as employees to try to make him happy.

Steinbrenner's demanding ways kept everybody in the organization on their toes, even when circumstances were obviously beyond their control. For Cashman, it was a lesson in crisis management regardless of the existence of an actual crisis.

He was the type that would call the office when the office opened and get a list from the receptionist who was in and who wasn't. I remember once I was stuck on the George Washington Bridge because an oil tanker exploded or something like that. I'm coming from Hoboken, New Jersey, and I was sitting on Route 95 for like three hours. Everything was shut down and you couldn't move at all. I was sweating bullets; there was no cell phone back then to call the office. There was such a fear of being late because if your phone rang and you weren't there, the accountability that you would receive from him was a real and present danger.

Don Mattingly was the face of the Yankees from 1983 to 1995, earning the title of captain from Steinbrenner in 1991. Aside from a brief arbitration squabble and a much-publicized controversy over the length of Mattingly's hair, the two enjoyed a relatively stable relationship, at least compared to those that had come before him.

Other than that little period of time with him and I, I was never bothered by The Boss. I always respected the owner; he owns the club. He owns the business, he owns the team, he pays your salary, so he has the right to say whatever he wants to a point. I always respected that.

He wanted to win; some people have different ways of getting to where they want to go. A prominent owner told me one time, "Sometimes you've got to fire people just to let them know you will." It sounds kind of rough because that somebody lost a job. But that's how some people run their organizations. He believed that people had to know they could get fired.

Jim Leyritz signed with the Yankees as an undrafted free agent in 1985, working his way through the farm system. He would go on to hit two of the biggest home runs of the mid-1990s dynasty, though Leyritz recalled his first-ever meeting with Steinbrenner, before anybody—including the owner—knew who he was.

I first met George in 1988 at a University of Florida basketball game. They showed Mr. Steinbrenner on the big screen and I told my friends, "Let's go say hello to Mr. Steinbrenner." They were like, "Jimmy, you don't do that." I said, "What do you mean?" and I went down there. I walked up to his security guy, Eddie, and I said, "Do you mind if I say hello to Mr. Steinbrenner?" I walked down three or four seats and I sat down next to him, introduced myself, and said, "Hey, Mr. Steinbrenner, how are you doing?" He said, "Oh, are you a Yankees fan?" I said, "No, sir; you put your name on my check."

When Leyritz was called up for the first time in June 1990, he had a pinch-hit single against Roger Clemens in his first game at Yankee Stadium.

When I came into the locker room, there was a bottle of champagne and a note from George that said, "I can't be here right now, but I remember Gainesville." I thought that was pretty cool.

Paul O'Neill was acquired in a trade with Cincinnati in 1992, though the deal—which sent Roberto Kelly to the Reds—was widely panned. Steinbrenner grew to love O'Neill, giving him the "Warrior" nickname that stuck with him for the rest of his career.

I felt the intensity of winning. I had heard all the stories, but I didn't witness any of that stuff. He seemed to mellow out as he got older. I always had so much respect for Mr. Steinbrenner because he kept those teams together.

He paid to keep that team together and continually give us a shot to win. He would bring in players. There aren't a lot of owners that will do that year in and year out;

a lot of owners run baseball teams as businesses. George had a sports mentality of winning—whatever it took. He would do everything, but he expected something in return—and that was to win.

Joe Torre was hired to manage the Yankees prior to the 1996 season, though having managed for three other teams, he was confident in his ability to handle Steinbrenner and his infamously short-tempered ways.

I was at the writers' dinner after I had been named manager but before I had actually managed. I said, "We're going to go out there and win, and if we don't win this year, we'll win next year or maybe the year after." Then I said, "Is he laughing?" I was comfortable with him.

This was a bonus opportunity for me; I had managed and gotten fired by the three teams I played for, so I had chalked it up that this was it. To get the opportunity, it was cool. You'd hear the rumors that he wanted Buck Showalter back, but that never bothered me. Even in '98 when we started badly, there were rumors that I was going to be replaced. He saw me at the Welcome Home Dinner and he said, "You're my guy." He was a presence. He was The Boss. I never forgot that. You had to take the whole package.

Tino Martinez helped beat the Yankees in the 1995 American League Division Series as a member of the Seattle Mariners, but an offseason trade brought him to New York, where he replaced Don Mattingly at first base. Martinez thrived in pinstripes, playing a key role in the team's four championship teams from 1996 through 2000.

He was The Boss. I thought he was great to play for, because we played hard as a team and we all wanted to win. Winning teams was all that he wanted. He hardly bothered us at all; if we had a bad stretch here or there, he would tell the media how upset he was with the way the team was playing, but whenever we needed a player to help us be better, whatever it took for us to win, he would go out and get it for us.

Joe Girardi played for the Yankees from 1996 to 1999, winning three World Series rings. In 2008, he was hired to manage the club, leading the Yankees to the 2009 World Series just one year before Steinbrenner's death.

You felt it when you weren't doing your job. You knew when he was in the building; people were like, "George is here!" You just felt the importance of winning every day and the demand for excellence. You felt that when you got out of your car in that lot and started to walk into the building; you knew it was time to win. That's what George brought.

Players didn't challenge Steinbrenner often, but when it happened, the owner developed a new level of respect for them. Bernie Williams recalled a year when Steinbrenner had decided to cancel the Yankees' Family Day festivities after the team had struggled on the field that week.

My kids were so excited about Family Day, so they were really disheartened when I told them that it had been called off. Mr. Steinbrenner saw something about us having a losing record on Family Day, and since we were in the middle of a pennant race, he decided to postpone it. I talked to Joe Torre and Joe said, "There's nothing I can do about it; if you want to do something, there's the phone—you can call him." So I did.

I called him and said, "Mr. Steinbrenner, I don't ask much from you, but I'm in a bind here because my kids were so excited about Family Day and going on the field with their dad. I know you postponed it, but if there's any way that you can reconsider your decision, that would be great." We ended up winning the next game, so he put it back again. People were scrambling, trying to get their families there for the next day. We had Family Day after all, which all came from our conversation.

Nick Swisher was traded to the Yankees after the 2008 season, but he was already familiar with the team's owner thanks to his days playing for Ohio State University, a school Steinbrenner held close to his heart. During a 2001 pregame meal at Damon's, a restaurant owned in part by The Boss, Swisher had an unexpected run-in with the Yankees owner.

I walk in the door of the restroom, and as I'm walking by, this older gentleman is walking by me as well—he shouldered me right out of the way. It was like I was in his way, and he wasn't moving, so he knocked me out of the way. I was like, "What just happened here?" He didn't even turn and look, and as I'm washing my hands, I look back and realize it's George Steinbrenner. I went back to table and said, "You guys don't know what just happened; I got shoulder-checked by George Steinbrenner in the bathroom!"

Sticking With It

Imagine a world in which Andy Pettitte is pitching for the Philadelphia Phillies, Bernie Williams is patrolling center field for the Detroit Tigers, Derek Jeter is manning shortstop for the Chicago Cubs, and Mariano Rivera is pitching to Jorge Posada with the Seattle Mariners.

If not for Gene "Stick" Michael, this dystopian scenario might have become reality for the Yankees.

Michael wasn't singlehandedly responsible for the Yankees dynasty in the mid to late 1990s, but the longtime executive played a key role in keeping all the aforementioned players in pinstripes.

"He had George Steinbrenner's ear, so in situations like should we trade a young Derek Jeter, should we trade Bernie Williams, he was the one who said no," Tino Martinez said. "He convinced The Boss to let these guys develop because he thought they were going to be great. Fortunately for all of us, The Boss listened to him."

Michael played 10 years in the majors, seven of them in pinstripes. A light-hitting, slick-fielding shortstop, Michael batted .229 in 973 career games, never establishing himself as a premier player. Upon his retirement in 1976, Michael joined the Yankees' coaching staff, beginning a 40-year post-playing career with New York.

Over the next few years, Michael would hold a number of roles. Whether it was as a major league coach, an administrative assistant in the front office, or manager of the Yankees' Triple A club, Michael impressed George Steinbrenner with his preparedness, insight, and talent evaluation.

"Gene's going full cycle," Steinbrenner told the *New York Times* in 1979. "He's been a coach. He's had management experience. He's outstanding as a person. He's a fine individual. We plucked him, put him in, and he took hold like a duck in water. He's front-office material, that's where he's going. Gene's got it all, he's got it all."

Michael had a good rapport with The Boss, which wasn't often the case for people drawing a paycheck from Steinbrenner. He wasn't your typical "yes man," often countering Steinbrenner's opinion in a way that was both forceful and respectful at the same time.

"Steinbrenner was good to work for, and he was good for me," Michael told the *Times*. "I admire him. I don't agree with him all the time. Anytime you make as many decisions as he does, you're bound to ruffle feelings. But you have to like what he does. He wants the Yankees to be the best and he plows back in the money to make the organization the best. It's first class with him."

Michael served as the Yankees' general manager in 1980, then shifted to the bench in 1981 as the team's manager. Michael led the Yankees to a 34–22 record in the first half of the strike-shortened season, but he was replaced by Bob Lemon after the club went 14–12 to begin the second half.

"You could see him being groomed as a guy who would rise through the organization," Bucky Dent said. "Stick was always a good baseball guy. I loved talking to him and being around him. His knowledge of the game was great."

Michael returned to the manager's office less than a month into the 1982 season, guiding the Yankees for 86 games that year before being replaced again in early August.

"I don't think Gene did a bad job, but I really believe he belongs up here in the front office," Steinbrenner told the *New York Daily News*. "He's a great evaluator of talent and did a wonderful job for me in 1980. We worked well together."

The next few years saw Michael take on a number of coaching and scouting roles, though he left the organization to manage the Cubs in 1986–87 before returning to the Yankees in 1988.

"George would always have him in the meetings as much as possible and always wanted to know his opinion on every single player we were talking about because he served so many different roles through the years," Hal Steinbrenner said. "George had such a good respect for him."

When Steinbrenner was banned from baseball in 1990 for his role in the Dave Winfield–Howie Spira controversy, one of his final acts was to name Michael as general manager, leaving the Yankees—who were headed toward a last-place finish—in good hands as The Boss departed.

"I have great confidence in him," Steinbrenner said at the press conference announcing Michael's new post. "No one is more knowledgeable in the organization."

"It's a good challenge, a big challenge," Michael said. "How many people would want to turn down this challenge?.... I'm not a rookie in this business. I'm not a know-it-all. As a team, within a year, you can become respectable. In two years, you can turn a team around."

It took more than two years, but without interference from the temperamental Steinbrenner, Michael was able to build the organization the way he saw fit.

"He was the one that kind of helped put the brakes on with trading minor league guys away," said Dent, who managed the Yankees in 1989–90. "I had left the organization, but you could see that they weren't going to trade away the nucleus of their kids and they were going to build within."

He drafted young players including Jeter, Pettitte, and Posada, gave Williams a chance to develop in the majors, and made an unpopular trade that sent Roberto Kelly to the Cincinnati Reds for Paul O'Neill.

"I think he saw in me things that I didn't even see in myself at the time," Williams said. "He was a great judge of character and a great judge of talent—and they're not the same. You can have great talent, but if your character is not very strong, you're not going to be able to make it in New York.

"It doesn't matter how much ability you have; you need to have that combination in New York because you need to have that Teflon skin and still care enough to want to do as good as you can do as a baseball player. Stick was an expert in seeing those qualities in people; not only the talent, but their ability to play in the city."

Michael rebuffed efforts by other teams to acquire the Yankees' young prospects, believing they could form the core of a championship club. Players such as Kelly, Jim Leyritz, Kevin Maas, Hensley Meulens, and Matt Nokes were given a chance to play, no longer looking over their shoulder or reading the papers for the latest trade rumors.

"Gene Michael brings me into his office and said, 'Hey, I don't want to put any extra pressure on you, but you're the first guy that we've brought up in a long time that has come through our entire system and is homegrown," Leyritz said. "'If you do well, you're going to open up the door for a lot of people. George is gone and I can build from within again.' He was so encouraging."

Michael was also one of the first executives to prioritize on-base percentage ahead of batting average, stressing the importance of long, grinding at-bats by his hitters in an effort to wear out opposing starting pitchers.

"He was Billy Beane before Billy Beane became Billy Beane," said longtime Yankees broadcaster Michael Kay, who first met Michael while covering the Yankees for the *New York Post*. "He was the first guy who was accentuating on-base percentage; he just didn't have Brad Pitt play him in a movie."

"He wanted balance in a lineup, he wanted walks and power," Joe Girardi said. "On-base percentage was really important to Stick. He loved patient hitters, he loved switch-hitters; he just loved having creativity in a lineup that made it really hard to pitch to."

Steinbrenner's ban was lifted prior to the 1993 season, but Michael managed to persuade him to stick with the plan to build from within. They had supplemented the roster with veteran free agents including Wade Boggs and Jimmy Key, but the days of trading blue-chip prospects for aging vets—Jay Buhner, anyone?—were behind them.

At least they were if Michael had anything to say about it.

"He was passionate, he would fight for principle," Brian Cashman said. "I saw some epic battles with him and The Boss where The Boss pushed in on him and accused him of something that wasn't accurate; he would defend himself and hold his ground. I was taught by Gene Michael to stand up for yourself."

The Yankees turned a corner in 1993, finishing 88–74, though the second-place finish left them out of the postseason for a 12th consecutive season. Michael knew the team was headed in the right direction, and with Steinbrenner back in the fold, it took some gumption for the GM to keep his plan in place rather than reverting to The Boss' old ways.

"He just knew players; he knew what pieces fit," said longtime *New York Daily News* baseball writer Bill Madden. "He had to really scramble to make those teams competitive in 1993–94 when they were at their lowest. He knew talent, but most importantly, he knew what players could play in New York and what players couldn't. When you look back at that team that he put together, they were all players that were not afraid of New York: Jimmy Key, Charlie Hayes, Joe Girardi, John Wetteland."

Michael's belief in the Yankees' homegrown talent began to pay off in 1994, when New York posted the best record in the American League prior to the mid-August players' strike. The Yankees ended a 14-year playoff drought in 1995, winning the first-ever AL wild card, but after a five-game loss to the Mariners, he was relieved of his GM duties, though he remained with the organization as a senior vice president and special advisor.

Steinbrenner might not have wanted Michael to be the GM, but that didn't mean he didn't want his two cents on all baseball-related issues.

"Steinbrenner respected people that had a backbone," Kay said. "If you stood up to him, I think he liked that; he looked at you as a worthy adversary. Gene Michael spoke his piece and the two of them had a really good connection. George really legitimately trusted Gene, and that Gene was always going to do the right thing by the team."

"George respected Stick because first of all, he knew he was a smart baseball guy," Madden said. "He was firm in his convictions, and he would not back down from George when George wanted to do crazy things. When George would yell at him, Stick would yell right back. Stick was one of the few guys in the whole organization who would stand up and tell him, 'You're full of shit, George. We're not doing this.'"

It was Michael who convinced Steinbrenner that Joe Torre was the right man to take over for Buck Showalter, who was run out of town after the 1995 season.

"I don't think I'm there unless Stick is in my corner recommending me," Torre said. "Stick was always a stand-up guy for me. He interviewed me to be the general manager and they offered me the job. He knew his baseball, he knew talent. He really did a great job for George. He could take the bumps and bruises."

Michael's ability to read the game was legendary. Prior to the 1996 World Series, he ran the Yankees' scouting meetings, giving hitters the lowdown on future Hall of Famers Greg Maddux, Tom Glavine, and John Smoltz.

"He told us what to expect in certain counts," Martinez said. "He knew exactly what the other team wanted to do, how they would try to get us out and how they would try to beat us."

Absent the pressure that comes with the general manager's title, Michael was able to lend his guidance and wisdom within the organization without fear of being fired. Torre referred to Michael as "real people," the type who could lighten a room while making everybody there just a little bit smarter.

"He was just a real mensch; he always had a smile on his face, always had a joke, was always lighthearted, never heavy-handed," Kay said. "He had seen it all and done it all, so he didn't really let himself get bothered by too much. I think that's why he was able to handle working as long as he did with George. He understood the rules of engagement and he didn't get angry at it. He knew how to handle it and he treated everybody with dignity and class."

As analytics invaded the game in the 2000s, Michael remained a talent evaluator who believed that his eyes were as discerning as any statistic.

"He could see a young player for a couple days and then break him down into what he does well and what he doesn't do well," Mark Teixeira said. "I just loved listening to him talk about talent. That was the old-school GM right there. It was all about the eye test. He didn't need any numbers."

Cashman embraced analytics, but he also relied on the traditional scouting methods he had learned under Michael's tutelage. He also absorbed another characteristic from Michael—guts.

When Cashman decided to trade David Wells for Roger Clemens in 1999, he knew the move would not be popular among a fan base that had grown to love the big lefty during the historic 1998 season. But just as Michael had done six years earlier with his trade of Kelly for O'Neill, Cashman stuck to his guns and made a deal he believed would be in the team's best long-term interest.

"He was willing to make the tough call and willing to execute a game plan that he felt was right," Cashman said. "If that meant sitting a veteran, releasing a veteran, whatever, he was never willing to do the popular; he was willing to do the hard. He was willing to walk the tougher road if it was the right road. That's true leadership."

Michael's contribution to the Yankees can never be overstated, and while he wasn't the manager or general manager during the team's five championships and seven AL pennants between 1996 and 2009, his fingerprints were all over those clubs that produced some of the greatest seasons in franchise history.

"I always had a great regard for his baseball knowledge, and secondly, how he handled the stress working for George that many years," Torre said after Michael's death in 2017. "He kept the thing afloat when George was away; he did more than that because he built a heck of an organization.

"He never craved attention. Looking at it, you'd never realize what an integral part of the Yankees organization that he was."

The Life of Brian

BRIAN CASHMAN NEVER WANTED TO BE THE GENERAL manager of the Yankees.

Why would he? During his early years with the organization, he had seen one GM after another endure the abuse heaped upon them by George Steinbrenner, ultimately costing them their job and, in many cases, their health and dignity.

"I never, ever aspired to being the general manager," Cashman said. "It was never a goal of mine; in fact, it was quite the opposite."

The subject opens a floodgate of stories from Cashman, each one a reminder of the chaotic atmosphere that engulfed the Yankees' front office during Steinbrenner's regime.

There was the time in 1987 that Steinbrenner had traded pitcher Joe Niekro to the Minnesota Twins for catcher Mark Salas, only to see Niekro return to Yankee Stadium one month later and shut out the Yankees for six innings.

"I'm in the office with [GM] Woody [Woodward] and The Boss is screaming at him on the speakerphone—they called it the Squawk Box back then—and he's yelling, 'This is what you're going to do, Woody!'" Cashman said. "All George kept hearing back was, 'Yes sir. Yes sir.' Woody was like a broken-down trail pony. George is blasting him and said, 'You're going to go down to the clubhouse after this game is over and you're going to take full credit for this trade. I had nothing to do with this trade! You did this trade!' He was just reading him the riot act, telling him how this was going to transpire."

Woodward reached into his desk drawer for some medication to deal with the stress—his nickname around the office was "The Pharmacist"—as Steinbrenner continued to berate him for a trade the owner himself had made.

"He was under siege," Cashman said. "I remember sitting in that room thinking, 'The Boss gets all the wins, and the GM eats all the losses.' Woody never had to go to the clubhouse and do the mea culpa on a trade he didn't really make because we came back in the late innings to win the game. But I remember vividly sitting in the room thinking, 'Wow, I would never want to be general manager of the New York Yankees.'"

Cashman first joined the Yankees as an intern in 1986, joining the organization on a full-time basis as a baseball operations assistant after graduating from Catholic University in 1989. Jim Bowden, a Yankees senior vice president when Cashman came aboard full-time, shared a story with *Sports Illustrated* in 2015 about Steinbrenner walking Cashman into an office where Gene "Stick" Michael, Lou Piniella, Bob Quinn, Dallas Green, and Syd Thrift were gathered.

"I want to introduce you to Brian Cashman," Steinbrenner said, according to Bowden, who would go later become GM of the Cincinnati Reds and Washington Nationals. "His dad is a good friend...and someday you'll all be fired and he'll be the general manager of the Yankees."

Everybody in the room laughed. Perhaps they should have taken The Boss seriously.

Cashman worked his way through the front office to assistant farm director, major league administrator, then ultimately assistant general manager, working four years under Michael and two for Bob Watson.

Just weeks prior to the start of spring training in 1998, Watson informed Cashman that he was stepping down as GM for health reasons; the job was simply taking too big a toll on his body. Watson had recommended that Steinbrenner hire Cashman for the job, and despite Cashman's attempts to persuade Watson to stay, the GM's mind had been made up.

"You've got a lot to think about, buddy," Watson told Cashman.

Steinbrenner soon called Cashman and asked if he could meet for lunch at the Regency Hotel, where the owner always stayed while in New York. The Boss told the 30-year-old Cashman, "I can go out there and recycle somebody to come in and do this job that's done it somewhere else, but I've been told by too many people—Gene Michael, Bob Watson, and others— that you can do this job. So I'm offering you to be the general manager of the Yankees."

Cashman knew he couldn't turn down the job, even if it was one he never wanted in the first place. Steinbrenner turned the conversation toward the contract, but Cashman didn't want one. Not yet, anyway.

"I said, 'Let's do a one-year deal handshake,'" said Cashman, who received a raise from $85,000 to $130,000 after taking the gig. "I felt like I needed to prove to myself, to the public, to our fans—and to The Boss—that I could do this. I didn't know if I could do it; I was scared to death and didn't know what I was getting into here. I wasn't stupid enough to turn the opportunity down, but I also felt it was the first day of the last run of my time with the Yankees, because when you take that chair, the next door is out."

Cashman knew he wasn't going to be the general manager forever, but as he prepared for the 2022 season, he was heading into his 25th year in the position, eclipsing Hall of Famer Ed Barrow as the longest-tenured GM in franchise history.

"That first year, I was doing everything in my power to do the job to perfection and not mess up," Cashman said. "I would stress about playing a game that night in inclement weather, but I can't control the weather. With time, you gain experience and you start to learn what you can control and what you can't control, so you stop worrying about things you have no control over."

The baseball part came easiest for Cashman, who had been given significant responsibility by Watson in his role as assistant GM. As front offices around the league were changing, Watson divvied up the other 29 GMs into two lists, putting Cashman in charge of communicating with the younger executives while he dealt with the veteran general managers.

"He said, 'I don't know who Kevin Towers is,'" Cashman said, referring to the former San Diego Padres GM. "'I'll take Pat Gillick, John Schuerholz, and Ron Schueler, you take this young whippersnapper Kevin Towers and this young guy in Oakland, Billy Beane.' Because Bob gave me such authority, it helped me hit the ground running. I was never preparing to be general manager in any way, shape or form, so this was like a lightning strike when I was offered the job. I was never thinking that job was a possibility."

Days after he officially assumed the GM position, Cashman completed a long-anticipated trade for second baseman Chuck Knoblauch. In late March, the Yankees signed Orlando "El Duque" Hernandez, who would go on to play a major role for the club that season.

The rest of the roster had been built by Watson and Michael, so when the Yankees bulldozed their way through the American League for an AL-record 114 wins (and 11 more in the postseason), many were reluctant to give the first-year GM much credit for the team's success.

Yet Cashman had been part of the front office that developed most of the team's homegrown stars; from Derek Jeter to Mariano Rivera to Andy Pettitte, all had flourished while Cashman was helping run the Yankees' farm system.

"I do feel I was part of the building of this franchise," Cashman told the *New York Times* in 2011. "I do resent it when people say that I inherited a lot of this stuff."

It was Cashman's relationship with Oakland's Beane that helped land Scott Brosius after the 1997 season, as the Yankees sent struggling lefty Kenny Rogers to the Athletics. Brosius had a strong 1998 season for the Yankees, winning World Series Most Valuable Player honors.

"Even though we won 125 games and lost only 50, it was probably the most stressful time in my entire life because I was doing something in the bigger chair that I had never done before," Cashman said. "As the season played out, I started to learn that I was really prepared for that position by Bob Watson for those two years prior."

Shortly before the Yankees were set to report to Tampa for spring training in 1999, Cashman began putting his personal imprint on the club. David Wells had been magnificent for the

Yankees during their historic season, becoming a cult hero among the fan base after throwing a perfect game.

Showing no concern for fan reaction, Cashman traded Wells, Graeme Lloyd, and Homer Bush to the Toronto Blue Jays for five-time AL Cy Young Award winner—and former Yankees nemesis—Roger Clemens.

"David Wells had done everything for us; he was a great Yankee and part of our '98 team, which was unstoppable," Cashman said. "I certainly thought—and was proven correct— that we needed something to allow us to stay motivated and focused. Roger Clemens had accomplished everything but a World Series title; a perennial All-Star, a perennial Cy Young Award contender, but he had never won a World Series."

Cashman had been told that Clemens' work ethic was "second to none," while the reports on the pitcher's makeup were "off the charts." With someone like Clemens joining the club, complacency was less likely to become an issue. It was time to shake things up.

"I made a tough choice, but as Gene Michael told me in countless conversations, when you're in a leadership position, you have to make difficult choices," Cashman said. "That decision was certainly controversial, but I felt like I had to do what I thought was right, not what I thought was going to make you popular as a leader. I was channeling my inner Michael Corleone; it's not personal, it's just business. And what's best for business is going to be best for the franchise."

The Yankees also re-signed Brosius, Cone, and Bernie Williams, bringing back three key contributors from the 1998 team. But it was the Clemens acquisition that opened people's eyes, making them realize that the youngest GM in the game wasn't afraid to make big moves.

"Cash had been around the Yankees for a long time, so he knew what Mr. Steinbrenner and the Yankee Way were all about," Tino Martinez said. "David Wells had a great year for us in '98, so it was a little bit shocking and exciting at the same time when we traded him for Clemens. It gave us a little bit of a boost that we weren't expecting in spring training."

New York won 98 games to earn another division title, then swept the Texas Rangers in the AL Division Series, bounced the rival Boston Red Sox in a five-game ALCS, and swept the Atlanta Braves in the World Series, steamrolling their way to an 11–1 postseason record and a third championship in four years.

New York returned largely the same roster for 2000, but Cashman made his impact felt again that season, trading for outfielder David Justice on June 29.

"It hit like a lightning bolt," Beane told *Sports Illustrated* in 2015. "I don't think anyone thought Justice was even available."

Justice had 20 home runs and 60 RBI in 78 games, as the Yankees won their third straight AL East title. After limping to the finish line with only three wins in their final 18 games, they survived a tough ALDS against the Athletics before beating the Seattle Mariners in a six-game ALCS. Justice, Cashman's prized acquisition, was named the MVP of that series.

The Yankees went on to win a third straight World Series, defeating the crosstown rival Mets in five games. Cashman had three championships in his first three years since taking over for Watson, an unprecedented start to a GM's career.

That's not to say that Cashman didn't hit his speed bumps. Winning three World Series rings certainly gave him a level of credibility with Steinbrenner, but that didn't stop The Boss from harassing him the way he had with every prior GM that worked for him.

The Yankees returned to the World Series in 2001, falling to the Arizona Diamondbacks in a classic seven-game series. The Bombers had been in the Fall Classic six times in eight years and won four championships, but Steinbrenner was the "What have you done for me lately?" type.

"After we lost the World Series, he said, 'You had your shot; now you're going to deal with things that I think we need to do,'" Cashman said. "All of a sudden, '03 and '04, things started to change with how things were running."

Steinbrenner went on a rampage, opening his checkbook to sign any player he believed would help the Yankees win their 27th World Series title.

Jason Giambi was signed prior to 2002, then the Yankees acquired Jeff Weaver and Raul Mondesi that summer. In 2003, the Yankees signed Hideki Matsui, then dealt for Aaron Boone and Ruben Sierra. The 2004 season saw even more roster movement; Pettitte signed with Houston, followed by Clemens, who changed his mind about retirement to pitch for his hometown Astros.

The Yankees traded for Kevin Brown and Javier Vazquez, then signed free agents Gary Sheffield, Kenny Lofton, and Tom Gordon. When Boone tore up his knee playing basketball in January 2004, Cashman swooped in and traded for Alex Rodriguez.

"Every trade I make is scary; I'm wired to think the worst and hope for the best," Cashman said. "Whether it is a free-agent signing or a trade, you're doing a deal because you hope it's going to benefit your franchise. Nobody cares about what you did last year or what kind of success you had prior; you have to do it again. You have to figure out how to make the playoffs, then how to win in the playoffs."

Only the Yankees weren't winning, at least not enough to satisfy Steinbrenner. New York lost the World Series to the Florida Marlins in 2003, though the Yankees' ALCS win over the Red Sox surely made Steinbrenner happy. Any joy derived from that memorable series dissipated the following year when Boston came back from a three-games-to-none deficit, winning four straight games to advance to the World Series, where the Sox put an end to the 86-year-old Curse of the Bambino.

Those postseasons were sandwiched by a pair of ALDS losses to the Anaheim Angels in 2002 and 2005, the latter of which marked the final year of Cashman's contract.

Steinbrenner had always enjoyed the separation of the New York and Tampa factions in the baseball operations department, though it wasn't always conducive for the man sitting in the GM's chair as he tried to do his job. Amateur scouting and the minor league operation ran out of Tampa, while the big-league club operated out of the Bronx office; on too many occasions throughout the years, one had no idea what the other was doing.

"The back pages would say, 'This is on Cash and [manager Joe] Torre,'" Cashman said. "Eventually I told him, 'If it's really on me, then I need to have the ability to do what I think is right. If not, I want you to find someone you're more comfortable with, because you don't trust me.'

"The separation was unhealthy; it was a bad dynamic. It pits employees against each other. You've got competing philosophies that are in conflict, so it just wasn't going to work. I tried to appeal to The Boss, who was big into the military chain of command. I said, 'No one has an operation like this. You can't have all these different personalities with different philosophies and expect it to somehow come together.'"

Cashman told Steinbrenner he was going to leave at the end of his contract, but The Boss charged some members of the organization with changing the GM's mind. When it became clear to Steinbrenner that Cashman was serious, he called him directly.

"He said, 'Why are you leaving me?' We had a long conversation. I told him, 'This is just not feasible. I can't keep starting a season with a roster that I didn't really put together in many cases.' He said, 'Then you stay and do it your way; I'll give you that authority.'"

Had Cashman walked away at the end of his contract, he would have had GM offers from other clubs within the hour. The Seattle Mariners, Los Angeles Dodgers, and Philadelphia Phillies were all interested in Cashman, while at least two or three other clubs had also been mentioned as potential landing spots.

"Cash still had people to answer to," Torre told *Sports Illustrated* in 2015. "But once he signed that deal, it changed his demeanor. It gave him the authority to really do his job."

Had The Boss not relented regarding the structure of the baseball operations department, the relationship might have ended. Push never came to shove, but Cashman's loyalty to the Yankees and their owner might have made that decision more difficult had Steinbrenner not given the GM the autonomy he so desired.

"I am a nobody without the opportunity that George Steinbrenner provided," Cashman said. "Despite it being a very difficult work environment, it's the only one I ever knew. I grew up in it. If he did not want me to go and he wanted me to stay, I would have a hard time telling him no and being able to sleep at night because of loyalty."

The Yankees' postseason struggles continued with first-round losses in 2006 and 2007, the latter of which marked the final year of Torre's tenure in the manager's office.

Joe Girardi was hired to replace Torre, but the Yankees failed to make the playoffs in 2008, ending their 13-year postseason streak. The disappointing performance of young pitchers Phil Hughes, Ian Kennedy, and Joba Chamberlain played a big role in the subpar season, which marked the final year at the old Yankee Stadium.

Cashman's contract was expiring once again, but he re-upped with a new deal after the 2008 season. His motivation appeared to come from media criticism as much as his desire to win, as some local columnists had started to question whether it was time for the Yankees to move on from Cashman after he had spent a decade as the GM.

"There's a lot more work to be done," Cashman said at the press conference announcing his return. "I'm a competitive person. I don't like what I see sometimes in the newspapers. I don't like that some people forget that I've been here since 1986, that I've been part of this franchise since it was no good or not very good; that I was part of the rebuilding process."

The same people that had criticized the Yankees for being too old were now hammering Cashman for his failed youth movement. It was time, some said, for the Yankees to bring somebody else in to clean up the mess Cashman had made.

"The storyline that's going to be written, if I left, I didn't agree with," Cashman said. "I wasn't going to let that story be written."

Steinbrenner's health was failing, so his sons, Hal and Hank, were now running the Yankees. The 2008–09 offseason felt like a classic Boss winter, as the Yankees spent $423.5 million to sign three free agents: left-hander CC Sabathia, right-hander A.J. Burnett, and first baseman Mark Teixeira.

The result was a 103-win season and the 2009 World Series title, the 27th in franchise history. Cashman's fingerprints were all over that "Mission 27" title in more ways than one; after loading up the roster with talent, Cashman flew to Atlanta in late June to give his underperforming team a piece of his mind.

"He definitely had more meetings than [that] one, but that's the one that worked," Teixeira said. "Those meetings are kind of worthless—until they're not. When you have a season that's not going the right way and you have your GM come and give you the business and then you win a World Series, that's a great story."

The Yankees returned to the postseason in each year from 2010 to 2012, but none ended with a parade down the Canyon of Heroes.

"Cash has a tough job," Girardi said. "When you're expected to win the World Series every year and if you don't, it's considered a disappointment. I don't care how much money you spend; it's not possible."

It might have been the natural passage of time or the prolonged success he had experienced, but Cashman grew comfortable enough in his own skin to speak his mind and take some leaps—literally, in some cases—in ways he never had before.

At a 2011 press conference to introduce new relief pitcher Rafael Soriano, Cashman told the assembled press he had been against the signing. In 2013, when asked by ESPN.com about Alex Rodriguez's latest tweet declaring himself ready to play following hip surgery—a contradiction to what the team had been saying—Cashman replied, "Alex should shut the f—k up."

Whether it was sleeping on a Manhattan street to raise money for homeless youth, rappelling down a 22-story building in an elf costume, or jumping out of a plane—twice!—to support the Wounded Warrior Project, Cashman's actions were showing a different, more liberated side of him.

"The beauty of Cash is that he is who he is," Teixeira said. "He says stuff that makes you cringe sometimes in the media, but it's because he's honest and because he's not really hiding anything. I'd argue that that the GM of the New York Yankees is as scrutinized as any Fortune 500 CEO out there."

With the retirement of the "Core Four" and others including Sabathia, Teixeira, and A-Rod, Cashman and the Yankees embarked on their next phase. They turned to "Baby Bombers" such as Aaron Judge and Gleyber Torres, supplementing them with established stars including Giancarlo Stanton and Gerrit Cole.

They also moved on from Girardi, hiring Boone to manage the club. Just as general managers once came and went with the wind under The Boss, the same was true for managers. In Cashman's two-plus decades in the GM chair, he has employed just three managers; Steinbrenner went through three managers in the 1982 season alone.

How has Cashman survived nearly a quarter-century in a job that once had a shelf life comparable to that of a gallon of milk? Trust.

"Hal looks at Brian the way that George looked at Stick; because Hal knows that Brian would never hurt the Yankees," longtime Yankees broadcaster Michael Kay said. "His first priority is doing right by the Yankees and, in turn, doing right by the Steinbrenner family. I've always said that Brian is almost like the fifth Steinbrenner kid. There's that kind of trust between Brian and the Steinbrenner family."

"Before the '90s when the Yankees started winning championships again, it was the Bronx Zoo; managers were getting fired left and right, GMs were getting fired left and right," Teixeira said. "When you find a guy like Cash that's willing to take all of the media heat, willing to take all of the fan heat, willing to say when he messed up—and then be able to hire great people on the field and let them do their jobs—I think the Steinbrenner family just trusts him and appreciates that about him."

Cashman's willingness to evolve with the game has also been an important factor. He embraced analytics without discounting scouts, looking at every angle before making a move.

"There's a mutual respect there and a lot of communication," Hal Steinbrenner said. "Ninety-five percent of the time, I'm going to do what he recommends. I'm not a baseball guy and I know how thorough he is. I am a very balanced person; I want to hear what the analytics people have to say, but I also want to hear what the pro scouts have to say. I value everybody's opinion and he does, too."

It has been more than a decade since George Steinbrenner died, yet Cashman's approach to his job remains as tireless and disciplined as it was when he was constantly answering to the most demanding owner in sports.

"He's put a process in place where he doesn't hurry his way through things, he doesn't try to take the shortcut; he's very meticulous and methodical in the way he does things," Kay said. "He's a guy who checks all boxes, and I think he got that from George Steinbrenner. He once told me, 'I work as hard as I do because I never want him to ask me a question that I wouldn't know the answer to. Those questions may never be asked, but I want to be ready to answer them just in case.' He still works at a level as if there was that specter of George Steinbrenner hanging over him. I don't think you ever lose that."

No Ordinary Joe

CLUELESS JOE.

The headline blared on the back page of the *New York Daily News*, with columnist Ian O'Connor declaring that Joe Torre had no idea what he was getting into by accepting the job as the Yankees' next manager.

Buck Showalter had turned the hapless Bombers around, getting the Yankees back to the postseason in 1995 after 14 years without October baseball. Yet after the season, George Steinbrenner had decided to move on from his manager at the end of his contract despite the team's return to relevance.

"I was a Buck Showalter guy, because he was the one that brought me up and he was very instrumental in getting me to be a switch-hitter," Bernie Williams said. "I had a debt of gratitude to Buck. He seemed to be on top of the world in '95, winning Manager of the Year with the Yankees. It was kind of a shocker to have him out of the team and out of the organization, then having Joe come in—especially when he didn't really have a reputation for being a winning manager."

Torre had experienced his share of adversity during his three previous managerial stints, getting fired by the New York Mets, Atlanta Braves, and St. Louis Cardinals—the three teams for which he played during his stellar career.

Just weeks after Torre took over as Mets manager in 1977, the club traded its ace, Tom Seaver. As manager of the Braves, Torre found himself in the middle of a power struggle, as a large contingent of the front office wanted Eddie Haas to manage the club rather than Torre. In St. Louis, Torre was initially offered the club's Triple A managerial job before Whitey Herzog decided to retire in the middle of the 1990 season.

When the Cardinals fired Torre just 47 games into the 1995 season, he assumed his days managing in the majors were over. Three strikes and you're out.

That offseason, the Yankees reached out to Torre about their vacant general manager position. It wasn't a job he necessarily wanted, but Torre flew to Tampa to meet with general partner Joe Molloy—Steinbrenner's son-in-law—and Gene "Stick" Michael, the outgoing general manager who had been shifted to a new role to focus on scouting.

"Knowing the answer, I asked the question anyway; I said, 'Is there any vacation time?'" Torre said. "Stick said no. I still wanted to manage, but the biggest thing was the time commitment. Working for George in that role, it's not like a baseball season and then you come back the next year; this was a year-round job. I was waiting for the birth of my daughter, and I didn't want to be away for that. It was flattering to get an offer; anytime you get fired a few times and somebody wants you, it's something that makes you feel good. I just didn't think it was the right time for that."

"Things happen for a reason. You don't know it at the time, so you have to play the hand and see what happens."

Torre thanked Molloy and Michael for the opportunity, offering his assistance if he could help as they vetted other candidates. As he headed back home from Tampa, he figured that would be his final conversation with the Yankees.

So when Arthur Richman, a former sportswriter and Mets executive who joined the Yankees as vice president of media relations in 1989, called Torre a couple weeks later to ask him if he would like to be put on a short list for potential managers with Davey Johnson, Tony La Russa, and Sparky Anderson, Torre was thrilled.

"I knew damn well I was on the bottom of that list, which didn't hurt my feelings," said Torre, who knew Richman from their days together with the Mets. "Just being on that list was good enough. "

La Russa accepted Torre's old job managing the Cardinals, while Johnson took the Baltimore Orioles' managerial gig. Torre was offered the Yankees job, though his brother Frank warned him that working for Steinbrenner would end in disaster—just as it had for everybody else who had managed for The Boss.

Torre didn't care. He believed in himself, and this being his fourth managerial job, he looked at it as a bonus opportunity.

The Yankees had a solid core of young players, though Derek Jeter, Andy Pettitte, and Mariano Rivera had yet to establish themselves as reliable major leaguers and Jorge Posada had yet to take a big-league at-bat. There were a number of proven veterans such as Wade Boggs, Paul O'Neill, Bernie Williams, David Cone, and John Wetteland to provide leadership, while new additions Tino Martinez, Joe Girardi, Tim Raines, Kenny Rogers, and Dwight Gooden had been brought in during the offseason.

"I went over there and I was nervous as a cat," Torre said. "Spring training was fun; I got there and looked around and saw all those starting pitchers. You manage as long as I did up to that point, you realize how important pitching is. You can't win the game unless you can get 27 outs, and in all the stops I had made as a manager, there were games that we just couldn't get the outs."

It took about a month for the Yankees to find their footing, but once they took over first place in the American League East on the final day of April, they never looked back.

"The first thing that those of us who read the paper saw back then was 'Clueless Joe,'" Jim Leyritz said. "Here was a guy who had been with three other teams and couldn't win. One of the things that I noticed right away with Joe was that he had a pretty good handle on Mr. Steinbrenner. A lot of us saw that and thought, 'Wow, he can handle George.'"

Torre's temperament proved to be perfect for the Yankees; his ability to remain calm in the face of adversity helped the team hold off the Orioles down the stretch after their lead—which was as large as 12 games in late July—had shrunk to just 2½ by mid-September.

"From day one, you felt his presence," Williams said. "He made you feel like even during a rough period, we were going to be OK. He was always the same guy. He had a great quality when it came to that."

Throughout the Steinbrenner era, managers had felt heat from The Boss following the slightest hiccup. Watching your division lead tighten by nearly 10 games might have been cause for dismissal at one point, but Torre had a way with Steinbrenner that none of his predecessors ever seemed to.

"Challenges and conflicts happen along the way, but he was cool, calm and collected," general manager Brian Cashman—

then the assistant GM under Bob Watson—said. "I always referred to him having 'calm bombs.' When things got worse, he would defuse rather than infuse. Instead of making it worse, he would make it better by defusing the whole situation. He had a great ability to create 'calm bombs.' We might have a real tense meeting come up with George Steinbrenner and we would be on a bad run with a great team, which didn't make any sense, but is a part of baseball. The Boss would call us all in and we would be on high alert, tension is through the roof, but Torre would open the meeting with some sort of joke that would just crack The Boss up and defuse the situation."

The Yankees went on to win the AL East in 1996, then got past the Texas Rangers in the AL Division Series. New York advanced to the World Series with a five-game AL Championship Series win over Baltimore, getting an assist from young fan Jeffrey Maier, who reached over the outfield fence to catch a game-tying home run that might have otherwise been an out.

"There was a lot of destiny going on there," Torre said. "It was a very resilient ballclub; they didn't have any superstars, but they all blended and played well together. A very unselfish group. The first playoff game against Texas, I had a decision to make between Darryl Strawberry and Cecil Fielder as far as who was going to be DH. Strawberry walked into the clubhouse and he was the first one I told about my dilemma, and he suggested I play Big Daddy because he could handle sitting on the bench better. That type of camaraderie made my job easier."

Torre, whose entire postseason career had consisted of a three-game NL Championship Series sweep at the hands of the Cardinals in 1982 while managing the Braves, was finally in the World Series 36 years after making his big-league debut.

The Yankees found themselves in an 0–2 hole after the Braves won the first two games at Yankee Stadium. Prior to Game 2, Steinbrenner stopped in Torre's office and told him it was a must-win game for the Yankees, but Torre didn't want to put that type of pressure on his players.

"I was so pumped up about just getting to the World Series at this point in time, because I had never been, other than sitting in the stands," Torre said. "I was as loose as I could be; we were in the World Series. I was half-kidding, but I was half-serious, too; I told him I thought we may lose Game 2, because we were flat as a pancake. We had gone about a week between the end of the ALCS and the first game of the World Series, which had been rained out. That week was torture to me, because I didn't know what to do. We practiced, but I didn't want to play a simulated game because I didn't want to get somebody hurt. We would practice, take a day off, practice again; we weren't game-ready when we started the World Series and it showed."

Torre told Steinbrenner that even if the Yankees dropped Game 2, they would go on the road and sweep the three games at Atlanta-Fulton County Stadium, then return home and finish the job in front of the home fans.

"He was easy to play for; a calming father figure," Girardi said. "Whenever you were around him, he had the ability to make you feel like everything was going to be OK."

The Braves won Game 2, but the Yankees went to Atlanta and swept all three games, sending the series back to the Bronx for Game 6.

"I didn't get nervous until we got home," Torre said. "Now we were one game away, and then I was nervous and jumpy as all get out."

The night before Game 6, Torre learned that a donor had been located to give his brother Frank a heart transplant. He and Reggie Jackson visited Frank in the hospital after the off-day workout, but given his brother's situation, the World Series was not at the forefront of his mind.

The Yankees finished off the Braves, winning their first championship since 1978. Torre was visibly emotional during the celebration, finally tasting the game's ultimate success after so many years.

"It was magical," Torre said.

That magic wasn't there the following season, as the Yankees were knocked out by Cleveland in the ALDS. That loss stuck with Torre and his players, who rattled off a remarkable run over the next three years, winning back-to-back-to-back World Series titles. Their record in the Fall Classic during that stretch was 12–1, cementing the dynasty's place in history.

"He was the consummate player's manager," Cashman said. "He was given a Secretariat, which is a once-in-a-lifetime type of horse, and he allowed the players to play. There's a saying I use all the time: 'Let them play and stay out of the way.' Joe was that type of manager. He was simple, engaging, connecting, [and] built a bond, a family atmosphere with his players.

"Joe Torre was probably no different a manager here than he was in Atlanta or in St. Louis or with the Mets; the only difference was that he had players this time, where before he never had the players, so he lost a lot of games. A manager is only as good as the players and the roster he is given. He was given a great roster every year he managed, and we were a 90- to 95-win team every year because of it."

The Yankees made it back to a fourth consecutive World Series in 2001, but the Arizona Diamondbacks stunned them in Game 7, ending their quest for a fourth straight title.

Despite a significant amount of turnover after 2001, New York returned to the Fall Classic in 2003, beating the rival Red

Sox in a classic seven-game ALCS to win the sixth pennant of the Torre era. The core of the team remained the same, though superstar newcomers such as Mike Mussina, Jason Giambi, and Hideki Matsui fit into the culture with ease thanks to Torre's steady command of the clubhouse.

"We didn't have meetings every month; he just put us out there and let us do the job knowing that we knew what we were supposed to be doing," Mussina said. "Even when it was going bad, there were no blow-ups, no flipping tables, no losing your mind. I don't even remember there being a raised voice during the seven years that I was there with him."

The Yankees experienced a historic collapse against the Red Sox in the 2004 ALCS, becoming the first team in baseball history to lose a best-of-seven series after winning the first three games. Torre's Yankees went on to lose in the ALDS in each of the next three years, after which the manager's contract had expired.

Torre was offered a one-year, $5 million contract, a deal that would have represented a 33 percent pay cut. For a manager who had experienced as much success as Torre had, the perfunctory offer was little more than a publicity move; Torre wasn't going to accept it, and the Yankees seemed satisfied to let him leave.

"Neither one of us knew how to say goodbye," Torre said. His final meeting with Steinbrenner and the rest of the front office was emotional, but it was clear that the time was right for him to move on.

Torre's final record with the Yankees was 1,173–767 in the regular season, with a remarkable 76–47 record in the postseason. The Yankees won four World Series titles and six AL pennants during his 12-year tenure, bolstering a résumé that landed Torre in the Baseball Hall of Fame in 2014.

Williams may not have thought getting rid of Showalter in favor of Torre was the best move for the Yankees in late 1995, but it didn't take long for the center fielder to understand that it was a franchise-altering decision that wound up rewriting history.

"Boy, was I wrong," Williams said. "He was the right guy for the job at the right time."

Family Business

GETTING INTO THE FAMILY BUSINESS CAN COME WITH PLENTY of pros and cons.

On the plus side, the prior generation has put an infrastructure in place to make the business successful, handing down a road map to follow.

The flip side, naturally, is the expectation to keep the business prosperous, living up to the standard set by your predecessor.

Welcome to Hal Steinbrenner's world.

The Yankees' managing general partner since November 2008, Steinbrenner has spent his life living in the shadow of his famous father, George. A 1991 graduate of Williams College, Steinbrenner has been involved with the Yankees in some capacity for more than 30 years, though his role was ancillary for a number of years while he worked in the family's hotel business.

"I was for the most part thrust into it right out of college, because my dad was out of baseball," Steinbrenner said, referring to George's ban from the game, which lasted from 1991 to '93. "Whatever I was planning on doing immediately after college got amplified when I moved to New York and lived there for a year. I was working with [Brian] Cashman; Stick Michael was the GM. It was definitely thrust upon me—happily so—but I just had to get into it a little bit quicker than I probably would have as far as the learning curve."

Even after his father returned from his ban, Hal's office was located just feet from George's at the Yankees' Tampa complex. Hal didn't have decision-making powers, but he would routinely get pulled into meetings and asked for his opinion.

"I was very involved just by proximity," Steinbrenner said.

When George's health began to fail in the mid-2000s, Hal and his brother, Hank, became more intimately involved in the baseball operation. Hank took the lead during the 2007–08 offseason, but a year later, it was Hal who was approved to be the club's managing general partner.

"I was old enough to know who I am and how I'm different than my father—and how we're alike," Steinbrenner said. "There has always been a lot of thought about how to keep this franchise great, how to keep the tradition alive and the history alive. This is not a job I would have—and I have always known this—if my name wasn't Steinbrenner, so I treat the job with a tremendous amount of respect. It's a privilege. It's not something I earned. That's just the way I go about my business, and I certainly always put a lot of thought into how to best do that."

The bloodlines were there, but the younger Steinbrenner took a different approach in running the Yankees than The Boss did during his tumultuous 35-year tenure as the club's head honcho.

"The Boss was very emotional and reactionary; he would make decisions in that environment—and in many cases, that would not be the best decision to be making in that type of environment," said longtime Yankees general manager Brian Cashman, who has had the unique experience of serving in that role under both Steinbrenners. "Hal is very deliberate; he wants to make an informed decision; he never wants to make an emotional decision. He wants to take his time to think through everything and have all the information in front of him and talk to as many people as he possibly can, so he's the opposite of his father in that way."

That is not an accident. Hal is measured, thoughtful, and methodical, loath to make a rash decision he will later regret. That he seems to be the polar opposite of his father is not a conscious choice he made, but rather the person he has always been.

"I certainly try to stay calm, and if you've got a problem, you've got to work through the problem," Steinbrenner said. "I'm not one to panic. I'm probably more optimistic than pessimistic, but I'm definitely not one to panic."

During his first 13 years as managing general partner, Steinbrenner has employed one GM and two managers. Under his father, those numbers would often be exceeded in one season.

"When The Boss got into an angry, emotional time where he was frustrated that the team wasn't doing what it was expected to do or something wasn't playing a certain way, boom!" Cashman said. "He became a tornado, and nothing was going to stop that until it spun its course. You would have to assess the damage after the fact."

Like Cashman, Joe Girardi had the opportunity to experience life under both Steinbrenners. He played for George in the late 1990s, then managed the Yankees from 2008 to 2017.

"I don't think Hal is nearly as emotional as George with every game," Girardi said. "Hal would come down and talk to me all the time, he would want to know things, but it was a different type of presence. Hal was more calming and relaxing; he never came down and slammed his fist on the table. George was about, 'You have to win today. I don't care what the circumstances are.' I love that attitude, but it's not possible to go 162–0."

The elder Steinbrenner's cyclonic nature was often interpreted as a passion and hunger to win. Whether his decisions translated into success—and for a lengthy stretch of his ownership, they did not—The Boss made it clear that he would not be satisfied until the Yankees were on top.

Because he doesn't possess the same impulsive—and sometimes reckless—traits that his father did, Hal is often criticized for caring more about the team's bottom line than its win-loss record. Cashman believes that Hal gets a "bad rap" from those critics, pointing out that owning a major league franchise in the 2020s is "a completely different type of game" than the one The Boss contended with throughout his tenure.

"The Boss didn't have revenue sharing, luxury tax, draft limitations, international signing spending limitations; one thing after another," Cashman said. "Every basic agreement that's come down the path has been designed to stop George Steinbrenner from doing what George Steinbrenner did in the past, which was maximize every opportunity he could find. Whether it was spending more than anybody else in the draft or for signing any international import for as much as he wanted—none of which was illegal—other clubs couldn't keep up with it.

"George built an empire here and made a lot of money from it. The Yankees were a premier franchise in the entire sports world, so the other clubs took notice and said, 'How can we take a piece of that pie?' Hal has had to deal with carrying that responsibility now in a whole new world order, so the Monopoly game that Hal plays is different than the Monopoly game George played."

Hal Steinbrenner was formally approved as the Yankees' managing general partner on November 20, 2008, taking control of the franchise his father had bought more than 35 years earlier. If he planned to take a different approach than The Boss had for so many years, that was not apparent during his first offseason in charge.

Cashman had already traded for Nick Swisher in mid-November with the idea of making him the Yankees' everyday first baseman. The team's need was in the starting rotation, where the young trio of Phil Hughes, Joba Chamberlain, and Ian Kennedy had underperformed that season, a year that saw the club's 13-year streak of postseason play come to an end.

Mike Mussina, Jason Giambi, Bobby Abreu, and Andy Pettitte were all free agents, freeing up a significant amount of cash from the Yankees' payroll. Just as his father had always done, Steinbrenner planned to put that money back into the team, giving Cashman the freedom to pursue the two top arms on the free-agent market: CC Sabathia and A.J. Burnett.

A few weeks after formally taking control, Steinbrenner approved a seven-year, $161 million contract for Sabathia and a five-year, $82.5 million deal for Burnett. The two pitchers were introduced at a December 18 press conference, giving Yankees fans an early holiday present.

A week later, the Yankees made a move that seemed straight out of The Boss' playbook, stunning the baseball world with the signing of Mark Teixeira to an eight-year, $180 million deal. The three free agents cost a combined $423.5 million.

"It was exciting," Steinbrenner said. "We had a good amount of money coming off the payroll, which was helpful. With the new stadium and all the expectations, when you have the ability to get talent like that, we went out and did it. A lot of fun press conferences that winter."

Winning the offseason was an annual rite of passage for The Boss, who seemingly coveted back-page buzz as much as—if not more than—he did on-field success. The Yankees were the clear offseason champions after their monstrous winter, but the team still had to back it up with its play.

Sabathia, Burnett, Teixeira, and Swisher did just that, joining forces with the "Core Four" of Derek Jeter, Mariano Rivera, Andy Pettitte, and Jorge Posada to win 103 games in the regular season. The Yankees then got past the Twins and Angels in the American League playoffs before disposing of the Phillies in six games, christening the new Yankee Stadium with the 27th World Series championship in franchise history.

For Steinbrenner, it was his first title as the primary decision-maker, justifying his offseason spending spree in the best way possible.

"It was very rewarding," Steinbrenner said. "There were so many people in the organization like Randy Levine that worked so hard to get that stadium. It was rewarding, but at the same time, it was surreal for me because I had just gotten into the job. I remember that last out well. I remember that night well; reflecting on everything that we accomplished that year was pretty special."

* * *

In the decade-plus that followed 2009, the Yankees never got back to the top of the baseball mountain. They reached the ALCS four times between 2010 and 2019, but every October ended with the same disappointment, watching other teams compete in the Fall Classic.

A stretch of that nature would have sent The Boss into a frenzy, causing him to throw money at any free agent willing to take it. That's not how the younger Steinbrenner operates, however. He chose to stick to the plan he and Cashman had devised, believing that you don't need to outspend the competition by wide margins to have success.

"I still am of the belief you shouldn't need a $200 million team to win a championship," said Steinbrenner, who has continued to hit that payroll mark every year in spite of his conviction. "There's just been too many other examples to the contrary. When we have money coming off the payroll, we put it back in. I think we've proven time and time again that we're going to do that in order to field a championship-caliber team."

Teixeira appreciated Steinbrenner's approach to ownership, which he described as being "hands off" for the most part. When the two men spoke, it was often about their families and life in general rather than baseball.

The idea that Steinbrenner cared more about the company's bottom line than the standings never sat well with Teixeira, who watched the front office make plenty of big-money signings during his eight years in pinstripes.

"There's definitely a job description for a GM, but there's not one for an owner," Teixeira said. "You have all different kinds of people that own sports franchises; some you never see, some are in the first row like Mark Cuban, right next to the bench, screaming at the refs all game long. There are owners that a player will never meet, and then there are owners that a player sees every single day. If I know that my owner is trying everything to win a championship and has my back and my teammates' backs, then I love them. When I was with the Yankees, we spent plenty of money and we tried to win. To me, Hal was a good owner from that standpoint."

When the Yankees endure a bad regular season stretch or face another early postseason exit, it has become standard operating procedure for local columnists, sports talk radio hosts, and fans to begin shouting the familiar-yet-tired refrain of "If George was still alive..." in an effort to highlight the younger Steinbrenner's perceived shortcomings.

Steinbrenner is not oblivious to the criticism he often faces, though he doesn't apologize for his approach.

"We have partners, banks, and bondholders, so clearly I've got a lot of responsibility to run the business as well as I can and be responsible," Steinbrenner said. "At the same time, the product I put out is not a car; it's a baseball team playing 162 games a year and hopefully more. There has to be a balance. I can't ignore the fact that this is a business and I have people I'm responsible to, including my family members; but at the same time, I'm also responsible to fans to put out on the field a great product that always has a chance to win it all."

Steinbrenner's Yankees have been the last team standing only once during his first 13 years at the helm. A stretch like that would have meant countless changes on and off the field under George—see the 1980s, for example—but Hal believes in his methodical ways, confident that his team will once again pop the final champagne bottle of the season soon enough.

"He's very confident in himself, which is one of the things that I appreciate most," said Swisher, who has worked as a special advisor to the club since his retirement. "Whatever the New York Yankees are doing, you know that with Hal

Steinbrenner there, he's going to be looking out for the best interest of the fans, the organization, and everything that comes along with the logo. He may do it in a little different fashion than his father, but that's not a bad thing."

PART 2

THE LEGENDS

8

Mount Rushmore

THE BASEBALL HALL OF FAME IS RICH WITH PINSTRIPED history, its plaque gallery loaded with five dozen men who once called themselves Yankees.

Of that impressive group, four are typically counted as the greatest quartet in franchise history: Babe Ruth, Lou Gehrig, Joe DiMaggio, and Mickey Mantle.

"They're the Yankees' Mount Rushmore," said Marty Appel, a longtime Yankees public relations director and author of *Pinstripe Empire*. "There's really no argument there."

Ruth was the first true star of the franchise, turning around the Yankees' fortunes after being purchased from the Boston Red Sox for $100,000 prior to the 1920 season. He hit 54 home runs in his first season with the Yankees, then 59 in his second. During his first five years in pinstripes, Ruth hit .370 while averaging 47 home runs and 131 RBI, producing video game numbers long before video games ever existed.

"To understand him, you had to understand this," former teammate Joe Dugan once said. "He wasn't human."

The Babe accomplished things never before seen on a big-league field, leading the league in home runs 12 times, including a then-record 60-homer campaign in 1927 that stood for 34 years. Ruth led the Yankees to their first World Series championship in 1923, the same season the club opened its palatial new ballpark in the Bronx. Ruth—nicknamed "The Sultan of Swat" and "The Great Bambino"—hit 714 home runs during his 22-year career, batting .342 with 2,873 hits, 2,174 runs scored, 2,214 RBI, and a .474 on-base percentage, eye-popping numbers that still somehow don't do justice to his dominance.

"It wasn't that he hit more home runs than anybody else," Spink Award winner Red Smith once said, according to the Hall of Fame's website. "He hit them better, higher, farther, with more theatrical timing and a more flamboyant flourish."

Ruth was a star pitcher for the Red Sox until Ed Barrow—the Boston manager who later became a Hall of Fame executive with the Yankees—decided his thunderous bat was more of a weapon than his talented arm. Ruth became a full-time outfielder once he joined the Yankees, wowing fans with his unprecedented power at the plate.

"People had to accept that he brought a dimension to the game that didn't previously exist," Appel said. "People who followed baseball from the turn of the century tended to say Honus Wagner or Ty Cobb was the greatest ever, that what Ruth has brought to the game is just an oddity and absurdity. Once the home run became an accepted part of the game, everything fell in line to say there's never been anybody like Babe Ruth."

Ruth played just 98 games in 1925, and while the Yankees struggled through their first losing season of the Ruth era, a new star emerged: Gehrig.

Inserted into the lineup after first baseman Wally Pipp was scratched with a headache, Gehrig made the position his for more than 14 years. His first two full seasons with the Yankees were solid, but in 1927, he and Ruth formed the most lethal one-two punch in the league, combining for 107 home runs, 338 RBI, and 307 runs scored as the Yankees won 110 games en route to the franchise's second World Series championship.

The two were as dissimilar as two men could be—Ruth lived his boisterous life to the fullest, while Gehrig prided himself on being a straight-laced family man—but together, they created magic on a baseball field the way no teammates ever had.

"I'm not a headline guy," Gehrig once said. "I always knew that as long as I was following Babe to the plate, I could have gone up there and stood on my head. No one would have noticed the difference."

Ruth and Gehrig combined to win three championships before the Babe left the Yankees at the end of the 1934 season, though Gehrig wasn't finished. Just as Gehrig had arrived a decade earlier to form a dynamic duo with Ruth, the Yankees welcomed a new phenom to the lineup in 1936—DiMaggio.

The 21-year-old made his presence felt immediately, making the All-Star team during his rookie year. Gehrig won the AL Most Valuable Player award in 1936, but DiMaggio was the talk of the town, his photo appearing on the cover of *Time* magazine.

DiMaggio had done the unthinkable. He had filled Ruth's enormous shoes, somehow establishing himself as a worthy successor to the Babe. Together with Gehrig, DiMaggio helped lead the Yankees to World Series championships in each of his first three years with the Yankees, continuing the dynasty that had started upon Ruth's arrival nearly two decades earlier.

Seven weeks after taking himself out of the lineup to bring his record consecutive-game streak of 2,130 to an end, Gehrig was forced to retire on June 21, 1939, as amyotrophic lateral sclerosis ravaged his body. On July 4, the Yankees held Lou Gehrig Appreciation Day, during which the Iron Horse delivered one of the most poignant speeches in American history.

"Fans, for the past two weeks you have been reading about a bad break," Gehrig said as he opened his remarks. "Today, I consider myself the luckiest man on the face of the earth."

Gehrig retired with a .340 average, 493 home runs, 1,995 RBI, 2,721 hits, 1,888 runs scored, two AL MVP awards, seven AL pennants, and six World Series rings. Gehrig died on June 2, 1941, exactly 16 years to the day after he had replaced Pipp in the Yankees' lineup, launching a Hall of Fame career.

DiMaggio carried the torch, leading the Yankees to a fourth consecutive championship while winning his first AL MVP award during that same season. With four titles in his first four seasons, DiMaggio—who earned the nickname "The Yankee Clipper" for his graceful outfield play—was already approaching legendary status.

Then came 1941.

DiMaggio put together a 56-game hitting streak, a record that has gone unchallenged since. Boston star Ted Williams hit .406 and had superior numbers in most categories, but DiMaggio, whose Yankees won 101 games to finish 17 games ahead of the second-place Red Sox, edged his rival in the MVP vote, winning his second such honor.

"In my heart I have always felt that I was a better hitter than Joe, which was always my first consideration," Williams wrote in his 1969 memoir, *My Turn at Bat*. "But I have to say that he was the greatest player of our time."

The Yankees won another World Series in 1941, then lost to the St. Louis Cardinals in the 1942 Fall Classic. DiMaggio missed the subsequent three years while serving in the Army

Air Force during World War II, but he returned in 1946, and while that season was a disappointment by DiMaggio's lofty standards, he bounced back in 1947, capturing his third AL MVP award and his sixth World Series title.

DiMaggio was part of three more championship teams from 1949 to 1951, bringing his impressive total to nine World Series rings.

Just as Gehrig had joined Ruth and DiMaggio had done the same with Gehrig, a new young star arrived in the Bronx during DiMaggio's final season in 1951—Mantle.

Mantle was the heir apparent to the 36-year-old DiMaggio, who announced in March that he would retire at the end of the 1951 season. Thanks in part to his three-year layoff during the war, Joltin' Joe didn't have the gaudy career statistics that Ruth and Gehrig had compiled, but his numbers weren't too shabby: a .325 batting average, 361 home runs, 1,537 RBI, 2,214 hits, 1,390 runs scored, and, perhaps most impressive, only 369 strikeouts in 7,672 career plate appearances.

DiMaggio played in 10 World Series during his 13 seasons with the Yankees, winning nine times, establishing himself as one of the greatest and most graceful winners in the game's history.

"Physical accomplishments, great as they may be, do not alone add up to what made Joe DiMaggio the national figure that he was," read the *New York Times* upon DiMaggio's retirement. "For Joe brought to the game not merely great prowess but great personal qualities. Modest to the point of self-effacement, he demonstrated on a ball field that it is possible to be at one and the same time a greatly feared competitor and an athlete of exemplary sportsmanship."

Now it was Mantle's turn to take the baton.

A native of Oklahoma, Mantle actually got his first taste of New York in 1950, spending the final few days of the season with the Yankees without getting into a game. In 1951, a 19-year-old Mantle played right field next to DiMaggio, doing his best not to gawk at his superstar teammate.

"Joe DiMaggio was my hero," Mantle once said, "but he couldn't talk to me because I wouldn't even look at him."

Mantle was sent back to the minors in mid-July, returning in late August. He played well enough to earn a spot in the lineup during the World Series, but Mantle suffered torn ligaments in his right knee after catching his spikes on a sprinkler, ending his season.

Mantle returned in 1952, making his first of 14 consecutive All-Star teams while helping New York to its second straight championship. The Yankees made it three in a row in 1953, and although Mantle's biggest statistical years were still ahead of him, the switch-hitter was already wowing the league with his raw power and tape-measure blasts.

The Yankees won seven pennants and five World Series titles during Mantle's first eight seasons in the Bronx as he averaged 31 home runs with a .314 average during that time. Mantle captured the league's Triple Crown in 1956 with a .353 average, 52 homers, and 130 RBI, winning the first of his back-to-back AL MVP awards.

"He was DiMaggio's heir apparent from the start," Appel said. "His presence, he had movie-star looks, muscles, never lifting anything heavier than a glass of beer; he just seemed to have it all. He was baseball's first television star. Everybody was buying TVs in the early '50s, and there he was on national TV every October; he was on the NBC fall schedule like *Bonanza* was."

The Yankees traded for Roger Maris prior to the 1960 season, adding a left-handed bat they believed was perfectly suited for Yankee Stadium. They were right; Maris edged Mantle in a tight AL MVP vote as the Yankees won another pennant.

Mantle hit .400 with three home runs and 11 RBI in the World Series, but the Yankees fell to the Pittsburgh Pirates in seven games, losing on Bill Mazeroski's walk-off home run.

The 1961 season saw Maris and Mantle engage in a home run race, with Ruth's record of 60 dangling in front of them. Fans and media alike were pulling for Mantle, believing he was a worthier successor to the Babe.

Mantle and Maris battled throughout the summer, but Maris ultimately pulled away in late September as Mantle dealt with a virus infection and an abscess in his hip caused by an injection. Mantle was only able to play in two World Series games, but the Yankees won anyway, their sixth championship in his 11 seasons.

The Yankees won another title in 1962 while Mantle earned his third AL MVP award. A broken foot sidelined Mantle for a significant part of the 1963 season, but he bounced back in 1964, putting together his last great season. Mantle hit .303 with 35 homers and 111 RBI, finishing second to Baltimore's Brooks Robinson for the AL MVP award, the seventh and final time he would place in the top three in the voting.

New York won its fifth consecutive pennant, and although Mantle hit three homers and had eight RBI in the World Series, the Yankees lost to the Cardinals in seven games.

Mantle was an All-Star three times over the next four seasons, but the Yankees never won another pennant before he announced his retirement on March 1, 1969—18 years to the day since DiMaggio had announced that he would retire after the 1951 season.

Like DiMaggio, Mantle retired at the age of 36, though his decision followed years of injuries and excessive alcohol use. Although he was no longer the same player, Mantle hit 40 home runs over his final two seasons, giving him 536 for his career.

"When he quit, he was third on the all-time home run list, so people weren't saying at the time, 'If he had only taken better care of himself,'" Appel said. "But you look back now and think, 'He was 32 in his last big year; what a tragedy.'"

Mantle was elected into the Hall of Fame in 1974 with 88.2 percent of the vote. He was inducted later that summer alongside his good friend and teammate Whitey Ford.

When Mantle's career was over, it closed the books on an incredible 48-year run for the Yankees. From Ruth to Gehrig to DiMaggio to Mantle, the club won 29 pennants and 20 world championships.

All four represent the Yankees in the Hall of Fame, but Ruth's legacy has endured the longest; the Babe is often cited as the greatest baseball player that ever lived.

"When you ask who is the greatest in each sport, you're going to say Tiger Woods or Jack Nicklaus; you're going to say Tom Brady, Joe Montana, or Jim Brown; you're going to say Wayne Gretzky or you're going to say Michael Jordan," Appel said. "These are all guys we saw. In baseball, 100 years later, it's a guy none of us ever saw. All we've seen are highlight films, so we never see him screw up—we only see him hitting home runs. The fact that his legend has endured for a century is remarkable."

Remembering Yogi

YOGI BERRA DOESN'T HAVE THE GAUDY NUMBERS OF SOME other baseball greats, but his career résumé ranks with the best the game has ever seen.

Ten World Series rings, three American League Most Valuable Player awards, and 18 All-Star selections highlight Berra's Hall of Fame credentials, but if you ask anybody who knew him, his on-field achievements pale in comparison to the man himself.

Rather than tell the tale of Berra's baseball heroics, let's allow those who knew Yogi on a personal level to share their favorite recollections of one of the greatest Yankees of all time.

Derek Jeter, Yankees shortstop 1995–2014
"Yogi Berra used to come in the locker room and every time we had won, he would come over and remind me how many rings he had. I used to joke with him and say, 'Well, you know it's a

little bit harder now because there's more rounds in the playoffs; you went straight to the World Series.' His response was, 'You can come over to my house and count the rings anytime you want.'"

Dave Winfield, Yankees outfielder 1981–90

"Those malapropisms that you read about, they were all true. One time during spring training, we're finished with the workout and we were going to run some sprints, so he said, 'OK, pair up in threes.' You just wanted to bask in the glow of Yogi. Winning all those championships, you would look at him and he was such a diminutive figure. Sometimes as you get older, you shrink a little bit, but you'd look at him and think, 'No way this guy could have accomplished everything he did.' He's the Bill Russell of baseball. He and his wife, Carmen, were wonderful people."

Paul O'Neill, Yankees right fielder 1993–2001

"We were at Old Timers' Day one year and he was kind of shuffling down the hall with Whitey [Ford]. They were starting to announce the names and I said, 'Yogi, you better speed it up. You have to be out there soon.' He said, 'Shut up kid, I'm sprinting.' When he showed up to my plaque induction and made an effort to say hello to my family, I'll never forget it. He was a special person."

Joe Torre, Yankees manager 1996–2007

"When he came back into the fold thanks to Suzyn Waldman, he would show up to spring training every year. I would get to the ballpark at 7:00 AM and he was already there, asking me, 'Where you been?'

"Most celebrity coaches pick and choose where they want to go, but Yogi made every trip in spring training. I would drive everywhere for the most part, so we would hang around and watch the guys back at camp, then head to the game in uniform. We'd make some longer trips, so Yogi would have to go to the bathroom.

"We would stop at a 7-11 so Yogi could use the bathroom, and he would get out of the car wearing his No. 8. People would look at him like, 'No, that couldn't be him.' He would just walk into 7-11, go to the bathroom, and come back out. It's one of the greatest visuals I can ever remember. He was oblivious to having to be self-conscious about doing things like that. He was a great individual and a dear friend."

Bernie Williams, Yankees center fielder 1991–2006

"One day in spring training, the day was already over for practice and workouts, and Yogi was just getting dressed in the coaches' room where I was sitting. He spent about 45 minutes to an hour with me, talking about his time in the big leagues, his experience and how different baseball was. It was an incredible one-on-one conversation with him in the locker room; I just felt like a little kid talking to my grandfather, listening to stories about the old family.

"I never really had an opportunity to talk to Yogi for such a long period of time; he was always gracious, saying hi and asking how you were doing, but it was always kind of in passing. To have that opportunity to sit down with him and hear all of those stories, soak in all of his knowledge, it was very special. I will always remember that moment as one of my greatest moments with a warm place in my heart."

Willie Randolph, Yankees second baseman 1976–1988
"Yogi would always come down and sit in the lobby early, so if the bus was at 1:00, Yogi would be down there at 11:30 just sitting there with a coffee, watching people. Guys who would go to the ballpark early would get a cab, so Yogi would always ask me, 'Hey, can I ride with you, shorty?' It's Yogi Berra! It's an honor that he would ride in a cab with me.

"We get in the cab and drive to the ballpark, but when it was time to get out of the cab, he would start laughing at me, get out of the cab, and take off. I'm like, 'I'm making a rookie salary here and you're Yogi Berra!' I would be going into my pocket to pay for the cab and he would just say, 'Thanks a lot, shorty.' He never, ever picked up a cab. He would just sit there laughing at me every time.

"He meant so much to me. He was there early in my career in almost every possible way; he managed me, coached me, he was my friend and mentor."

Nick Swisher, Yankees right fielder 2009–2012
"My grandfather passed away in 2008, and I told Yogi, 'I'm going to adopt you as my grandfather.' Whether we were sitting in the lunchroom drinking a cup of coffee or if we were sitting on the bench talking about hitting, there was a simplicity with which he lived his life. Yogi had a smile on his face every single day. It was just a blast to be around him."

Bill Madden, veteran *New York Daily News* baseball writer
"We're in Cleveland, it's his first year as manager. I came down to breakfast and Yogi was sitting alone by himself, having breakfast in the coffee shop. He calls me over, he says, 'Sit down, Sauce'—we used to call each other 'Sauce' because we

all went out drinking together every night. I sit down and Yogi has already had his scrambled eggs, bacon, toast, and coffee. The waitress comes over and I just order an English muffin. We talked for about an hour, the check comes, and I pick up the check. It's $35, so I said, 'How did this come to $35?' He looked at me without missing a beat and said, 'It must have been the English muffin. They've got to import that.'"

FORD TOUGH

Any conversation about the greatest Yankees in history begins with the same names: Babe, Lou, Joe D., and Mickey.

They're known as the Bronx Bombers for a reason, right?

"You could say the Yankees' Mount Rushmore should have a place for Whitey Ford and Mariano Rivera, but we don't think in terms of pitchers for some reason," said Marty Appel, author of *Pinstripe Empire*. "Whitey was remarkable; you compare him to everybody else of his time and he was sort of in a league of his own."

Born and bred in New York City, Edward "Whitey" Ford won his first nine decisions after making his debut in July 1950, helping the Yankees to a World Series title as a rookie. Ford missed the 1951 and 1952 seasons while serving in the Army, resuming his career in 1953.

On teams that included Joe DiMaggio, Mickey Mantle, Yogi Berra, Phil Rizzuto, and Roger Maris, Ford—a blond-haired southpaw who was given the nickname "Whitey" in the minors by Lefty Gomez—quickly became one of the Yankees' most important players, leading the club to four consecutive American League pennants and two World Series championships between 1955 and '58, going 62–25 with a 2.41 ERA during that four-year stretch.

"I don't care what the situation was, how high the stakes were—the bases could be loaded and the pennant riding on every pitch, it never bothered Whitey," Mantle wrote in his 1985 book *The Mick*. "He pitched his game. Cool. Crafty. Nerves of steel."

Ford and the Yankees lost the 1960 World Series, but they bounced back the following year under new manager Ralph Houk, posting one of the finest seasons in baseball history. Unlike Casey Stengel, who pitched Ford every fifth day, Houk asked the left-hander if he would prefer pitching every fourth day. Having never won 20 games in a season during his first nine years with the Yankees, Ford jumped at the opportunity.

Ford went 25–4 with a 3.21 ERA and a career-high 283 innings pitched, winning his only AL Cy Young Award. Catcher Elston Howard gave Ford another nickname, noting his cool, calm demeanor in the face of any situation: The Chairman of the Board.

"It was a Guidry-like year," Appel said, referring to Ron Guidry's brilliant 1978 season. "He really knew how to work hitters and how to use his full repertoire. He was just a master."

As remarkable as Ford's season was, he was overshadowed by the home run race between Mantle and Maris, the latter of whom broke Babe Ruth's long-standing record by hitting 61 homers.

With Ford as their ace, the Yankees won five straight AL pennants from 1960 to 1964, winning the World Series in 1961 and 1962. The left-hander threw 14 scoreless innings over two starts in the 1961 Fall Classic, earning MVP honors.

By the time Ford retired in May 1967, he had 236 wins, more than any other pitcher in Yankees history. New York won 11 AL pennants and six World Series titles during Ford's career; he started Game 1 of the World Series a remarkable eight times. Ford's 10 victories, 22 starts, 146 innings pitched, 94 strikeouts, and 33 consecutive scoreless innings all remain World Series records.

"He had such enormous self-confidence; it carried over to the whole team," Appel said. "It was like, 'Well we've got this one; Whitey is pitching.' He had that New York swagger, which translated into self-confidence."

10

Center of Attention

EVERYBODY KNOWS ABOUT THE YANKEES' "CORE FOUR" OF homegrown stars, but should the group have been expanded beyond Derek Jeter, Mariano Rivera, Andy Pettitte, and Jorge Posada?

In the eyes of many, it was a "Fab Five" of core players that contributed to the Yankees' incredible success from the late '90s into the early aughts.

The fifth player in this equation, of course, is Bernie Williams, the Yankees' longtime center fielder and a focal point of New York's lineup during its championship run under manager Joe Torre.

"Bernie was great at baseball, but he was not a big personality," longtime Yankees broadcaster Michael Kay said. "I think a lot of the blame of why he might be underappreciated probably lands at his feet because he was just that guy. He was just Bernie."

In truth, the "Core Four" moniker was created in 2009, when Jeter, Rivera, Pettitte, and Posada helped lead the Yankees to the 27th World Series title in franchise history. That was three years after Williams had played his final game, hence his exclusion from the group and its catchy new nickname.

The 2009 title was technically the fifth championship for each of them, though Posada appeared in only eight games for the 1996 team and was not included on the postseason roster that fall. Williams retired with four World Series rings, hitting in the heart of the Yankees' lineup throughout their astonishing run from 1996 to 2003.

Between 1996 and 2000, Williams hit .324 with an impressive .410 on-base percentage, averaging 26 home runs, 107 RBI, 108 runs scored, and 14 stolen bases while receiving votes on American League Most Valuable Player ballots in all five of those seasons. He won four consecutive Gold Glove awards and was selected to four straight All-Star teams from 1997 to 2000.

"When it came to pressure situations, I trusted Bernie as much as you could trust anybody with men on base because you knew he wasn't going to get himself out," Torre said. "Bernie was a very special player. I think he gets overlooked; people took him for granted sometimes. But I don't think the guys in the clubhouse did; they relied on him a great deal."

A track star during his high school days in Puerto Rico, Williams turned his focus to baseball, signing with the Yankees on his 17th birthday. He made his minor league debut in the Gulf Coast League in 1986, beginning a five-year journey through the team's farm system.

Williams had his ups and downs in the minors, but he showed enough promise to be considered one of the Yankees' top prospects. Initially a right-handed hitter exclusively,

Williams began switch-hitting during the 1990 season, adding another aspect to his game as he experienced success from both sides of the plate.

The Yankees promoted him in July 1991 to fill in for an injured Roberto Kelly, and although Williams spent the remainder of the season in the majors, the Yankees sent him to the minors one week and five at-bats into the 1992 season, hoping to finish off his development.

"Mr. Steinbrenner came into the locker room and he personally took the time to talk to me," Williams said. "He said, 'We understand that you're a very young player, and it's not in your best interest to sit here on the bench. You need to get more development, so you're going to go down and play your heart out, play hard, and we'll see you out here again soon. Is that clear?' I said, 'Yes sir.'"

Williams spent the majority of the first four months of the 1992 campaign at Triple A, but when he was recalled in August, his minor league days were officially behind him.

It seemed that Williams' future in the Bronx was bright, but a sluggish start to the 1993 season left his place with the Yankees in limbo. George Steinbrenner, known for his patience with underperforming players, was pushing general manager Gene Michael to trade the 24-year-old. One potential deal would have sent Williams to the Montreal Expos for Larry Walker, who was slated to hit free agency at the end of 1994.

"George wanted to make it happen," said Brian Cashman, who was working his way up the front office at the time. "George didn't get along with the owner of the Expos, so Gene knew he was protected because George wouldn't call the owner. When George said, 'Where are we at with the Expos?' Gene said the Expos backed out and wouldn't do it. That was false; the Expos were willing to do it, but Gene wouldn't trade Bernie for a pending free agent in Larry Walker because of Bernie's service time." Williams admits that he suffered from "uncertainty and anxiety" during those early years of his career, as Steinbrenner was known for trading young players away in exchange for proven veterans.

"He was very successful in putting a competitive team on the field on paper, but the chemistry may not have been there," Williams said. "When you have a whole group of players coming from different organizations, sometimes chemistry wasn't completely there."

Trade rumors were a part of Williams' life, but that came with the territory when you were a young player in the Bronx. As players such as Pat Kelly, Jim Leyritz, Hensley Meulens, and Kevin Maas began tasting success in the majors, it strengthened Michael's resolve to let the club's homegrown players develop in pinstripes.

"They gave them the opportunity, so they paved the way for me," Williams said. "It kept escalating to the point where we had a team that at its core was filled with people that were coming from the organization rather than getting people from other places."

Williams showed gradual improvement in 1993 and 1994, but his true breakout came in 1995, when he hit .307 with 18 home runs and 82 RBI. The Yankees—who had the best record in the AL when the '94 season was cut short by a players' strike—returned to the postseason for the first time since 1981, getting contributions from a pair of young pitchers named Pettitte and Rivera.

The following season, Torre took over for Buck Showalter, a manager to whom Williams felt a debt of gratitude for helping him make the transition to switch-hitting. New York handed the starting shortstop job to the 21-year-old Jeter, who went on to win AL Rookie of the Year honors.

Just as the Yankees had chosen to keep Williams rather than trading him for Walker or another seasoned veteran, the front office held on to Pettitte, Jeter, and Rivera, all of whom had been involved in trade talks at one point before they showed what they could do.

Williams thrived in his first season under Torre, batting .305 with career highs in home runs (29) and RBI (102), anchoring the lineup as the Yankees won the World Series, their first title since 1978. He earned ALCS Most Valuable Player honors, batting .474 with two home runs and six RBI in the five-game triumph over the Baltimore Orioles.

"When you have a team of people that are growing up together, it was a big difference when we started creating a core of players that were there year in and year out," Williams said. "Even if they were young, we had an opportunity to grow together as a team and create this rapport and this camaraderie and this chemistry that was, in my opinion, one of the most important keys to our success."

At 27, Williams was an established player, but with veterans such as Wade Boggs, Paul O'Neill, Tim Raines, and David Cone on the roster, he didn't consider himself to be a leader on the club.

Torre disagreed with that assessment.

"I think it was my first or second year, I told Bernie, 'You're a leader on this team,' and he said, 'I am?'" Torre said. "I told him, 'Yeah. You take your position every single day; to me, that's leadership. You come out and give me everything you've got every day.'"

Williams wasn't a leader in the rah-rah sense, nor was he the fiery type who would get in a teammate's face if he saw something he didn't like. Instead, Williams would spend his pregame time sitting in his corner locker or in a back room in the clubhouse strumming away on his guitar, an activity that brought him peace as he prepared for that night's game. That is, if he wasn't taking a nap.

"There's a certain relaxation you need to have in order for your body to respond to what you want it to do," Torre said. "You have to relax and get yourself mentally ready to go out there. Bernie would be playing the guitar, and if he was in a slump I would walk by and say, 'Why don't you hit with that thing?'"

Williams didn't need much help in that department. He hit .328 with 21 homers and 100 RBI in 1997, then won the AL batting title in 1998 with a robust .339 average. His timing couldn't have been better; Williams was a free agent at the end of the Yankees' historic 1998 championship season.

The Yankees were holding firm to a five-year, $60 million offer to Williams, believing they could sign slugger Albert Belle in the event that Williams departed. But Belle received a huge offer from the Orioles, while the Boston Red Sox had been aggressive in their pursuit of Williams, offering him a seven-year pact worth more than $85 million.

Facing the prospect of losing Williams *and* Belle, Steinbrenner blinked after a face-to-face meeting with Williams. They agreed to a seven-year contract worth a guaranteed $87.5 million, keeping the popular center fielder in the Bronx.

"It came down to the fact that I wanted to be a Yankee," Williams told reporters after signing his new contract.

Red Sox general manager Dan Duquette was understandably miffed at the end result, believing he had been close to signing Williams less than 24 hours before the Yankees boosted their offer.

"'What it came down to is that I'm not sure Bernie ever really wanted to leave the Yankees,'" Duquette told the *New York Times*. "And when George Steinbrenner realized that one of the best all-around players the Yankees have had since Joe DiMaggio was ready to leave, he wouldn't let that happen.'"

Williams lived up to his new contract immediately, batting .323 with an average of 25 home runs, 108 RBI, 107 runs scored, and a .410 on-base percentage during the first four years of the deal. According to the Society for American Baseball Research, Williams' 1999 season made him just the fifth Yankees hitter to score 100 runs while driving in at least 100 RBI in three separate seasons. The other four: Babe Ruth, Lou Gehrig, Joe DiMaggio, and Mickey Mantle. Pretty good company.

"He wasn't a dynamic superstar, but he was a superstar," Kay said. "A switch-hitter that hits for power, gets clutch hits, and hits in the middle of the order? That's invaluable."

The Yankees won the World Series in 1999 and 2000, then reached the Fall Classic again in 2001 before losing in heartbreaking fashion to the Arizona Diamondbacks in seven games.

"We started getting into these crazy expectations of being in the World Series every year," Williams said. "If we didn't get there, it was a bad year for us. What kind of team has those kinds of expectations? We took that very seriously, even though it was next to impossible to accomplish. Just to have that attitude, it made the team culture one of always pursuing excellence and not settling for being mediocre. The ultimate prize was to win the World Series; that's where our sights were. The fact that we had a legitimate shot at getting there every year, it was nothing short of remarkable."

The Yankees returned to the World Series in 2003, coming up short again, this time against the Florida Marlins. That was the last time Williams would play for a title, as the Yankees were stunned by the Red Sox in the 2004 ALCS, then lost in the ALDS in each of the two subsequent years.

Williams was offered a minor league contract by the Yankees prior to the 2007 season, but he chose to decline it. He didn't attend a game at Yankee Stadium in 2007 or '08, finally returning to take part in the closing ceremonies in the ballpark's final game. Williams was the final player introduced during the hour-long pregame ceremony, receiving a thunderous ovation from the crowd that had showed him so much love throughout his career.

Williams' reception from the sellout crowd was louder than any other pinstriped legend that night, but despite sitting out two seasons, Williams hadn't completely given up on the idea of playing again.

"I think I'll probably keep thinking that I can play at 50," Williams said. "I may never retire officially."

During spring training in 2009, Williams showed up to Yankees camp to work out the kinks in an attempt to play for Puerto Rico in the World Baseball Classic. He never suited up in a big-league game again, and although he still hadn't officially announced his retirement, Williams appeared on the Hall of Fame ballot in 2012.

Williams fell off the Hall of Fame ballot after two years, and although he wouldn't have a plaque in Cooperstown, the Yankees announced in 2014 that one would be hung in Williams' honor in Monument Park. Prior to the 2015 season, the team went one step further, revealing that Williams' No. 51 would also be retired.

One month before those two honors would be bestowed upon him, Williams signed a minor league contract with the

Yankees and immediately—finally—announced his official retirement.

"To set the record straight, Bernie is a member of the 'Fab Five,'" Cashman said at the press conference. "He is a member of that fabulous five that got produced from our system that led to many of these championships."

On May 24, 2015, Williams joined the list of legends honored in the Bronx, his number hung up on the Stadium wall for the rest of time.

"It was just validation of all the years that I spent with the team and to know that you're really considered a big part of a championship team—and not only once, but having the opportunity to go six times and win four of them," Williams said. "This is what you work for as a player. When you're playing sandlot baseball as a kid, you're always imagining yourself being in a situation like that. The fact that I was not only able to get there, to have all those rings, it was a magical career that people can only dream about. It became a reality for me and I feel very grateful and very proud of that."

Cashman may have viewed Williams as a member of the "Fab Five," but history will always remember Jeter, Rivera, Pettitte, and Posada as the "Core Four." Posada called Williams "the key" to the quartet ever getting the chance to shine with the Yankees, noting that prior to Williams, young players had typically been traded before they could ever establish themselves.

"If he didn't pan out, I don't think the Jeters, the Posadas, the Pettittes, and Mariano Riveras would have been there," Posada told the YES Network in 2020. "We would have been gone."

Even after putting together a legendary career in pinstripes, Williams still marvels at the fact that it happened at all.

"For whatever reason, I stayed under the radar. I survived all the attempts for trades and releases, being sent to the minors," Williams said. "The fact that I stayed in the Yankee organization for as long as I did, I consider it nothing short of a miracle."

Williams' biggest fans might feel snubbed that their hero isn't recognized in the same manner as his "Core Four" teammates, but No. 51 isn't bothered by the omission.

"I was never really resentful of that, because I always noticed that every time they would talk about the Core Four, they always mentioned my name as an outsider; that meant I was always mentioned," Williams said.

"I have a memory bank filled of all these great moments; to me, to be mad or sad or feel anything other than positive about this thing is just a waste of time.

"For me to have the opportunity to have the success in the same organization that I signed with as a minor league player and go all the way through, get to the big leagues and have your whole career with that team as an instrumental part in their success, I couldn't ask for anything more."

11

Simply the Best

FROM BARSTOOLS TO SOCIAL MEDIA TO CABLE TELEVISION, sports present an opportunity for a debate on virtually any topic. MJ or LeBron? Montana or Brady? Koufax or Gibson?

You could sit here and come up with hundreds, possibly thousands, of similar questions. If the question "Who is the best closer in baseball history?" arises, however, there isn't any debate to be had.

Mariano Rivera. That's the answer. Don't try to argue.

How good was Rivera? One word tells his entire story: unanimous.

"The one unanimous Hall of Famer that we have," said Jim Leyritz, a former teammate of Rivera's.

The right-hander's 652 career saves are the most in history, while his postseason record—42 saves in 47 opportunities, a minuscule 0.70 ERA, and five World Series rings—elevated him to a legendary level.

"You can't win a game unless you can end a game," said Joe Torre, who managed Rivera from 1996 to 2007. "You can't freeze the ball in our game, so you better have somebody who can get those outs."

Unlike some phenoms who catch the eye of scouts at an early age and have great expectations thrust upon them as teenagers, Rivera never even imagined a career in professional baseball while growing up in Panama.

Rivera dreamed of becoming the next Pelé, though a career as a mechanic or a police officer seemed far more realistic. As a teenager, he had caught the eye of a local scout while playing shortstop, so Yankees international scouting director Herb Raybourn took a look at Rivera the next time he was in Panama. Rivera had good hands and solid range, but his bat was suspect, causing the Yankees to pass on him.

A year later, Raybourn saw Rivera for a second time, only this time he was pitching. Rivera was unaware he was even being scouted, but it took no more than 20 pitches for Raybourn to know he wanted to sign him. Rivera signed for a $2,000 bonus.

Elbow surgery in 1992 sidelined Rivera, keeping either of that year's expansion teams—the Colorado Rockies and Florida Marlins—from selecting him in the expansion draft.

By 1995, Rivera was called up to the majors for the first time, making his debut on May 23. Rivera made four starts before being sent back to the minors on June 11, though at least he had company; his teammate, shortstop Derek Jeter, was also being sent back to Triple A.

"We were devastated; we were almost in tears," Rivera said. "I remember sitting in Bennigan's in Englewood, New Jersey, right by the hotel that we were staying at. The feeling that we were feeling that day, we didn't want to feel that again, ever. We pushed ourselves. We said, 'We're coming back and we were going to come back for good.'"

Rivera did return in 1995, starting six more games while also working out of the bullpen. When the Yankees reached the postseason—their first time there since 1981—Rivera found himself on the AL Division Series roster, though nobody knew that he would prove to be New York's breakout performer against the Seattle Mariners.

He threw 3⅓ scoreless innings in Game 2, setting the stage for Leyritz's 15th-inning heroics. Rivera retired all four batters he faced in Game 3, then got two outs in Game 5 without allowing a run, giving him 5⅓ scoreless innings in the series.

The Yankees lost in the decisive fifth game, but they had discovered something in the process: Rivera was really, really good.

"We didn't know who he was," said Tino Martinez, the Mariners' first baseman who would join the Yankees in 1996. "The scouting report was that he throws a lot of fastballs. When they took him out, we were like, 'Thank God they took that guy out.' He had good stuff, but nobody at that time knew that he would be what he became."

Not even the Yankees knew that. Rivera opened the 1996 season pitching in middle relief, but it didn't take too long for Torre—who had taken over for Buck Showalter after the 1995 season—to realize the type of weapon the right-hander could be.

"We're all talking in the dugout like, 'Who is this guy? Why is he pitching in middle relief?'" said Jason Giambi, who played for the Oakland Athletics that season. "He was unbelievable. Then you see him become a setup man and he got even better."

Rivera became one of the best relief pitchers in the game, though he wasn't even pitching in the closer's role. Torre routinely deployed him to pitch the seventh and eighth innings, then held his breath as John Wetteland pitched the ninth.

"He started off as just kind of a low-leverage guy and he just soared," catcher Joe Girardi said. "It got to the point where it was just, 'Get Mo in here and it's lights out.' He was so dominant."

The Yankees won the World Series that fall, while Rivera— who posted a 2.09 ERA and 130 strikeouts in 107⅔ innings— finished third in the American League Cy Young Award vote, a rarity for a setup man.

"It was the best I've ever seen," Martinez said. "It was almost like Little League; we would play five or six innings, and once we had the lead, the game was over. He was lights out; it wasn't five out of 10 times that he did well; it was every single outing, just 1-2-3, 1-2-3. We knew after five or six innings of the game, we were going to win; that never happens in baseball with any other pitcher. That's how dominant he was."

Torre handed him the closer job in 1997 after Wetteland departed as a free agent, though Rivera experienced some bumps during his first two months in the role.

Then came that fateful June day in Detroit, when a simple game of catch with Ramiro Mendoza changed the course of Rivera's career, the Yankees franchise, and all of baseball history.

Rivera unleashed a throw to Mendoza, who was caught off guard by the ball's sharp movement. Mendoza told Rivera to stop playing around, only Rivera wasn't playing.

Rivera was throwing the way he always had, but the ball wouldn't stay straight. A few more throws were enough for Mendoza, who walked away out of a fear of getting hurt.

Rivera had been gripping his fastball the same way since he first learned to pitch as a child, yet suddenly it was behaving like an entirely different pitch. The same thing happened when he threw to bullpen catcher Mike Borzello that night, so they called in pitching coach Mel Stottlemyre. The grip was the same. The mechanics were the same. The results were noticeably different.

"I was petrified," Rivera said. "Closers have to know exactly where the ball is going; where you're throwing the pitch, what the ball is doing, and be in control of that. I wasn't in control of that. I had no control of the pitch."

Rivera, Stottlemyre, and Borzello went out to the bullpen early the next day, trying to solve the riddle that had been presented to them. Movement on a fastball is usually a positive, but Rivera—a pitcher with immaculate command—had no idea where the ball was going when it left his hand. No matter what Stottlemyre suggested, the ball moved in ways it never had before.

Rivera has called the cutter his "gift from God," and while he has never been able to explain how or why it suddenly appeared, he has never questioned it.

"It was because I just became the New York Yankees closer; I needed something special for me to be successful," said Rivera, whose faith has always been an integral part of his life. "The Lord wanted to give me a platform that no man can give me. That's why he gave me that pitch. I learned how to use it to be effective, and to bring glory to His name. That's the reason why he gave me that pitch."

Rivera's cutter immediately baffled professional hitters, vaulting the right-hander into the upper echelon of closers. Even when teams had video to study, the pitch exploded on hitters in a way they had rarely seen before.

Once Rivera learned how to command his new gift, he became as unhittable as any pitcher in the game.

"That pitch made big leaguers look like they never played the game of baseball," Rivera said. "When they were swinging at that pitch, it looked like they didn't know what they were doing."

Hitters through the years would echo that sentiment.

"As helpless a feeling as a professional baseball player that I've ever had," said Mark Teixeira, who was 1-for-9 in his career against Rivera before becoming his teammate in 2009. "It almost takes a miracle for a left-handed hitter to square up Mariano Rivera. As a lefty, that ball is cutting so late, my mind is not programmed as a hitter to adjust to a late cutter like that. It's like, 'system error' if you try to punch it into your computer. I was like, 'I've got no shot here; I just hope I don't strike out.'

"So many fans ask me who was the toughest pitcher I ever faced, and it's always a super easy answer: Mariano Rivera. I like to joke that that's why I signed with the Yankees, so I wouldn't have to face him anymore."

Like Teixeira, Nick Swisher had the misfortune of facing Rivera before joining the Yankees. Swisher was 1-for-5 against the closer, calling his cutter "an illusion" for a hitter awaiting the pitch.

"I don't want to say he's like a magician, but when you're hitting, it's impossible for your eyes to make contact bat-to-ball at those speeds," Swisher said. "What you're doing is noticing where the ball is coming out of the pitcher's hand, and in your mind, you're trying to get your barrel to that point before the baseball does.

"With Mo, when the ball comes out of his hand, unlike a lot of other pitchers who may be throwing two-seam pitches, four-seam fastballs come at you looking like a cue ball in a game of pool. There's no seams on it; you don't see anything, so you're taught that when you see no seams, that ball is moving straight. Mariano had the amazing ability of creating that same visual to the hitter as a four-seam spin, but it would move.

"So in your mind, you think the ball is on the inside third of the plate, but what's really happening is that ball is about four inches deeper into your hands as a left-handed hitter than what your eye is telling you. That's what made it so difficult; in your mind, it should be in one spot, but he has the ability to manipulate the baseball so much to move it to put it in another spot. Every single pitch I stepped to the plate, he threw me a cutter and I still couldn't be consistent enough to put the barrel on it. That's unbelievable. It's inexplicable."

Opposing hitters weren't the only ones that had to stay on their toes when Rivera was on the mound. His catchers also knew what pitch was coming, but given the explosive nature of his pitch, receiving the cutter took an incredible amount of concentration.

"You had to remind yourself not to relax, because if you did, that that cutter would be by you," said John Flaherty, who caught Rivera from 2003 to '05. "I've never caught a guy whose mechanics were so easy and smooth; he lulled you to sleep as a hitter, but he could lull you to sleep as a catcher, too. He would usually pepper your glove wherever you put it, so I always kind of told myself, 'Don't relax too much here, because he can make that happen.' He was the easiest guy to catch as far as pitch selection; cutter in, cutter away, and the occasional sinker. He was incredibly under control and confident out on the mound."

Rivera was as sure a thing as there was in baseball. Yes, he would blow a save from time to time, but every time it happened, neither the Yankees nor their opponent could believe what had just taken place.

"He was a security blanket," said Girardi, who caught Rivera from 1996 to '99, then managed him from 2008 to '13. "Every baby has that one blanket; that was Mo. I could sit and watch and 99 percent of time, it was going to turn out really good."

Rivera's cutter ranks among the most impressive pitches in baseball history, yet his greatness was the result of more than his unhittable weapon. As talented as he was physically, it was his ability to put the past behind him that separated him from virtually every other closer in history.

Every time he came to the ballpark, it was impossible to tell whether he had breezed through the ninth inning the night before or suffered a gut-wrenching blown save. Teammates would marvel at his consistent demeanor, especially in the aftermath of a devastating defeat.

"The biggest thing that he taught me, after I would blow a game or something like that, he would come over to me in the clubhouse and say, 'It's over. It's done. Get rid of it,'" said right-hander Tanyon Sturtze, who shared a bullpen with Rivera from 2004 to '06. "If it was a really bad loss, maybe he would wait until the next day when we were playing catch and say, 'OK, what did you learn? Now it's done. We can't change it, we're not going to get that ball back and throw that pitch again. It's about today. We have to win today.' Having that mentality was so important, especially becoming a reliever after so many years as a starter."

The Yankees won three straight World Series titles from 1998 to 2000 with Rivera as the closer, then reached the Fall Classic again in both 2001 and 2003. Even when he blew the save in Game 7 of the 2001 World Series, he came back the next season and was as good as ever. Ditto after 2004, when he blew two saves against the Red Sox in the AL Championship Series, helping Boston end its 86-year curse in stunning fashion.

"He respected his opponents, and on the rare occasion that somebody bested him, it was like, 'OK, I'll get you tomorrow,'" general manager Brian Cashman said. "He understood the deal; this is a competition, and you can't win them all. You wish everybody had that type of makeup."

As he reached an age when most players begin to face the harsh reality that they aren't what they once were, Rivera somehow seemed to get better.

"To have a closer last as long as he did and never change the kind of pitcher he was, that's unusual," Torre said. "Sometimes guys will say, 'I'll add a splitter' or whatever, but he stayed the same guy as far as stuff. Pitchers usually need to make adjustments because they lose a little something along the way, but he never did."

In the four seasons between the ages of 38 and 41, Rivera posted a 1.71 ERA, keeping that mark below 2.00 each season. He helped lead the Yankees to the 2009 World Series title—his fifth championship—at the age of 39, saving five of New York's 11 postseason victories while allowing one run in 16 innings.

"We had had a lot of years in between championships," said Andy Pettitte, a fellow member of the Yankees' "Core Four" group. "We were all older; we were all up in our late thirties at the time. A lot of people were saying we'd never be able to win another championship with the group of guys that we had, and so to be able to do it again in '09, for me, and I think for the older guys there for sure, it was as special as our first one was."

Rivera had planned to retire at the end of the 2012 season, but he suffered a torn ACL while shagging fly balls in early May, prompting him to return in 2013.

"Me and Alex [Rodriguez] were standing next to each other and Alex saw it happen," Teixeira said. "He screamed out an expletive, grabbed me, and just said, 'Mo! Mo!' The entire field stopped. It was a super sad and almost surreal day for the team, but nobody doubted that Mo would come back just as good as ever. He said, 'I'll be fine.'"

Rivera was more than "fine," saving 44 games while posting a 2.11 ERA in his age-43 season. The only disappointment for Rivera in his final year was that the Yankees didn't qualify for the postseason, though the certainty that the season was ending in late September allowed Girardi to script a memorable conclusion to the closer's career.

September 26 was to be the final game at Yankee Stadium that season, as New York—which had been officially eliminated from wild card contention the previous night—would play its final series in Houston. The Yankees trailed the Tampa Bay Rays 4–0 in the eighth inning, though the score was a mere footnote.

With runners at first and second, Girardi called on Rivera, who made quick work of Delmon Young and Sam Fuld, stranding the two runners on base the way he had done for nearly two decades.

As the Yankees came to bat in the bottom of the inning, Rivera returned to the clubhouse to cool down, knowing he was heading back to the mound for the ninth. That's when it hit him.

"I was sitting in the training room and these scenes crossed my mind like a picture, like a movie from 1990 when I left Panama to all the processes that I went through to that point," Rivera said. "It was amazing."

Rivera came back for the ninth, retiring Jose Lobaton on a ground ball and Yunel Escobar on a pop fly to second base.

"I said, 'Man, this is it,' 'Rivera said. "We were out of the playoffs. This is it. This is the last time that I will pitch here at Yankee Stadium. Now, I'm all messed up; my heart, my mind, my body, everything was messed up. Everything was crumbling."

Rivera didn't notice right-hander Matt Daley warming up in the bullpen, or he might have telegraphed what was coming next. The Yankees were making a pitching change, only it wasn't Girardi making the walk out from the dugout: it was Jeter and Pettitte.

Pettitte signaled to the bullpen for a new pitcher to come into the game, bringing a smile to Rivera's face. Rivera handed Pettitte the ball and embraced his longtime teammate and friend, breaking down and crying uncontrollably on Pettitte's shoulder. Pettitte kissed Rivera on the head, then Jeter hugged Rivera, who was still sobbing. Rivera wiped the tears from his eyes and began to walk off the field, tipping his hat to the sellout crowd.

Girardi and his coaches met Rivera at the front of the dugout for more hugs, while the crowd chanted "Mariano" during a four-minute standing ovation. One by one, Rivera's teammates walked to him for hugs of their own; as emotionally drained as Rivera was, he soaked it all in, aware he would never again experience anything like this.

"That moment was the icing on the cake," Rivera said. "That moment was the moment in my career as a baseball player. Having my two brothers standing with me on the mound and closing my career, that was special. That was special. Even if I could write it, it could never be that good, the way it happened."

Rivera retired with more saves than anybody in the history of the game, but the respect of his teammates and opponents alike meant more to him than any statistic ever could. In 2019, he became the first player to be elected unanimously to the Baseball Hall of Fame, a feat not even Jeter could match the following year, falling one vote shy.

Three Yankees relievers were selected to represent the AL All-Star team in the first five years after Rivera's retirement, but even with some of the league's best relief arms, New York quickly realized that nobody dominated as consistently as Rivera had.

"It was just incredible what he did and what he accomplished; it was almost a guarantee," Hal Steinbrenner said. "It didn't always turn out that way, but it usually did. Once he retired, it opened our eyes again as to what the ninth inning of a game is normally like for most teams. That's not a knock on any of the closers we have had since him, but it's a tough damn job that he made look ridiculously easy."

PART 3

THE CAPTAINS

Leading by Example

Four years before he retired from baseball and delivered one of the most emotional speeches in sports history, Lou Gehrig finally stepped out of Babe Ruth's sizeable shadow.

The Iron Horse was named captain of the Yankees on April 12, 1935, filling a role Ruth had been stripped of following a very brief tenure in 1922. Everett Scott stepped in as captain during the 1922 and 1923 World Series, but Gehrig became the first full-time pinstriped captain in more than a decade.

"A diamond hero in his own right, Gehrig experienced what amounted to obscurity in the glare of the popularity that clung to Ruth," James P. Dawson wrote in the *New York Times*. "In his appointment as captain is seen a move at last to popularize the player who has been practically unnoticed through the ten years that Ruth reigned."

It had been widely expected that once Ruth was no longer with the Yankees, Gehrig would assume captain's duties. When

Ruth departed for the Boston Braves prior to the 1935 season, that's precisely what happened.

"Ruth being the bigger star probably made the choice of Gehrig difficult for all those gap years," said Marty Appel, author of *Pinstripe Empire*. "How can you name Lou Gehrig when Babe Ruth is on the team? Of course, Babe wasn't exactly a leader by example; he went out and played his own game. Gehrig certainly showed year after year that he was, in fact, a role model and a leader on the field, and being a first baseman, he was more into the action than Babe was daydreaming in the outfield."

The role of captain had changed over the years; according to the Yankees, the club had seven captains between 1903 and 1921, as baseball's rules required teams to designate an active, uniformed player as captain to perform the tasks of a modern-day manager, such as changing pitchers, positioning fielders, and arguing with umpires. By the mid-1910s, managers had assumed many of those duties, rendering the role of captain largely ceremonial.

"Gehrig just had that embodiment of strong, silent leadership," Appel said. "Once the position evolved to the guy they would all follow, Gehrig was an obvious choice. Part of it was physical; athletes always respect big, strong guys. You look at those newsreels of Gehrig without his uniform shirt on, he was Tarzan. He was a remarkable physical specimen. Unlike Miller Huggins, players gravitated toward a figure like that."

Gehrig captained the Yankees to three straight World Series titles from 1936 to 1938, but as his body began to break down from amyotrophic lateral sclerosis—the disease that would later be named for him—the first baseman displayed a noble act of leadership by removing himself from the lineup on May 2, 1939, bringing his record streak of 2,130 consecutive games to an end.

"I haven't been a bit of good to the team since the season started," Gehrig told reporters. "It would not be fair to the boys, to Joe [McCarthy], or to the baseball public for me to try going on. In fact, it would not be fair to myself, and I'm the last consideration."

13

The Fallen Captain

FOR ALL THE LEGENDARY FIGURES THAT DONNED PINSTRIPES from 1939 to '75, none had ever been named to succeed Lou Gehrig as the next Yankees captain.

In 1976, that all changed.

George Steinbrenner learned in early March that his two-year suspension from baseball—which followed a guilty plea for making illegal contributions to political campaigns, including that of former President Richard M. Nixon—had been reduced to 15 months, allowing the Yankees' owner to return to the game.

The Boss quickly gathered his complete senior staff for a meeting at the Carlyle Hotel, wanting to make sure he was up to speed with everything happening within the organization. Manager Billy Martin was going through the Yankees roster when Steinbrenner stopped him.

"Steinbrenner said, 'Billy, this is up to you, this is your call, and sometimes these things are good and sometimes they don't work out, but I think we should have a captain on this team,'" said Marty Appel, who was in the meeting as the team's director of public relations, later authoring *Munson: The Life and Death of a Yankee Captain.* "I think we know who we're talking about, and it should be Munson, but it's your call entirely.' Billy said, 'Well George, we never had a captain in my time, and we won a lot of pennants.'"

That's when Appel chimed in with a bit of a history lesson for Steinbrenner.

"I sheepishly raised my hand and said, 'Well, I think it ought to be mentioned that when Lou Gehrig died in 1941, Joe McCarthy said the position of captain will die with Lou; that there will never be another Yankee captain.' Nobody in the room knew this."

Steinbrenner, always a quick thinker, replied, "Well, if Joe McCarthy knew Thurman Munson, he would know this was the right guy and this was the right time."

"I'm thinking to myself, 'Brilliant,'" Appel said. "This is why he owns the team."

Martin was charged with the task of informing Munson of his new role, one that hadn't been filled during the lifetime of any player on the Yankees roster. When asked why neither he, Joe DiMaggio, Mickey Mantle, Whitey Ford, Phil Rizzuto, nor any of his other Hall of Fame teammates had ever been granted the captaincy, Yogi Berra once replied, "We were all captains."

Those Yankees were also always winning, capturing 19 American League pennants and 13 World Series championships in the first 25 years following Gehrig's retirement in the middle of the 1939 season.

By 1976, the Yankees were going on their 12th year without a trip to the World Series, and given the introduction of divisional play in 1969, getting to the Fall Classic was a more arduous process than simply winning the most games in the AL.

Steinbrenner believed the Yankees needed a leader. And he believed Munson was that man.

"Thurman was kind of reluctant at first; he thought it would mean bringing the lineups out every day and maybe even wearing a 'C' on his uniform, so he didn't have any interest in that sort of stuff," Appel said. "He was assured, 'No, it's sort of just like you've always been; you lead by example. This time you're just going to have the title.'

"Given how hard he played, his teammates were just embarrassed to play any less than he did, with grit and toughness. That was on display every day because the position he played required that kind of grit and toughness. He was the de facto captain even before he was officially named."

Already a four-time All-Star, Munson had become a fan favorite with his gritty style of play, one that had landed him in a brawl with Boston's Carlton Fisk a few years earlier. The Yankees of the mid-1970s had a certain brashness, and Munson was the personification of that edge.

"He was one of those old-school guys," Bucky Dent said. "One of the fiercest competitors I ever played with."

"He has just the right cockiness," Martin told reporters after naming Munson captain. "He's a born leader."

Munson's tough-guy persona wasn't reserved for opponents; he was just as hard on his own teammates, demanding excellence while doing his best to keep things light during the grind of the long season.

"He had a little sarcasm," Dent said. "You would be standing around the cage and you might be struggling a bit; he would walk up to you, look at you, and say, 'Are you trying?' It was his way of trying to loosen you up—then he would just turn around and walk away. He was a great teammate, he played hurt; he was just one of those grizzly guys that loved to play the game."

Willie Randolph, a rookie with the Yankees the year Munson was named captain, would constantly marvel at the catcher's ability to play through pain.

"You hear this cliché all the time, but Thurman led by example; he got beat up a lot, man," Randolph said. "He was an old-school, grumpy catcher. He played every day, he got hit in the knees, got hit by foul balls, he collided with guys all the time. He was just one of those guys where, if you were on his team, unless you had a broken bone, you were playing.

"All he would do is give you that look. He had that gruff, stern personality; he wasn't warm and fuzzy. But if he saw you as a gamer, as someone who played every day like he did, he would give you the shirt off his back. He taught me a lot about toughness."

Those lessons were accompanied by a modicum of fear. No matter how banged up Randolph's body was, the rookie was careful never to let Munson see him getting work done in the trainer's room.

"I would never, ever let him catch me on the training table, even if I was just getting a hamstring rub or something," Randolph said. "If Thurman walked into the room, I would jump off the table, because he would give me that look and say, 'What is this? You're 21 years old! What the fuck are you doing on the table?' I never wanted to disappoint him."

Despite Randolph's fear of being scolded, Munson was not a particularly vocal leader inside the Yankees clubhouse. Like some who would follow in his footsteps—Don Mattingly and Derek Jeter come to mind—Munson was more of a lead-by-example captain than one likely to deliver a pregame speech in order to rally the troops.

"There were too many strong personalities on that team, so it was sort of unnecessary for Thurman to do that," Appel said. "I don't think those guys required that. It was kind of self-disciplined."

Munson's approach to dealing with the New York media was something teammates watched closely. He wasn't outwardly hostile toward the press, but he was far from cooperative.

"The other players looked at him and would see how he would be tough on all of us," said longtime *New York Daily News* baseball scribe Bill Madden. "I think that was another reason why they admired him, because he really didn't take shit from anybody. He was his own man.

"George was afraid of Munson and the players saw that. He would rip players in the paper regularly, but he never touched Munson. Munson was the third rail; you didn't touch him."

Munson won the American League Most Valuable Player award in 1976, while the Yankees returned to the World Series for the first time since 1964. The Bombers were swept by the Cincinnati Reds in the Fall Classic, but that experience served the Yankees well in the ensuing years.

It was Munson who urged Steinbrenner to sign Reggie Jackson as a free agent after the 1976 season, telling the owner, "Go out and get the big man. He can carry a team like nobody else." Once Jackson had signed, however, Munson took a disliking to the slugger's attitude, especially after his legendary June 1977 *Sport Magazine* interview in which he claimed he, not Munson, was "the straw that stirs the drink."

Jackson later sent backup catcher Fran Healy to suggest to Munson that he had been misquoted. The captain fired back, "For four fucking pages?"

Differences aside, Munson and Jackson were key contributors for the Yankees in 1977 and 1978, as New York won back-to-back World Series titles, their first championships since 1962.

Munson joined Johnny Bench as the only catchers in history to win a Rookie of the Year award, an MVP, a Gold Glove, and a World Series title during their career. (Buster Posey of the San Francisco Giants would later join that exclusive list, which now consists of those three backstops.) He was making his presence felt in every way possible, both on and off the field.

"He was more of a behind-the-scenes type leader; that was a team that controlled themselves and governed themselves," Madden said. "[Lou] Piniella might call a clubhouse meeting sometimes, but in that clubhouse, Thurman was the guy. Contrary to what Reggie said, Thurman did stir the drink."

Jackson and Munson eventually mended fences, learning to appreciate each other as teammates.

"We talked about it over a beer a few times," Jackson told the *New York Times*. "We got it settled. And hitting in front and behind each other, hitting when it counted, we grew to respect each other."

Munson's widow, Diana, told *Yankees Magazine* in 2019 that after the 1978 World Series was over, Munson made a special request to Steinbrenner. He didn't want a World Series ring; he wanted a World Series trophy.

"George sent him the trophy," Diana told the magazine. "And it wasn't the little one that kids have. It was the real deal. And it said, 'Thurman Munson, Captain of the New York Yankees.' That was a moment. He broke down. It all came forward for him. All of the hard work, all of the naysayers, all of the people that didn't think he could do it."

Munson and the Yankees were experiencing a championship hangover of sorts in 1979, entering August trailing the first-place Baltimore Orioles by 14 games despite a respectable 57–48 record. Following a win over the Chicago White Sox at Comiskey Park on August 1, Munson flew himself home to Canton, Ohio, for the Yankees' off day.

The Yankees had been dreaming of a late-season comeback similar to the one they had pulled off the prior season against the Red Sox. New York won three straight games entering that off day, giving them eight victories in their past 12 games. Little did they know when they left Chicago that their season—and their lives—would never be the same again.

"You kind of thought that they were going to be able to pull another '78; they were starting to play well," Madden said. "Thurman, [Bobby] Murcer, and Piniella were staying at Murcer's house in Chicago that weekend. They stayed up all night drinking after the Sunday game, and they all had this meeting of the minds that they thought they could pull off another '78.

Munson had taken up flying for the sole purpose of commuting home to see his family on days off, but piloting had become something of an obsession for the 32-year-old. He spent the late afternoon hours of his off day practicing take-offs and landings at the Akron-Canton Airport, but his third landing went awry, causing his Cessna Citation to crash short of the runway.

Munson's neck was broken in the crash, and while his two passengers were able to escape the plane, he was not. Munson died in the accident, sending shockwaves throughout the baseball world. Nowhere did his death have a bigger impact than inside the Yankees clubhouse, where teammates were forced to deal with the harsh reality of his loss.

"When I heard the news, I just fell to my knees," Randolph said. "It hit me like a ton of bricks; you don't believe it. It was like, 'I was just with him yesterday; he can't be gone. That can't be true.' You just didn't believe what you were hearing."

Dent was finishing an early dinner at Windows on the World, a renowned restaurant atop 1 World Trade Center, that evening. When he finished, a car attendant broke the news to him that Munson had perished in a plane crash.

"My knees buckled, and I started crying," Dent said. "It was probably the most difficult thing that I've ever had to deal with, trying to play after losing a teammate like that who was so much a part of your club."

The Yankees chose to play their scheduled game on August 3, as his widow, Diana, had told Murcer that was what Munson would have wanted his team to do.

A photo of Munson adorned the outfield scoreboard, alternating with words written by Steinbrenner himself:

OUR CAPTAIN AND LEADER HAS NOT LEFT US—TODAY, TOMORROW, THIS YEAR, NEXT...OUR ENDEAVORS WILL REFLECT OUR LOVE AND ADMIRATION FOR HIM.

The Yankees took the field as Terence Cardinal Cooke delivered a prayer, then Robert Merrill sang "America the Beautiful." Eight players stood at their positions, but the area behind home plate remained empty, a nod to Munson.

"The shock of it all, you can equate it to the unthinkable—losing a child," Appel said. "Could you imagine anything worse than that? That was the feeling in the clubhouse; they had lost a blood brother. It wasn't just a teammate, and it wasn't just somebody they respected; it was somebody who was really family to them. It was like losing someone in your family."

Everybody on the field that Friday night—the eight players standing at their positions, both teams standing at the top of their dugout steps, even the umpires—remained frozen, as if somebody had hit the pause button on a VCR. The crowd of 51,151 stood on its feet and cheered in memory of the fallen captain for eight minutes, while those who knew Munson best wiped away tears with the sleeves of their pinstriped jerseys.

"I will never forget the scene when they're playing the national anthem, and George had ordered home plate to be empty," Madden said. "It was just an eerie scene; they're all standing at their positions with their heads bowed. Reggie was sobbing, Piniella was crying. From then on, it was just an emptiness in that clubhouse. You could just feel it was not the same, and everybody knew it would never be the same."

"Reggie was probably crushed as much as anybody when Thurman passed," Randolph said. "Everyone thought they didn't like each other, but they got along. They didn't hang out, but there was a mutual respect for each other. Reggie was as torn up as anybody when Thurman passed; he was crying like a baby in the outfield when we had the moment of silence."

Public address announcer Bob Sheppard thanked the crowd for its "wonderful response," then Jerry Narron made the walk from the dugout to the plate, where he squatted down in the dirt that Munson and his achy knees had called home for the past decade.

"It was a long, stressful day," Dent said. "We all wanted to play, but it was weird because when we ran out on the field, they left home plate empty. You kept looking back there thinking, 'Where is he? Come on, let's go; run out there.' It was just a really difficult, difficult night to play."

But they played, then did the same on Saturday and Sunday. Munson's funeral was Monday, so Steinbrenner chartered a plane and flew the entire team to Canton for the service. Piniella and Murcer were among those to deliver eulogies.

"Whatever he was to each one of us, he should be remembered a man who followed the basic principles of life," Murcer said. "He lived with his wife, Diana, and his three children; he led his team to two world championships; and he loved the game, his friends, and, most of all, his family."

Steinbrenner had said the Yankees would forfeit that night's game if they didn't make it back to the Bronx in time, but they did. Some players would have preferred not to play, but just as they had three days earlier, the Yankees followed the words of Diana. This is what Thurman would have wanted.

"To this day, I don't see how we got through that," Randolph said. "We played that same day, and we were literally on fumes."

The Yankees trailed 4–0 at the seventh-inning stretch, but Murcer pulled New York back into the game with a three-run home run against right-hander Dennis Martinez in the bottom of the seventh. Still behind by a run in the ninth, Dent led off the inning with a walk, then Randolph laid down a sacrifice bunt, only to see left-hander Tippy Martinez throw the ball away, allowing the runners to reach second and third with nobody out.

Murcer stepped to the plate and lined a hit to left field, scoring both Dent and Randolph for the winning runs.

"Everybody was so tired," Murcer told reporters after the game. "I think we were playing on the spirit of Thurman. I think that's what carried us through the game. I know it did me."

"Really emotional," Dent said. "It was a big night for Bobby Murcer, because they were really good friends and he had a big game that night. It was a really uplifting night for him."

The Yankees had pulled off a miraculous comeback, and although the game meant little in the standings, it meant everything to Munson's teammates.

"I remember when I got to home plate, we all just kind of collapsed in each other's arms; it was a big hug pile," Randolph said. "We were carrying each other to the dugout, we were so exhausted. It was a fitting tribute to our fallen captain; Thurman would have wanted us to play."

"I think that was something that Thurman would have enjoyed," said Ron Guidry, who pitched a complete game that night. "He would not have wanted us to just lay down and not play like we were supposed to."

The emotions that carried the Yankees through that weekend would remain with them for quite some time, but unlike the previous year, when they overcame a 14-game deficit to chase down the Red Sox, there would be no comeback that season.

"It took us a good year and a half to get over that," Randolph said. "I had never, ever experienced a teammate passing, especially when it's someone close to you like that. We were just shocked; we were literally in shock for a good year or so. There was just a malaise in the clubhouse for a very long time."

The contents of Munson's locker were cleaned out and sent to his family, but the locker remained untouched for the next 30 years. When the Yankees moved into their new ballpark on the other side of 161st Street, Munson's original locker was moved with it and placed in a museum inside the new Stadium. Munson's No. 15 was also retired, and a plaque was posted in Monument Park in his honor.

"It was a great tribute to him, but it was sad; every time I would walk by it, he would pop in my mind," Randolph said. "It was so hurtful to be reminded of a great player who, if he had stayed with us, I think would have been a Hall of Famer."

AN IMPOSSIBLE TASK

When Lou Gehrig stepped away from baseball in 1939, the Yankees didn't name another captain for 37 years, finally tabbing Thurman Munson for the role in 1976.

So when Munson died in a tragic plane crash in August 1979, nobody knew whether the Yankees would name a replacement. Two and a half years later, the Yankees answered that question, choosing third baseman Graig Nettles as the team's new captain only weeks before spring training was set to commence.

"I have no idea what a captain does," Nettles admitted at a luncheon announcing his new role. "But it's a great honor, and I hope I can uphold the tradition. Maybe I can help as a liaison between players with problems and the manager or front office."

"There was nobody who could step into that role after Thurman," said Marty Appel, a former Yankees public relations director and author of *Pinstripe Empire*. "I think Nettles handled it well. I don't think anybody felt it was too soon."

Nettles, who was acquired in a trade with Cleveland in 1972, was entering his 10th season in pinstripes when he was chosen to succeed Munson, making him only the third Yankees captain in 43 years.

"Both of them were kind of in the same mold; they were tough, hard-nosed players," Bucky Dent said. "Gritty players with a sarcastic way about them. If I was picking someone to be captain after Thurman, Nettles would have been the guy."

"We didn't think George would ever name another captain again," longtime *New York Daily News* baseball writer Bill Madden said. "But George was always looking for things that would get a lot of press. Nettles was coming to the end of his career, but he was the natural guy. He was the last of the old guard."

The 37-year-old third baseman had a sarcastic way about him and had his issues dealing with the press. Then again, Munson hadn't exactly been a media darling, so perhaps Nettles was a natural to assume the role left vacant by his good friend's passing.

"The edict for Gehrig had not only been broken, but it had been broken successfully," Appel said. "Munson had proven a value as captain, winning MVP and leading the Yankees to the World Series for the first time in 12 years the year he became captain. That might have happened even if he hadn't been named captain, but still it was a good exclamation point to the season and to his being named captain. George always had in mind that it turned out to be a good thing, so let's keep it going as deemed appropriate. I didn't think Nettles was much of a captain, but I guess he was the right guy at that right time."

Nettles was one of the few players Steinbrenner typically avoided bashing through the press; the owner respected his fearless nature, which raised Nettles' stature within his own clubhouse.

"Nettles and Thurman were really close; they were always hanging out together," Willie Randolph said. "Nettles had seniority, and in a lot of ways, he was like Thurman. He didn't say much, he didn't talk much in meetings, he never stood up and said much, but he was smart and he was in tune with what was happening in the clubhouse. He was a total lead-by-example guy."

Dave Winfield had been with the Yankees for one year at the time Nettles was named captain, a move he said "didn't really make a difference" inside the clubhouse. Winfield hadn't been around during the Munson years, but he understood that Nettles' link to the previous captain and the Yankees' 1977–78 championship teams made him an obvious choice.

"He had a connection to the previous culture of winning and people who have been around," Winfield said. "He wasn't the most talkative or collaborative; he just did his thing at third base. Having him as captain didn't really change anything. Management just appointed captains as they saw fit."

Nettles "had a different kind of personality," according to Randolph, though for those that didn't know him well, that might not have been viewed in a positive light.

"He had a good sense of humor, but if you didn't know Graig, you probably didn't like him too much," Randolph said. "He had a quick wit, but it could be biting and edgy. Once you knew him and his humor, you were cool with him. He had everyone's respect."

Nettles' captaincy lasted only two seasons, as the third baseman was traded to the San Diego Padres days before the 1984 season was set to begin.

14

Double Duty

Two and a half years after Thurman Munson died tragically in a plane crash, George Steinbrenner felt the time was right to name a new captain.

His choice was third baseman Graig Nettles, who had been with the club for a decade and was a respected veteran inside the clubhouse. Willie Randolph had been under consideration, but the 27-year-old was passed over for his 37-year-old teammate, one of Munson's closest friends on the team at the time of his death.

Randolph didn't take The Boss' decision as a slight. He had been the Yankees' second baseman for six years, and although he was younger than many of his teammates, he knew that he had grown into a role as one of the team's leaders thanks to his hard work and determined style of play.

He had also been a favorite of Billy Martin during his first four years in pinstripes, earning Randolph the trust of his manager at an age when most players of that era would keep quiet and try to blend into the background.

"He treated me like the unofficial captain by giving me a lot of responsibility," Randolph said. "Even amongst a lot of veteran guys, he treated me as one of the leaders, a guy that players looked to."

A smooth-fielding second baseman with a knack for getting on base, Randolph didn't post big power numbers for those late-1970s teams. But his superb defensive skills and sound approach at the plate helped him make the American League All-Star team in each of his first two seasons with the Yankees, who acquired him in a December 1975 trade with the Pirates.

Randolph was intense as a young player, but he internalized things, doing his best on most days to be seen and not heard. He was the Yankees' starting second baseman at the age of 21, but with a number of established veterans on the roster, Randolph spent the early months of the 1976 season getting a feel for the landscape.

Munson, who had been named captain in April of that year, noticed Randolph's serious demeanor and decided he needed to loosen up the Brooklyn native, who was playing in his hometown for the first time as a pro.

"Thurman would needle me around the cage all the time; I thought he didn't like me early on, because he was always on my ass," Randolph said. "He would call me 'Rook' all the time. I would take seven or eight swings in the cage, and he would run me out of there. It wasn't until I finally stood up to him—and I was crazy to do that, because he would have broken me in half—that I said, 'What's the deal?' He looked at me and said, 'Relax, rookie. If I didn't like you, I wouldn't mess with you! You're one of us!'"

Randolph admits he "had a little chip" on his shoulder, uncertain in the early going whether the veterans on the club were going to accept him as an equal. Munson's words had the desired effect; Randolph was able to exhale after that, helping him settle into his new baseball surroundings. But the incident had a longer-lasting impact on Randolph, as well.

"From that day on, I felt like a Yankee, and Thurman made me feel that way," Randolph said. "That was what a captain was supposed to be. That stayed with me. Anytime a guy walked into our clubhouse, I made them feel welcome. I made them feel like they were a part of what was going on."

When Bucky Dent was traded to the Yankees in 1977, he and Randolph formed a sure-handed double-play combination, helping the Yankees to two straight World Series titles. They didn't have the flash (or power) of Reggie Jackson or the grittiness of Munson, but the pair provided steady defense and did enough things well at the plate to contribute to those "Bronx Zoo" championship teams.

Randolph took mental notes on the way more experienced players went about their business, studying everything from their pregame routines to the way they handled the media. Chris Chambliss, Roy White, Lou Piniella, and others were the models of what a big leaguer looked like to Randolph, who was embarking on what he hoped would be a lengthy major league career.

"So many veterans taught me how to play the game when I got there as a 21-year-old; all those guys had a piece of molding me in some way," Randolph said. "I wasn't as volatile as Lou, but the competitor in him, the way he competed every day, that sunk in. There was a lot of pressure playing in New York and it got very intense at times, but we had fun. On the bus, on the plane rides, we knew how to keep things loose."

Nettles served as captain for the 1982 and '83 seasons, but his relationship with the team grew rocky toward the end, prompting a trade that sent him to the San Diego Padres during the final week of spring training in 1984.

The Yankees went without a captain for the next two seasons, but Randolph didn't need a title to fulfill the responsibilities of the job.

"I felt like I was an unofficial captain, because when Nettles left, I was starting to feel comfortable in that role," Randolph said. "We had some veteran guys on the team, but the way I went about my business, the way I posted and played, I wanted to set that example. I learned that from Thurman, from being around a guy like Roy White. I learned how to lead, be accountable, and help your teammates from them."

One of those young teammates watching and learning from Randolph was Don Mattingly, who had played 91 games in 1983 before assuming full-time first-base duties in 1984.

"All of those guys were lead-by-example types," Mattingly said of players such as Randolph, Nettles, and Piniella. "I didn't feel like they were going around the room talking, making speeches or any of that kind of stuff. I thought they were all guys that went out, did their job, did their work, were professional, just the way they went about their business. They were my guys who taught me how to be a pro and what it's like to be a Yankee."

Prior to the 1986 season, Steinbrenner decided it was time to name another captain. Well, two of them, to be more precise.

He met separately with Randolph and Ron Guidry in early March, informing them that he wanted to make them co-captains of the club. After the two players discussed the situation themselves, they both sat down with The Boss and accepted the roles as the first co-captains in team history.

"When we met with George yesterday, he told us what a team leader should do—help guys in bad times, enjoy the good times with them," Guidry said after being introduced in his new role. "If guys complain about the food in the clubhouse after games or about the plane flights, come to us and go through channels.

"You have to go through the lieutenant and the first lieutenant and the corporal. Mr. Steinbrenner is a stickler for going through channels. It's been done differently, but it's been bad for both people involved. You can talk to him. You'd be surprised how easy it is to talk to him. We talked to him for 30 minutes yesterday. He told us what he wanted, we told him what we wouldn't be. We're not going to be a middleman."

Woody Woodward, the team's vice president of baseball administration who would be promoted to general manager later that year, said of Randolph and Guidry, "Both are proven winners, both are proven all-stars, both are first-class citizens."

The "proven winner" part might have been the biggest impetus for Steinbrenner to give Randolph and Guidry their new roles.

"Both of them had a link to Munson, which was really important," said longtime Yankees broadcaster Michael Kay, who also covered the team as a beat writer for the *New York Post* and *New York Daily News*. "By the time they were named captains, the team was a long way away from the last championship in 1978. They were trying to keep that last vestige of that greatness; that last connection to the championship pedigree. I think that had everything to do with it. George wanted it on the same linear plane from Munson to Nettles to Guidry and Randolph. It was really important to connect the team to '77–78, because the further they moved away from that, the bigger deal it became to keep it alive."

The selection of Randolph and Guidry had an even simpler explanation for veteran *New York Daily News* baseball writer Bill Madden: "George was running out of old Yankees."

"They were the two main guys left, and George didn't want to slight either one," Madden said. "George wanted to keep this captain thing going; he always got a lot of publicity in the papers for it and people would always make a big deal about a new captain, the tradition of Thurman and Gehrig."

"At one point, he was giving out captaincies like Chiclets," said longtime general manager Brian Cashman, who was just breaking in with the club as an intern in 1986. "Thurman Munson was a captain, Nettles was a captain, Guidry was a captain, Willie Randolph was a captain. Everybody was a captain at some point."

Whatever motivated Steinbrenner to make the move, Randolph welcomed the opportunity. Not only was he joining an exclusive list of men to hold that title, but he was the first African American player to serve in the role.

"I took a lot of pride in that," Randolph said. "There hadn't been Black players with the Yankees before Elston Howard, who was my first early mentor. As a young player, 21 years old, he taught me how to be classy, dignified, and a team player. Roy White was a guy who took me under his wing and taught me how to be a Yankee, what it meant to be a Yankee.

"To have that happen the way it did and be the first African American captain of the Yankees, it was a tremendous honor. It was the same way when I became the first African American manager in the history of the Mets. It's just a feeling of pride; feeling like you're part of that African American legacy."

Randolph was indeed the first African American captain of the Yankees, but the decision to name Guidry as a co-captain was also historic; no pitcher had ever served in the role in franchise history.

"We wondered about a pitcher as a co-captain,'" Woodward said at the time. "That's a little unique. But then Hank

Steinbrenner said, who makes up the largest percentage of the ball club—the pitchers. Why shouldn't they be represented? One regular, one pitcher—it's a natural."

Randolph had considered himself the unofficial captain of the Yankees since Nettles' departure in March 1984, so when he was granted the title along with Guidry, very little changed in terms of Randolph's approach on or off the field.

"Gator and I had been there the longest; we had this run of playing winning baseball and we had a relationship where it was unspoken in ways that we understood how to motivate and get the most out of our teammates," Randolph said. "To have George put that trust in us and give us that honor meant something. Most pitchers are not captains for the most part, but because of the respect that Gator commanded in the room and the way he went about his business, he was someone that could handle that role."

Months after Randolph and Guidry were named captains, Roy White—who played with both in the 1970s before becoming a Yankees coach in the early 1980s—told the *Village Voice* that he had seen a transformation in Randolph from a "quiet kind of shy young man" into the leader that he had become.

"Willie is a leader on the club and is a lot more verbal about it than people realize," White said. "In the clubhouse, in the dugout, on the bus, he talks to guys, gets on them. He's very good with the younger players."

Although the 1980s wound up being the rare decade in which the Yankees didn't win at least one World Series title, the club performed admirably during the Randolph/Guidry captaincy despite an ever-evolving roster. With an offense paced by Mattingly, Dave Winfield, Rickey Henderson, and a rotating cast of characters, New York won 90, 89, and 85 games between

1986 and '88. Aside from Randolph and those three players, no other player started on Opening Day in all three of those years. "It made me focus even more on being the leader, being there every day and helping my teammates," Randolph said. "Back then, we had a lot of guys come through the pipeline. We did a lot of trading and signed a lot of free agents, so there was a lot of turnover. I always felt it was my responsibility to welcome everybody and try to teach them the Yankee way."

Guidry's career wound down, as is often the case for pitchers in their mid to late thirties, and with no other starters stepping up to lead the rotation, pitching became the primary issue keeping the Yankees from the playoffs.

Guidry retired at the end of the 1988 season, having thrown just 56 innings that year. A four-time All-Star, the lefty finished his career with a 170–91 record, a 3.29 ERA, and the 1978 AL Cy Young Award.

Randolph's Yankees career ended after the 1988 season, when New York signed free agent Steve Sax away from the Los Angeles Dodgers. Randolph, who had battled some injury issues, went on to sign with the Dodgers. He played for the Oakland Athletics, Milwaukee Brewers, and New York Mets before retiring after the 1992 season.

The Yankees brought Randolph back as a coach in the mid-1990s, where he won four more World Series rings as part of Joe Torre's coaching staff. He was named manager of the Mets in November 2004, making him the first African American to hold that role in club history. After missing the playoffs in 2005, Randolph managed the Mets to the NL Championship Series in 2006, but they missed the postseason again in 2007, and he was fired halfway through the 2008 season.

Randolph's No. 30 was never retired by the Yankees, but he was honored with a plaque in Monument Park on June 20, 2015.

"To think that I'll be out there forever with players like Babe Ruth, Lou Gehrig, Joe DiMaggio, Mickey Mantle, and Yogi Berra, it's hard to believe," Randolph said. "It was an amazing ride."

There have not been co-captains since Randolph and Guidry, as Mattingly and Derek Jeter have been the only players to hold that role since the pair retired. Randolph and Guidry remain close friends, co-hosting the annual Yogi Berra Museum charity golf event.

"To be able to share that with him and help lead the team was just tremendous," Randolph said. "To this day, we're like Mutt and Jeff; we're like brothers."

Carrying the Torch

Before the word "captain" became synonymous with Derek Jeter, there was another pinstriped icon with that title: Donnie Baseball.

Don Mattingly—also nicknamed "The Hit Man" for his prowess at the plate—was among the most popular players in Yankees history, which was no surprise given his blue-collar, hard-working approach to the game.

But unlike other captains such as Jeter and Thurman Munson, Mattingly wasn't associated with championship teams in the Bronx. He debuted with the Yankees in 1982—one year after they reached the World Series—and retired after the 1995 season, just before Joe Torre came on board and led New York to four titles in five years.

"He was kind of a shining star on some really bad Yankee teams," said Mark Teixeira, who counted Mattingly among his favorite players while growing up in Baltimore. "He kept the

Yankees relevant even then, when most people were writing them off."

The Yankees posted winning records in each of Mattingly's first six full seasons, but without the benefit of a wild-card system, it was never quite good enough to win the American League East. Even in Mattingly's MVP season of 1985, the Yankees' 97 wins were only good enough for second place, sending New York home for another early winter.

"I loved playing there," Mattingly said. "I love the toughness of the city, the demanding part of fans in New York. They pushed you to be better; they pushed you to keep performing. I loved that part."

Performance was not an issue for Mattingly during his first half-dozen years with the Yankees. He averaged 27 home runs and 114 RBI from 1984 to '89, hitting .327 while being selected to six AL All-Star teams.

In 1984, Mattingly outlasted teammate Dave Winfield .343 to .340 to win the AL batting title, making him the first Yankees player to earn that distinction since Mickey Mantle in 1956.

The best of Mattingly's seasons came in 1985, when he hit .324 with 35 homers, 48 doubles, and 145 RBI, winning the AL Most Valuable Player award. He finished second in MVP voting the following season after hitting .352 with 31 homers and 113 RBI, but the Yankees placed second in the AL East in both seasons.

In 1987, Mattingly matched a major league record by hitting a home run in eight consecutive games. He also established a new big-league record with six grand slams that season; remarkably, those were the only slams he would hit in his entire career.

"Anytime you catch a streak and you're going good, getting your hits, you're just trying to ride that as long as possible,"

Mattingly said. "Just stay on that wave as long as you can ride it. You know there's going to be a stretch coming that you get out of sync and you run into a group of pitchers that give you trouble and you don't see them good. All of a sudden, now you're in a funk. There really is no stress during that period, because you're just seeing the ball so good, you're relaxed, and you feel like you can hit anybody."

Such times didn't last forever for Mattingly. The 1989 and 1990 seasons were arduous for Mattingly and the Yankees, who finished with 74 and 67 wins, respectively. Mattingly missed 60 games in 1990 with a back injury, an issue that would linger for the remainder of his career.

He reported to spring training in 1991 hoping to manage his balky back, looking for a bounce-back season after posting the worst numbers of his career. A couple days into camp, manager Stump Merrill told Mattingly he was being named captain, the first player to hold that title since Ron Guidry and Willie Randolph—who served as co-captains from 1986 and '88—had left the team.

"I was obviously honored, but I don't know if I quite knew the magnitude of the Yankee history of the captains," Mattingly said. "I knew [Graig] Nettles, who was one of the older guys when I first came up; you look up to those guys. Then Gator and Willie, two other guys I looked up to who were captains. That was really my kind of guidepost."

Merrill had discussed the idea with Mattingly during the offseason, but the two kept it quiet until the team assembled in Fort Lauderdale, Florida. George Steinbrenner had been banned from day-to-day management of the club in the middle of the 1990 season, so the theatrics that might have accompanied such an announcement were nowhere to be found.

"It wasn't a big ceremony or a press announcement," Mattingly said. "I didn't pay attention to that stuff. They just kind of told me and that was it. I didn't really look at it as a job; I just had to continue being myself."

The pomp and circumstance might have been absent, but the response from Mattingly's teammates was overwhelmingly positive, a sign of respect for the longest-tenured player on the club.

"Who else could you name captain?" Randy Velarde told the *New York Times*. "When you think of the Yankees, who do you think of? Don Mattingly. It's ideal that Stump did it."

At 30 years old, Mattingly should have been in the prime of his career. The back issues that hampered him in 1990 were manageable, but while he found a way to play 152 games in 1991, his production wasn't up to the lofty standard he had set for himself.

Even as his back took its toll on his offensive abilities, Mattingly's intimate knowledge of hitting helped him fight through the injury. Mike Mussina made his big-league debut with the Orioles in 1991, facing Mattingly a total of 16 times over the next five years. Mattingly went just 4-for-15 with one RBI and no extra-base hits against Mussina, but the pitcher had an uneasy feeling every time he pitched to the longtime Yankee.

"The guys who were willing to use one foul line to the other foul line, they were the toughest guys to get out; you can throw a great pitch and they'll just flick it over there, you throw a bad pitch and they'll drive it someplace else," Mussina said. "The guys who always want to drive it and feel like their job is to hit 35 homers and drive in 110 runs are easier to get out. They might cause more damage when you mess up, but they're going to get on base less often because they're trying to do more than guys like Mattingly, Paul Molitor, Robin Yount, or Ichiro.

They're tough to get out because they'll hit it over the shortstop as easy as they'll hit it to the right fielder, and they don't care."

Mattingly's guile and approach were keeping him moderately productive, but his effect on the Yankees went beyond the batter's box. If Mattingly's physical limitations weren't going to allow him to be the offensive force he had been throughout the mid to late 1980s, he would find other ways to impact the Yankees in a positive way.

"Donnie was a gamer; his whole thing was leadership by example," said Bernie Williams, who debuted in 1991. "He would be in the trainer's room hours before the game started because he was nursing injuries that affected his preparation, but he never complained once. He had to deal with things coming from the front office, doubting his ability even though his back was giving him problems. He was always gracious, ready to play and ready to contribute."

Mattingly's impeccable defense had won him five consecutive Gold Glove awards from 1985 to '89, a streak that ended during his injury-plagued 1990 campaign.

His bat might not have been the same because of his back troubles, but Mattingly's glove remained the gold standard at his position, earning him four more Gold Gloves between 1991 and '94.

More importantly, it became immediately obvious that the decision to name him captain was the right one.

"Leadership comes in different forms, and he led by example," said Brian Cashman, who was working his way up the Yankees' front office at the time. "He was not a vocal guy, but just the way he went about his business at all times was pure class, pure commitment. He set a standard of what it's like to display excellence in a Yankees uniform both performance-wise and how he engaged with our fans and the press. Just the way he wore the uniform and presented himself, he was the consummate professional."

Just as his predecessors Nettles, Randolph, and Guidry had helped guide him through major league life during the early days of his career, it was time for Mattingly to pay it forward to the next generation.

"In 1990 when I first got called up, I walk into Yankee Stadium and my locker is next to Donnie's," Jim Leyritz said. "At the time, Donnie was Mr. Baseball; he was the superstar. The first words he said to me were, 'Kid, if you've got any questions, don't be afraid to ask. You're not going to make it here unless you ask questions.' He helped me learn what it was like to play in New York and to be a New York Yankee. Donnie could have been a snob; he was a superstar and the hero of New York. But he just was so down to earth and so open, he just loved talking about baseball. It's in his blood."

Williams was one of many young players who viewed Mattingly as the prototype for a professional baseball player, but the captain's reach with the rookie went far deeper than that.

Early in Williams' first stint with the Yankees, a few veteran players were, in his own words, "hazing and bullying" him. Once Mattingly got wind of it, he made sure that such antics came to an immediate stop.

Over the next few weeks, Mattingly took Williams under his wing, even showing him tough love during a particularly difficult stretch for the rookie. The captain sat down with Williams in the back of the bus and told him exactly what he needed to do to take his game to the next level. Nobody had ever explained things to Williams in those words, and coming from a player of Mattingly's ilk, the advice meant the world to the youngster.

"Donnie was always there to give an encouraging word to the young players," Williams said. "I so appreciated him taking time out of his routine to sit down with a rookie and show him the ropes. I'm really grateful to have had the opportunity to have him as a teammate and my captain before he retired. That was a great learning experience for me. He was very instrumental in making me the player that I was with the Yankees."

Mattingly's lead-by-example approach came naturally for him; being the team captain didn't change who he was or how he prepared to play the game. The Yankees saw fit to name him to that role based on what he had done during the first seven years of his career; why change anything?

The work ethic that helped Mattingly go from a 19th-round draft pick in 1979 to a league MVP just six years later was constantly on display—whether Mattingly knew it or not.

"At the old stadium, the batting cages used to be behind the right-field fence in the asbestos tunnel," Leyritz said. "I used to take the subway home every night from the game, so I would walk across the field to go through the back entrance to get to the subway. I remember leaving one night after Donnie had a couple hits, and all of a sudden I hear the pop of the tarp behind the batting cage. It was Mattingly. He didn't have a bat in his hands; all he was doing was watching pitches, watching pitches, getting his timing down. The next day, I saw him at his locker and I said, 'What were you doing?' He said, 'I don't care if I went 2-for-5, I was so far off, I had to get back my timing.' That's why he was the captain."

Mattingly's influence wasn't limited to rookies, either.

When Paul O'Neill was traded to the Yankees prior to the 1993 season, he had already been an All-Star and won a World Series during his eight years with the Cincinnati Reds. O'Neill had heard about Mattingly from people around the league, but because interleague play wouldn't be introduced for another four years, he had never seen him play in person.

"He had so much respect from everybody because he wasn't the typical first-round pick that just flew through the minor leagues," O'Neill said. "He worked. He was a likable person that you wanted to root for. Don Mattingly was what I knew about the Yankees. Everything I had heard about him, he was that person. I learned so much from 'Cap' by just talking and watching him hit."

The 1994 Yankees were 70–43 when a players' strike brought the season to a grinding halt on August 11. With a 6½-game lead, New York was in prime position to end its 13-year postseason drought, but the season never resumed. The labor war caused Commissioner Bud Selig to cancel the rest of the season, robbing Mattingly of his chance to finally experience the playoffs.

When baseball resumed in 1995, the Yankees carried the momentum of that interrupted season, going 79–65 in the 144-game campaign. That earned New York the first-ever AL wild card spot, sending Mattingly to the postseason for the first time in his career.

"He was having issues with this back the last few years, but we were so happy to finally get to the playoffs while Donnie was still there in his last year," O'Neill said. "I'll never forget, he said, 'I just want there to see how I play under these circumstances.'"

The Yankees beat the Seattle Mariners in the first two games of the AL Division Series at Yankee Stadium, getting five hits from Mattingly, who homered in the Game 2 victory. The series headed to Seattle for the next three games, and after Mattingly went hitless in a Game 3 loss, he went 4-for-5 with two doubles and two RBI in a losing effort in Game 4.

The series came down to a winner-take-all Game 5. With the score tied 2–2 in the sixth, Mattingly lined a two-run double against right-hander Andy Benes, leaving the Yankees 12 outs from a trip to the AL Championship Series.

"I think everybody sort of rallied around him," Williams said. "Baseball is a funny sport in the sense that people try to play it cool; they understate the obvious, so some things are left unsaid. In '95, it was certainly obvious from a team standpoint that we really wanted to do well for Donnie, because he had never been to the postseason. We knew that he was going through all these pains and aches in the twilight of his career, so everybody was like, 'Let's do this for Donnie.'"

Seattle came back to tie the game in the eighth against David Cone, ultimately sending the contest into extra innings. The Yankees took a lead in the 11th on Randy Velarde's RBI single, but the Mariners came back against righty Jack McDowell in the bottom of the inning, winning the game and the series on Edgar Martinez's walk-off two-run double.

Mattingly finished the series 10-for-24 (.417) with four doubles, a home run, and six RBI. Playing on the biggest stage in the game, Mattingly looked like his old self: the strong, healthy player who had tortured opposing pitchers for those six magical years in the 1980s.

"We lost, but he had a tremendous series," Williams said. "We did not lose because of him. It was great to see him play at that level with so much on the line."

Game 5 turned out to the final game of Mattingly's career. The record five-year, $19.3 million contract he had signed in 1990 had expired, and although Mattingly wasn't ready to announce his retirement, he said he would sit out the 1996 season.

He declined an offer to play for the Baltimore Orioles in July 1996—wouldn't that have been something?—and hadn't ruled out the idea of playing again in 1997, but after watching the Yankees win the World Series with Tino Martinez manning first base, it was time to go. He contemplated a return as late as Thanksgiving, but his back continued to be an issue (not to mention his wrist, elbow, and knees), prompting him to walk away from the game that had defined his professional life.

"I hadn't really retired, but just stepped away, and I had some talks with teams that were calling about me playing again," Mattingly said. "I thought about it, but it didn't feel right. I played my whole career with the Yankees, and I'm glad it happened that way."

Mattingly revealed his decision at a press conference on January 22, 1997, where the Yankees announced that his No. 23 would be retired. His number would hang in Monument Park along those of legendary figures such as Babe Ruth, Joe DiMaggio, and Mantle, players whose excellence had resulted in so many championships. For all of Mattingly's accomplishments, he remains the only player with a retired number in the Bronx who never celebrated a World Series title.

"I don't know if that's necessarily a good thing," Mattingly said with a laugh. "I was honored, for sure. When you play there long enough, you learn more about the history of the team and understand what those numbers mean out there. As a kid from a fairly small town who wasn't a high pick and nobody thought that much of, to end up out there is pretty amazing."

16

A Natural Leader

WHEN MARK TEIXEIRA SIGNED WITH THE YANKEES PRIOR TO the 2009 season, he arrived at George M. Steinbrenner Field for his first spring training in pinstripes, uncertain what type of atmosphere he was walking into.

There were stars everywhere, and more media types than Teixeira had seen in his days with the Rangers, Braves, and Angels combined. It would have been easy for the newcomer to feel overwhelmed by his new surroundings, but Teixeira received a piece of advice from one of his predecessors that set the tone for his eight-year run in New York.

"Tino Martinez was in camp as an instructor and he told me, 'The best piece of advice I can give you is this: just do what Derek does,'" Teixeira said. "I didn't puff my chest and rip my shirt off after big hits, dance around the bases. I wanted to model my Yankees existence after someone that had done it really well for a long time."

When it comes to the modern era, nobody has done it better than Derek Jeter, who spent all 20 years of his major league career starring for the Yankees during one of the most successful runs in franchise history.

"I tried to play the game the right way," Jeter said. "I tried to play hard every single day; I felt as though that was my responsibility."

Long before Jeter was named captain by George Steinbrenner, the former first-round draft pick was a kid whose future in the Bronx remained uncertain. Jeter had gotten a taste of the majors in 1995, appearing in 15 games during two cups of coffee with the Yankees.

"He had a presence about him," Don Mattingly said. "He had confidence, but it was quiet and respectful."

Jim Leyritz recalled working out with Jeter at the Yankees' spring facility in Tampa in January 1996, watching the 21-year-old grind through an arduous program on the field and in the batting cage.

"He's taking 150, 200 ground balls, throwing as hard as he can, then taking 300, 400 swings in the cage," Leyritz said. "I'm like, 'Dude, you do realize it's January.' He said, 'This is my routine; this is what I do every single day.' It was impressive. I worked hard, but not quite like that."

The plan heading into 1996 was for Jeter to assume the starting shortstop duties from Tony Fernandez, who had struggled through an injury-riddled 1995 campaign. Jeter's spring was less than impressive, and with Fernandez suffering a severe elbow injury in late March, the Yankees had no safety net for the rookie.

Clyde King—a close advisor to George Steinbrenner— told The Boss that he needed to find a new shortstop. A deal was worked out that would have sent a young pitcher named

Mariano Rivera to the Seattle Mariners in exchange for Felix Fermin, but other members of the front office—namely vice president of scouting Gene Michael and assistant general manager Brian Cashman—helped talk Steinbrenner off the ledge, persuading him to give Jeter a chance.

"It was more about Jeter than Mariano," Cashman said. "We said, 'We've committed to this and we're going to go with this.' We disagreed with Clyde's assessment and didn't think we needed to trade for Felix Fermin. It was really less about saving Mariano and more about staying on line to commit to Jeter taking over."

The rest, of course, is history.

Jeter won American League Rookie of the Year honors that year, helping the Yankees to their first World Series title since 1978.

"He was a leader right from the first year he was there," Joe Torre said. "Even in August and September that first year, there were more veteran players really looking to him to do something during games because he had earned that trust on the type of player he was early on."

In 1998, Jeter made his first All-Star team and the Yankees won their second championship under Torre, part of a memorable 125-win season that put them in the conversation for the greatest team of all time.

"His maturity was incredible from day one," Martinez said. "Just the way he went about his business day in and day out, his preparation, his love for the game, his accountability. You knew he would be a great leader all those years and he developed into one, but he was a pretty good, quiet leader in years one and two, as well."

Jeter quickly established himself as a clutch player and a role model that kids could look up to. More importantly, the young superstar had become a leader within his own clubhouse, a room filled with accomplished veteran players.

"I put him in the same category as Donnie," Leyritz said. "He was not a rah-rah guy that would get in people's faces, but if you saw his work ethic, you knew that this kid was mature from a very young age. I think that just resonated within that entire clubhouse."

Leyritz left the Yankees after the 1996 season, but he returned in the middle of 1999, traded from the San Diego Padres back to New York for the stretch run. A lot had happened in the Bronx since Leyritz had departed, but when he walked back into the clubhouse, there were plenty of familiar faces. The one Leyritz was most intrigued to see was Jeter, who was no longer the fresh-faced rookie he had played with three years earlier.

"The one thing I wanted to know about Derek Jeter was when I came back in '99, had all of his success gone to his head?" Leyritz said. "My first game back in July, we were in Texas and it was blazing hot. I went to the field that day for early batting practice and sure enough, Jeter was out there taking all these ground balls, taking all these extra swings. He had not changed his routine whatsoever. I really respected that so much."

By the end of the 2000 season, Jeter had four World Series rings, was a three-time All-Star, and was voted the Most Valuable Player of both the 2000 All-Star Game and World Series—not to mention one of the most popular athletes in the world.

The Yankees hadn't named a new captain since Mattingly departed at the end of the 1995 season, though Torre relied on some of his veterans to help him police the clubhouse or get a message across when necessary.

"Early on in the first couple years, I used Joe Girardi for that," Torre said. "There's no question that if you get called into the principal's office, it's not going to have the same impact as somebody in the locker next to you sending a message that you need them to take seriously. If I do it, it sounds like criticism; if you get it from another player, that's the respect for each other that is important."

For those who had an opportunity to watch Jeter work every day, it was easy to respect the way he approached his job. But even players in the opposing dugout found themselves impressed by Jeter, whose respect for the game and his opponents was reciprocated by those even on the Yankees' greatest rivals.

"I kind of looked at Jeter the way I looked at Donnie. He was a competitor," said Mike Mussina, who played against Jeter as a member of the Orioles from 1995 to 2000 before signing with the Yankees in 2001. "He's the guy who is going to run out every ground ball like you're supposed to. He's the guy that's going to play hard every time. That's why he had success, hit .330, and played shortstop for the Yankees in their World Series–winning seasons."

The Yankees reached the World Series again in 2001, thanks in part to Jeter's brilliant flip play in Game 3 of the American League Division Series against the Oakland Athletics.

"As an opposing player, you knew Derek was great," Jason Giambi said. "You would watch him, he always got big hits, did it on the biggest stage in the playoffs, made big plays; he was that storybook you would read as a kid."

"Anytime you have someone mention your name with playing the game the right way, that makes you feel good," Jeter said. "It's humbling. A lot of organizations, I tried my best to try to beat them throughout the years. For them to have respect for how you played the game, it makes you feel really good."

Although the Yankees lost to the Arizona Diamondbacks in a classic seven-game World Series, Jeter added another chapter to his legacy with his "Mr. November" walk-off home run in Game 4.

The 2002 season saw the Yankees get bounced by the Angels in the ALDS, but they came charging out of the gate in 2003, opening the season with 23 wins in their first 29 games.

They were the hottest team in baseball. Until they weren't.

Torre's club lost 17 of its next 26 games, finishing May with a 32–23 record. The Yankees beat the Detroit Tigers in a 17-inning marathon at Comerica Park on June 1, then headed to Cincinnati for a rare interleague series against the Reds at Great American Ball Park.

The Yankees were still in first place, but their lead, which had been as high as five games before the end of April, was down to just a game and a half. George Steinbrenner was not pleased, but he had an idea that he believed would help light a fire underneath what he viewed as a lackluster team: he was naming Jeter as the team's new captain.

"I felt this could give us a spark," Steinbrenner said at the time.

Steinbrenner informed Jeter of his decision, though the owner didn't even tell Torre. The manager learned the news from Cashman, now the team's general manager.

"We were stumbling around a little bit when George decided to do this," Torre said. "I don't think Derek was crazy about the idea, to be honest. He took it because he respected George, but he liked just going out there and playing baseball without having the captain thing around his neck."

On June 3, prior to the opener against the Reds, the Yankees called for a press conference in the bowels of the ballpark. Steinbrenner was not present for the announcement, sending his son, Hal, and son-in-law Steve Swindal—both general partners—and Cashman, who was now the GM, to represent the club.

"It meant a lot, because I know it's a title that is not thrown around too lightly in our organization," Jeter said. "Prior to The Boss naming me the captain, there were whispers that may happen. When he called me and he asked me if I was OK with being named captain, the one thing he told me was, 'Listen, I don't want you to change anything. I want you to continue to handle yourself how you've handled yourself up until this point. That's why I'm naming you the captain.'"

"It's a lot of responsibility and Derek certainly knew that," Hal Steinbrenner said. "It's not something we give out every year; it's a special person. It's not like Derek became the captain after his third year here. It's earned. The history of it is pretty significant when you look at the players that have been captain."

Torre and third-base coach Willie Randolph—a former Yankees captain—were also there for the hastily arranged press conference, one that would have felt more appropriate roughly 650 miles to the east at Yankee Stadium.

"I don't think anything is going to change," catcher Jorge Posada said at the time. "I've always looked at him that way anyway. The only surprise is, why in Cincinnati?"

The locale of the announcement proved to be little more than a footnote in Jeter's story. Although baseball teams don't all have captains the way teams do in the National Football League or National Hockey League, the naming of Jeter to the role felt natural. He was in his eighth full season as a Yankee, was signed through the 2010 season, and had the admiration and respect of every player in his clubhouse.

There would be no pushback, because as Posada said, virtually every player on the team had already viewed Jeter as the de facto captain, anyway.

"He certainly fits what you would want a captain to be," Torre said. "The number one thing about being named captain is that there was nobody on that ballclub that resented that. Before you name somebody captain, I think that's an important ingredient to have. He certainly had that."

Bernie Williams, the longest-tenured player on the team, believed a number of people on that team could have filled the role, but there was something about Jeter that made him the ideal candidate.

"I think he had a special appeal because of his talent and the fact that he had established himself as a very popular and well-liked person in the sports community in New York," Williams said. "He was the guy that every girl wanted to be with and every guy wanted to hang out with. The city of New York was his oyster. He was really committed to the game and winning was the most important thing for him. He made it very appealing for Mr. Steinbrenner to make him the captain."

Jeter heeded Steinbrenner's words and didn't change a thing after being named captain. The Yankees lost four of the first six games following the announcement, but they got hot soon enough, winning 17 of their final 20 games in June.

The Yankees didn't run away with the AL East, though they won the division by a comfortable six-game margin over the rival Red Sox. The two teams met again in the American League Championship Series, slugging it out over seven games before Aaron Boone hit his infamous walk-off homer against Tim Wakefield in the 11th inning of Game 7 in the Bronx.

Boone had been dealt to the Yankees at the trade deadline on July 31, giving him fewer than three months as Jeter's teammate. He had watched Jeter from afar while playing in the National League with the Reds—yes, Boone was on the opposing team the day Jeter had been named captain—but it wasn't until he had a chance to observe him on a daily basis that Boone understood what really made Jeter great.

"He played the game with tremendous confidence," Boone said. "He was always prepared. He was tough as nails. He played through things and he posted. He was just a rock of consistency in the kind of person he was, how he prepared and how he played. He certainly set an example that way."

The work ethic Leyritz had observed on the back fields in Tampa in January 1996 hadn't wavered. Jeter knew he might not be the most talented player on the field at all times, but he swore that nobody would ever work harder than he did. That attitude rubbed off on his teammates, especially once he officially had the captain title.

"His leadership style was his work ethic," Giambi said. "You were like, 'If Derek's out there, how can I not be?'"

Work ethic is one thing. What Jeter did went beyond that. Just ask Tanyon Sturtze.

Sturtze was on the mound for the Yankees in the 12th inning on July 1, 2004. The opponent was the Red Sox, and although New York had lengthened its division lead over its rival to 7½ games by winning the first two games of the series, a sweep was there for the taking.

Boston had runners at second and third with two out when Trot Nixon hit a high pop-up that Jeter tracked down near the foul line in short left field. After making the catch while running at full speed, Jeter wound up just feet from the wall, his momentum carrying him into the stands.

Jeter held on to the ball for the third out, emerging from the seats with a bruised and bloodied face. The Yankees went on to win the game in the 13th inning.

"First of all, I said, 'Holy shit! I hope to hell he's OK.' The second thing was, 'I can't believe he caught the ball,'" Sturtze said. "The third was, 'I'll never let anything happen to this guy.' If you're going to sacrifice your body for me for something like that, it's only the right thing for me to do to show the same respect and make sure I did the same for you. That's the kind of leadership that he always showed by doing things like that."

"It reminds you of the things that Derek did every night," said John Flaherty, who delivered the game-winning hit that night. "Nothing was going to stop him from catching that ball. He knew he was going to get hurt and it didn't matter."

As well respected as Jeter was, his status within the game grew in the mid-2000s. He wasn't the best player in the game—that title, which had belonged to Ken Griffey Jr. and Barry Bonds throughout the 1990s, had transferred to Albert Pujols and Alex Rodriguez—but he didn't have to be. Jeter was a model of consistency, and he was only getting better after his 30th birthday.

The Yankees had entered a strange time in terms of roster construction. After having so much success with their homegrown core, the club seemed to make a flashy acquisition on an annual basis. Mike Mussina, Jason Giambi, Hideki Matsui, Gary Sheffield, and Jose Contreras signed on as free agents, while A-Rod, Kevin Brown, Randy Johnson, and Javier Vazquez were brought in via trade. Newcomers tend to have an adjustment period, but Torre relied on Jeter's steady presence to help his new stars adapt to the Yankee way.

"I always felt and tried to communicate that you don't play the game for writers to write nice things about you or to hear nice things said about you on television or radio; you play the game for the guy in the locker next to you," Torre said. "You're the only ones that know how hard it is to do what you do. If you wanted to get a point across to somebody, after a very short time, Derek was an easy messenger for me."

"He would take the time to talk to guys," Giambi said. "He understood what it meant to be in New York and be in the spotlight."

The spotlight was never hotter than in October 2004, when the Yankees suffered the greatest defeat in franchise history—and baseball history, for that matter. The Red Sox came back from a 3–0 deficit in the 2004 ALCS, winning four straight games to steal the AL pennant.

The stunning loss could have sent the Yankees into a tailspin, but they returned to the playoffs in each of the subsequent three seasons. The chemistry that defined the late-1990s dynasty was no longer there, but Jeter's steady presence helped the Yankees through three straight first-round postseason knockouts.

Torre and the Yankees parted ways after the 2007 season, ending their successful 12-year run. Girardi took over as manager, and just as Torre had relied on Girardi to help police the clubhouse, the new manager did the same with Jeter.

"You'll hear all kinds of coaches and managers say that the best clubhouse or locker room is one run by the players," Girardi said. "It means more when Derek says something to you than when I say something to you. When your teammates demand and expect excellence, you know that they're prepared every day. You know they're ready to play every day. It's all about winning, and that's who he was. I never really had to worry about the clubhouse."

Jeter wasn't an in-your-face type of leader. Team meetings weren't his thing, but if there was a message he wanted to get across, he wasn't afraid to relay that—out of the media's view.

"As you get a little bit older and you're around a little bit longer, you may be a little bit more vocal behind the scenes," Jeter said. "I wasn't a guy that spoke just for the sake of speaking; I spoke when I had something to say—and I did a lot of it behind the scenes."

Having added free agents Teixeira, CC Sabathia, and A.J. Burnett prior to the 2009 season, the Yankees finally returned to their first World Series since 2003, giving them a chance to end their nine-year title drought. Experiencing your first postseason in pinstripes can be a nerve-wracking time for a player and Jeter knew that, so he did his best to keep his teammates loose leading into the biggest games of the year.

"Whether you're at home or on the road, you've got a bunch of free time and a bunch of nervous energy," Teixeira said. "We would just be banging balls in the cages for hours and hours on a workout day. Derek would quietly walk by and say, 'Hey guys, if you haven't figured it out yet, you're not going to figure it out.' It kind of calmed us down a little—and he was right."

The Yankees beat the Philadelphia Phillies in six games, winning the 27th championship in franchise history—the fifth of Jeter's career. Jeter played four more years before announcing that 2014 would be his final season, sparking a league-wide retirement tour complete with tributes and gifts at every stop along the way.

Jeter's final game at Yankee Stadium meant nothing to the standings; the Yankees had already been eliminated from postseason contention. Yet the ballpark was sold out, with the Bronx faithful cramming into the stadium to bid farewell to one of the greatest players they had ever seen.

The captain responded in the most appropriate way possible, delivering a game-winning single in the bottom of the ninth. He would have traded that moment in for one last chance to play in October, but despite the lack of stakes, Jeter found a way to make his final game in pinstripes as memorable as any he had ever played.

"It was vintage Derek Jeter," Girardi said. "That was the only time that I ever saw him out of sorts a little bit. He couldn't find his batting gloves that day. He was a stickler for detail; he knew where everything was all the time, but that day it was like, 'Hey, he is human. There is something that can get to him a little bit.'"

Jeter finished his career with 3,465 hits, a .310 average, 14 All-Star appearances, five World Series rings, and the respect of an entire sport.

"When it comes to leading by example, you could not do better than Derek Jeter," Hal Steinbrenner said. "His work ethic, the way he conducted himself, the things he said, there's never better. There may have been some as good, I'm sure, but there's never been better."

17

The New Home Run King

As one era ends, a new one begins.

That was certainly the case for the Yankees during the second weekend of August 2016, as the club bid farewell to Alex Rodriguez one day, then welcomed Aaron Judge to the Bronx less than 24 hours later.

On Friday, August 12, Rodriguez played the final game of his polarizing, tumultuous, and remarkable career. The Yankees had made the decision to release A-Rod from the final year-plus of his contract, which was slated to run through the end of the 2017 season.

But the 14-time All-Star looked like a shell of his former self for most of 2016, his body unable to produce the same prodigious power that had helped him bash 687 home runs through his first 21 seasons. Perhaps the performance-enhancing drugs he had used at different points in his career—Rodriguez had copped to using PEDs during his three-year stint with the Texas Rangers from 2001 to '03, later earning a 162-game suspension in 2014 for his involvement in the Biogenesis drug scandal—had finally caught up with him, or perhaps Father Time simply decided that the 41-year-old's days in the majors were up.

Whatever the cause of Rodriguez's sudden demise, his final game at Yankee Stadium on that rainy Friday night in the Bronx felt like the end of a chapter, one that peaked with New York's 2009 World Series championship. The Yankees had been sellers at the trade deadline only two weeks earlier, convinced of the need to get younger. The farm system was loaded with talent, so general manager Brian Cashman decided it was time to see whether any of his highly touted prospects had what it took to succeed at the major league level.

Just hours after the Bronx crowd had ushered A-Rod out with thunderous applause and a number of standing ovations, the Yankees recalled two of those young players: Judge and first baseman Tyler Austin.

Both players were in the starting lineup on Saturday, the same day the Yankees were celebrating the 20th anniversary of the 1996 World Series champs. That team, of course, was loaded with homegrown talent including Derek Jeter, Bernie Williams, Andy Pettitte, and Mariano Rivera, so it was only fitting that two youngsters the organization felt would help get it back to the mountaintop were making their debuts with those legends in attendance.

Judge's journey to the Bronx began in June 2013, when the Yankees selected him with the 32nd pick in the MLB draft, using a compensatory pick they had received after Nick Swisher signed with Cleveland as a free agent.

A three-sport star at Linden High School, Judge had been drafted in the 31st round by the Oakland Athletics in 2010, a team rooted less than 100 miles from his hometown. He turned down the chance to sign—not to mention recruitment by a number of high-profile football schools—to attend Fresno State on a baseball scholarship.

"When you get the opportunity like that, getting drafted—especially by Oakland, a California team, pretty close to home—it was tempting," Judge said. "At the time, I just didn't think I was ready or mature enough mentally or physically to start pro ball."

Scouts agreed with Judge's self-assessment. One Yankees scout who had seen him play in high school said Judge was "almost like a newborn giraffe," but the outfielder began to become comfortable with his size once he got to Fresno State.

"He was a completely different guy," said Keith Snider, an area scout for the San Francisco Giants. "It looked like he put on at least 15–20 pounds from his senior year into his freshman year, and his swing got nice and short to the ball. It was night and day."

Judge played in the Cape Cod Baseball League after his sophomore year, giving him an opportunity to compete against many of the country's top college players. John Altobelli, his manager with Brewster that summer, was astonished on a daily basis watching the powerful Judge take batting practice.

"It looked like he was hitting Pro V1 golf balls out of the ballpark," Altobelli said.

Altobelli had the benefit of writing Judge's name into his lineup. For the other managers, they were forced to watch their pitchers try to get him out. Chatham manager John Schiffner even reached out to his buddy Matt Hyde, an area scout for the Yankees, telling him about what he had seen.

"Schiffner called me up and said, 'We just played against Brewster, and they've got a kid who is the biggest player I've ever seen on a baseball field'" Hyde said. "'He's got power, but he also stole a base against us and he's an incredible athlete.'"

Another Yankees scout filed a report that gave Judge an 80 for raw power, the highest possible grade on the 20–80 scouting scale. He also gave him a 65 for his arm, a 50 for his speed, tabbing him as a future 55 hitter and future 70 power guy. Damon Oppenheimer, the Yankees' VP of amateur scouting, was intrigued.

"When we see sevens and eights, it's like diamonds," Oppenheimer said. "[Bryce] Harper, [Mike] Trout, A-Rod kind of guys."

Judge only hit five home runs in 32 games that summer, but it was apparent the tools were there to go along with his impressive size and athleticism. He blossomed in his junior year, hitting 12 homers with a .369 average and 1.116 OPS in 59 games. Nine Yankees scouts filed reports on Judge over the course of the year, each one coming back with the same impression: he was a first-round pick.

The biggest concern was the very thing that made Judge stand out above most of his peers: his massive size.

"He obviously doesn't fit the normal mold," said Jim Hendry, special assignment scout for the Yankees and former GM of the Chicago Cubs. "There aren't a lot of people in history 6-foot-7 or 6-foot-8 that became outstanding major league hitters. Whether it was Frank Howard, Dave Winfield, or Richie Sexson, the common denominator for me is when you're that big, you're going to have some issues with certain parts of the strike zone. Do you have the athleticism and the makeup to overcome that?"

The Yankees had three picks—Nos. 26, 32, and 33—in the first round, and while there was a hope within the front office that Judge would be on the board when it was their turn to pick, it was no certainty. The Arizona Diamondbacks (who owned the 15th and 36th picks) and San Diego Padres (13th pick) were both interested in Judge, while the Yankees had only met with him once or twice, never giving the player an impression that he was high on their list.

San Diego passed on Judge at 13, selecting Mississippi State outfielder Hunter Renfroe. Ditto for Arizona at 15, as the Diamondbacks chose Braden Shipley, a right-hander from the University of Nevada.

The Yankees liked Judge, but they also coveted Notre Dame third baseman Eric Jagielo. If they passed on Judge at 26, the Yankees would have to hope that five teams would do the same before New York's next pick at 32. Arizona was hoping for the same, and as the first round moved along, even Judge believed he was headed to the Diamondbacks with the 36th pick.

"We were nervous," Yankees national crosschecker Brian Barber said. "We had three picks, and we spent months leading up to it with scenario after scenario after scenario of how we could maximize those picks. Those minutes leading up to it, the 20 minutes between 26 and 32, the heart rate was definitely elevated."

"Usually, you get a call from your agent ahead of time saying, 'We just spoke to this team, and we think they're going to take you with this pick.' I didn't hear anything," Judge said. "The funny thing is, moments before that pick, I actually almost got up and went to the bathroom. I kind of had an idea of where I was going to go, so I figured I'd go to the bathroom here in the next couple picks, then come back and hopefully get drafted. Right before I stood up to go to the bathroom, they said, 'With the 32nd pick, the Yankees take Aaron Judge.' It took me by surprise."

Less than a week later, Judge was invited to take batting practice with the Yankees prior to a game in Oakland.

"The first thing that stood out the most was his size," said Joe Girardi, the Yankees' manager from 2008 to '17. "The second thing that stood out was how far he hit the ball. The third thing that stood out? How respectful he was. His personality, how mature he was; you had a feeling that this kid had a chance to be really, really special."

"The whole day, I was just trying to stay out of their way," Judge said. "I had Andy Pettitte, Mariano Rivera, Robinson Canó, CC Sabathia, and all these guys that I've watched growing up.... They were coming up to me saying, 'Hey Aaron, how are you doing? Andy Pettitte. Great to meet you.' I was like, 'Andy, I know who you are. You don't have to introduce yourself.'"

About a month later, Judge and the Yankees agreed to an over-slot bonus of $1.8 million, officially launching his professional career.

"I was excited, but I knew this was just the beginning," Judge said. "It's never guaranteed; even though you signed that contract and you're playing for a professional team, there's no guarantee you're ever going to make it to the major leagues."

Judge hit .308 with 17 home runs and a .905 OPS in 131 games at two levels of Class A ball in 2014, then performed well in the Arizona Fall League, prompting the Yankees to start him at Double A Trenton in 2015. But first, Judge received an invitation to big-league spring training, thrusting the 22-year-old into a clubhouse with the likes of A-Rod, Sabathia, Mark Teixeira, and Carlos Beltran.

Judge wasn't even a rookie yet, but even in a room filled with Hall-of-Fame-level talent, he stood out. His size brought about comparisons to Miami Marlins slugger Giancarlo Stanton, the National League MVP runner-up in 2014.

Some players had seen him take BP in Oakland back in 2013, but watching it on a daily basis on a quiet back field during spring training gave the Yankees a close look at what they had.

"Power is what people like to talk about, especially with a guy of his size," said Billy Eppler, an assistant GM with the Yankees at the time. "Watching him take BP is fun; it's like going to a long-drive contest. But watch him go get a ball in the gap, watch him throw, watch him do the other things. Everybody wants to see a bomb in the batter's box, but we just want him to have a quality at-bat and win every pitch."

Judge took advantage of his surroundings, constantly observing Teixeira's routine and picking Beltran's brain. He knew he was headed for Double A to open the season, but as long as he was in big-league camp, Judge had a goal.

"I just want to give them something to think about," Judge said that spring. "Try to soak up as much as I can, talk to everybody, learn as much as I can. Put on a show and make it tough for them to send me across the street [to the minor league complex]."

As expected, Judge was sent back to minor league camp to prepare for his Double A season, but he had opened some eyes during his time with the big club. The idea of him becoming the next great homegrown Yankee wasn't so far-fetched, even if it wasn't going to happen in 2015.

"Even as a little kid, you want to grow up and be one of the legends, one of the greatest of all-time," Judge said. "One of my dreams is to be one of the next great ones, but I know I have to work hard every day to work toward that goal. This is where we all want to be. Getting a taste of it here, I want more. Now I have to go out there and get it."

Judge continued to impress at Double A, hitting .284 with 12 home runs and an .866 OPS in 63 games before earning a promotion to Triple A Scranton/Wilkes-Barre. That level proved to be a little tougher for Judge, who hit .224 with eight homers and a .681 OPS in 63 games.

Having drafted Judge in 2013, the Yankees didn't need to add the outfielder to the 40-man roster that offseason in order to protect him from the Rule 5 Draft. Because of that, he wasn't called up when rosters expanded in September, though his struggles at Triple A may have suggested that Judge wasn't quite ready for prime time.

"It's good that he's going through it," Cashman said. "You'd rather have that stuff happen in the minor leagues as they make adjustments and figure out what they have to do on a daily basis to stay positive."

Judge opened the 2016 season back at Triple A, showing vast improvement from his first stint in Scranton. The Yankees overcame a dreadful start to the season, and although they climbed back to the .500 mark by the All-Star break, they were unable to carry that momentum into the second half. Cashman made the un-Yankee-like decision to be a seller at the trade deadline, dealing away Beltran, relievers Aroldis Chapman and Andrew Miller, and starter Ivan Nova, collecting a group of prospects to reload the farm system.

Gary Sánchez, the Yankees' top catching prospect, was called up on August 3, displacing Brian McCann as the everyday catcher. Sánchez got off to a solid start, hitting .357 with a .951 OPS during his first week as the starter.

Following the A-Rod drama, the Yankees turned the page with the promotion of Judge and Austin, who joined Sánchez and Luis Severino as part of the youth movement in the Bronx.

The two newest "Baby Bombers" made quite a first impression.

With two out in the second inning, Austin belted a solo home run against Matt Andriese of the Tampa Bay Rays, becoming the fourth player in franchise history to go deep in his first big-league at-bat.

Four pitches later, Judge became the fifth.

Judge launched a 446-foot blast to center field, depositing the ball in a spot that had only been reached by two other players in Yankee Stadium's first seven-plus seasons. Austin and Judge were the first teammates in history to homer in their first career at-bats in the same game.

Alex who? With two swings, Judge and Austin had helped the Yankees move on from the A-Rod era, giving fans the hope that the newcomers would help form a core for the next great championship team.

Judge repeated the feat in his second game, joining Joe Lefebrve (1980) as the only players in Yankees history to homer in each of their first two games.

"I don't think you can expect a homer every day. I think that would be a record," Girardi joked after the second game. "It seems like every time he hits a ball in the air, people get excited."

Judge had multi-hit performances in three of his first five games, starting his career 7-for-18. The good vibes dissipated quickly, however, as he went 3-for-35 (.086) with one home run and 20 strikeouts over the final 11 games in August. September wasn't much better; Judge went 5-for-31 (.161) with one home run in 11 games before an oblique strain ended his season on September 13. In total, Judge struck out 42 times in 84 at-bats.

"Obviously, he's struggled with strikeouts," Cashman said following Judge's injury. "But part of the process is to get him up here, get these growing pains out of the way, speed up the adjustment process."

Eager to address the issues that hampered him during his first month in the majors, Judge flew to New York that offseason for a three-day session with hitting coach Alan Cockrell. They worked on mechanics, but the primary focus was Judge's approach at the plate—namely identifying the pitches against which he could do the most damage. It took until the end of spring training for Judge to secure a spot on the Opening Day roster, but once he made it, he took advantage of the opportunity.

By the end of April, it was clear that Judge had figured something out. The rookie—his September injury kept him from reaching official rookie status in 2016—hit .303 with 10 home runs, 20 RBI, and a 1.161 OPS in 22 games, though he did strike out 24 times in 76 at-bats.

The Yankees were willing to live with the strikeouts if the other at-bats were going to be as productive as they were. But even as he graced the cover of *Sports Illustrated* next to the words "All Rise!" in May, Judge wasn't taking anything for granted. He didn't even get an apartment in New York, staying either at a hotel or in Brett Gardner's guest room.

"I don't want to put all my cards that I'm going to be in New York and then I go to Triple A," Judge told the magazine. "Maybe next year, if everything goes well."

Things went exceedingly well for Judge. The 25-year-old led the majors with 30 home runs at the All-Star break, hitting .329 with 66 RBI to spark talk of a Triple Crown run. He had already eclipsed Joe DiMaggio's team record for home runs by a rookie, and there were still two and a half months to play in the season. The Yankees had even carved out a section of seats in right field in his honor, introducing the "Judge's Chambers," which looked like a courtroom jury box and featured a select group of fans each night dressed up in judges' robes and white wigs.

Even as he became the toast of the town and one of the best stories in the game, Judge knew how quickly things could turn. He kept a note on his phone that simply read ".179," a reminder of his 2016 batting average with the Yankees.

"This game will humble you in a heartbeat," Judge said as he prepared for his first All-Star Game after garnering more votes than any player in the AL. "So I just try to keep going out there and play my best game every day, because I could hit .179 in a couple weeks."

Judge launched 47 home runs over three rounds to win the Home Run Derby at Marlins Park, cementing his newfound superstar status. The following day, Commissioner Rob Manfred said Judge was the type of player "who can become the face of the game," noting both his talent on the field and appeal away from it.

Judge struggled out of the break, ironically hitting .179 with seven homers and 67 strikeouts in 44 games to start his second half.

"I saw frustration," Girardi said. "I didn't see him getting down. I never saw him stop working. I never saw him not believe in himself."

September was a different story, as Judge smacked 15 home runs and hit .311 with an eye-popping 1.352 OPS. He broke Mark McGwire's rookie home run record of 49, finishing the season with 52. He was a unanimous AL Rookie of the Year winner, finishing as the runner-up to Jose Altuve of the Houston Astros in the AL Most Valuable Player vote.

The Yankees also made an improbable run to the AL Championship Series, where Altuve and the Astros—with a little help from a now-notorious garbage can—beat them out for the AL pennant. Judge set a new postseason record with 27 strikeouts in 12 games.

Judge underwent arthroscopic shoulder surgery after the season, but he was ready to go by Opening Day the following March. In late July 2018, Judge experienced the first serious injury of his big-league career, sustaining a fractured right wrist after being hit by a pitch, shelving him for seven weeks.

An oblique injury cost him two months in 2019, while shoulder soreness and a stress fracture in his first right rib cost him time during spring training in 2020. The pandemic delayed the start of the season by more than three months, giving Judge time to heal, but an August calf injury sent him to the injured list for two weeks of the 60-game campaign.

Judge's injuries weren't of the chronic variety, but rather a series of flukes. There was no degenerative knee or a nagging hamstring that constantly gave him problems, but the tag of being an "injury-plagued" player was becoming part of his narrative.

Judge did his best to put that behind him in 2021, playing 148 games, his highest total since his breakout 2017 season. He made the All-Star team for the first time since 2018, finished fourth in AL MVP voting, and won his second Silver Slugger award.

"When you're a leader on the team, you have to be out there with your soldiers," Judge told *Yankees Magazine* prior to the 2022 season. "That's the most important thing. For me, not getting hurt at all was a big-time thing. If not for COVID, I would have played in 158 games. I feel like if I'm out there, I'm going to put up the numbers that will help my team win. If you're missing time, you can't help your team win that much.

"You can support your teammates and be a great cheerleader, but that's not going to have a direct impact on how many games you win.... For me to be out there and not have some freak accident where I dive for a ball and break a rib or get hit by a pitch and miss a few months, it was a good season."

With one year to go until Judge's free agency, the Yankees began talks about an extension to keep him in pinstripes for years to come. Not wanting to be distracted by contract issues during the season, Judge set an Opening Day deadline to reach a deal, but the two sides were unable to come to an agreement.

The Yankees took the unusual step of revealing their final offer: seven years, $213.5 million. Combined with his 2022 salary—the two sides had filed arbitration numbers at $17 million and $21 million, respectively—it would have meant an eight-year deal worth somewhere between $230.5 million and $234.5 million.

The $30.5 million average annual value of the extension would have put Judge slightly ahead of Mookie Betts ($30.4 million) and behind only Mike Trout, whose $35.5 million average annual value was the highest in history for a position player.

Judge had placed a massive bet on himself. Yes, he had remained healthy for nearly all of 2021, but he was set to turn 30 on April 26, and one injury of note could have potentially cost him millions of dollars.

"I don't mind going to free agency," Judge said after the details of the rejected deal became public. "At the end of the year, I'm a free agent. I can talk to 30 teams, and the Yankees will be one of those 30 teams. It's always nice to try to wrap something up, the sooner the better. But we weren't able to get it done. Now it's on to baseball."

With one home run through his first 13 games, some wondered whether the contract situation was indeed serving as a distraction for Judge. Any concerns were alleviated soon enough, as Judge belted five home runs in the final seven games of April, looking like a slugger on a mission.

Judge blasted 12 more home runs in May and 11 in June, giving him 29 homers through 77 games. Even more importantly, the Yankees were steamrolling their way through the league, going 56–21 in those games to build a 12½-game lead in the AL East.

The Yankees and Judge were prepared to go to an arbitration hearing over their $4 million difference, but the two sides settled at the midpoint of $19 million shortly before the hearing had been set to begin. The deal included a $250,000 bonus for winning the AL MVP award—he was already an overwhelming favorite by that point—and another $250,000 for winning World Series MVP honors.

"Now we can get back to focusing on baseball games and trying to bring a championship back here to New York," Judge said. "I'm glad we were able to get through that process. It took a little longer than expected, but thankfully we're past it. Time to focus on winning some games."

That had hardly been a problem for Judge and the Yankees. On July 7, Judge hit his 30th home run of the season; the following day, the Bombers beat the rival Red Sox to improve to 61–23, boosting their division lead to 15½ games. It also marked the second time in Judge's career that he compiled 30 home runs prior to the All-Star break.

The 2022 season was going as well as Judge and the Yankees could have possibly imagined. He was setting himself up for a huge payday, but that wasn't his focus. The Yankees were the best team in baseball, creating expectations that New York would end its 13-year championship drought.

"Whenever we're walking through Yankee Stadium, we see the championships up there," Judge said at the All-Star Game.

"We see the old photos of all these guys being in pressure situations. That's what I want. I want to be in those pictures."

By the end of July, Judge had hit 13 more home runs, bringing his total to 42. The idea of him hitting 62 home runs—which would break Roger Maris' record for both the Yankees and the American League—was becoming very realistic.

"Like I've said a thousand times, I'm focused on winning baseball games right now," Judge told MLB.com. "The stats and stuff like that, we can talk about that at the end of the year."

Two weeks later, Judge smashed his 46th home run of the season, reaching the 100-RBI mark in the process. He became the fastest player to reach 100 RBI since Miguel Cabrera in 2013 and the first Yankee to drive in 100 runs in fewer than 109 games since Alex Rodriguez—the same player who was released on the day Judge had debuted in August 2016—in his 2007 AL MVP campaign.

Judge was thriving, but the Yankees were fading. New York lost 14 of its first 18 games in August, thanks largely to an offense that failed to get anything going unless Judge was doing the damage.

The team seemed to straighten itself out with five straight wins, but a three-game losing streak followed, raising concerns that the Yankees might squander their large lead. Judge hit his 50th home run in the third of those defeats, becoming just the 10th player in baseball history to record multiple 50-homer seasons. He was on pace to hit 63 home runs, but the team's uneven performance made it impossible for Judge to focus on his personal triumphs.

"It's just another number," Judge said. "It's great, but I'm kind of upset we lost. It's a close game we could've won.'"

As September arrived, the Yankees' lead had shrunk to six games, the smallest it had been since early June. Three days later, it was down to four games, causing widespread panic around New York.

Judge wasn't just hitting home runs at a prodigious pace; he was also leading the AL in batting average and RBI, giving him a shot at the Triple Crown. How much were the Yankees relying on Judge? During the second half of the season, Judge's slash line was .349/.502/.784, while the rest of the offense posted a line of .223/.292/.360.

"As a kid, you'd look up and you'd see Albert Pujols hitting .330 every year and consistently putting up the RBI numbers," Judge said. "So for me, grading a hitter has always been about average. I might be old-school, but it's, can you hit or can't you?"

Eight wins in the next 10 games pushed the lead back to six, as Judge continued his season-long home run binge. Two home runs on September 13 gave him 57, then another two-homer night on September 18 left him one away from the magic number of 60.

Judge wasted no time, launching a solo shot against the Pirates in the Yankees' next game to spark a ninth-inning comeback win.

"I haven't really been thinking about numbers or stats and stuff like that," Judge said. "I'm going out there trying to help my team win. At the time, it was a solo shot in the ninth, still down by a couple of runs. But this team, we've always had a never-say-die attitude. We fight until the end."

"I'm out of adjectives," Yankees manager Aaron Boone said. "It's just really impressive."

Two of Maris' sons—Kevin and Roger Jr.—were on hand for Judge's 60th, and the latter had decided to attend every game until Judge broke his father's record. The Yankees had 15 games remaining, making it *fait accompli* that Judge—who joined Maris, Babe Ruth, Barry Bonds, Mark McGwire, and Sammy

Sosa as the only players to hit 60 in a season—would set a new AL mark.

"When you talk about Ruth and Maris and Mantle and all these Yankees greats, you never imagine as a kid getting mentioned with them," Judge said. "It's an incredible honor and something I don't take lightly at all. We're not done."

Now just one home run away from Maris, Judge went into a power slump. He went 34 plate appearances—each of them prompting networks to break into their regular programming—without a home run.

In the seventh inning of the Yankees' September 28 game at Toronto's Rogers Centre—the night after the Yankees had clinched the AL East and earned a first-round postseason bye—Judge finally caught Maris. He had seven games to hit No. 62, and for a player who had gone deep once every 9.13 at-bats, the baseball world held its breath for the record-breaking blast.

The Yankees had their final three-game series at home from September 30 to October 2, but Judge went 1-for-7, walking five times while striking out six times. Fans jeered Orioles pitchers after each walk—and each ball, for that matter—hoping their decision to attend the game would be rewarded with the history-making blast.

If Judge was going to pass Maris, it was going to be at Globe Life Field in Arlington, Texas, where the Yankees were set to close the season with four games against the Rangers.

Texas' pitchers challenged Judge, who went 2-for-9 with no walks in the first two games. With only two games left, Judge knew his chances were running out.

Enough was enough.

With his parents and wife watching from the stands, Judge led off the second half of the October 4 doubleheader with a shot to left field against right-hander Jesus Tinoco, finally allowing the slugger to exhale.

"I can't lie," Judge said. "The past couple of games, I looked up in the seventh inning and I'm like, 'Dang, I've only got one more at-bat. We'd better figure this out.'"

The Yankees rushed out of the dugout to meet Judge near home plate, congratulating their teammate on his incredible accomplishment. Judge's chase for 62 was finally over.

"I tried to enjoy every single moment," Judge said. "I didn't think about, 'Hey, they're all on their feet to see you hit a home run.' I tried to think about, 'Hey, they're here to see an exciting ballgame and see something special.' Having that mindset helped me stay pretty calm, but there was definitely a little pressure in there."

Maris Jr. was on hand to congratulate Judge, whom he said he now considers the true home run king. He never mentioned the PED cloud that hung over the heads of Bonds, McGwire, and Sosa, but his message was clear.

"He should be revered and celebrated as the single-season home run champ, not just the American League home run champ," Maris Jr. said. "I can't think of anyone better that baseball can look up to as Aaron Judge, who is the face of baseball, to actually do that."

When all was said and done, Judge finished the season with a .311 average, 62 home runs, and 131 RBI, though he missed out on the Triple Crown, finishing second to Luis Arráez of the Minnesota Twins in the batting race.

Judge led the AL in home runs, RBI, runs scored (133), walks (111), on-base percentage (.425), slugging percentage (.686), OPS (1.111), OPS+ (211), and total bases (391). He was voted as the AL MVP, earning 28 of the 30 first-place votes, though the season ended in disappointing fashion once again as the Astros swept the Yankees in the ALCS, extending New York's title drought to 13 seasons.

"The motivation throughout the year, man, it goes to my teammates," Judge said. "I said that all year; they constantly pushed me day in and day out to just show up and play, because I see the hard work they put in. I've got to show up, just like them. Without the special crew we had this year and the past couple of years, I know I definitely wouldn't be in this position."

Judge's preseason bet on himself had paid off, as he entered free agency as the No. 1 player on the market. The Yankees, whose seven-year, $213.5 million extension offer seven months earlier now seemed absurdly low, knew it would take significantly more money to retain their franchise player.

The San Francisco Giants, desperate for a star to build around, had their sights set on Judge, who grew up just 100 miles away in Linden, California. Could a monster offer bring the slugger home? The Giants were going to find out.

Hal Steinbrenner met with Judge shortly after the Yankees' ALCS loss to the Astros, trying to get a sense of what it would take to keep Judge in pinstripes. The Yankees' initial offer to Judge after the season was for $296 million over eight years, an average annual value of $37 million that would make him the highest-paid position player in the game, eclipsing Mike Trout.

But Judge, who was set to turn 31 the following April, wanted nine years. And San Francisco was going to give it to him. So, as it turned out, were the San Diego Padres, who threw their hat in the ring during the winter meetings, hoping to shock the world by signing Judge.

The intrigue of Judge's free agency came to a head during those meetings in San Diego. Steinbrenner, on vacation in Italy, had a phone conversation with Judge that proved to the be the tipping point in the negotiations.

Steinbrenner asked Judge point-blank whether he wanted to be a Yankee. When Judge said he did, the owner asked him what it would take to get a deal done.

"Hal Steinbrenner would be the Mariano Rivera of these negotiations," Cashman said.

It wasn't long before the sides had agreed to a nine-year, $360 million deal to keep Judge in the only major league uniform he had ever worn.

"I feel like he certainly belongs in pinstripes," Boone said. "A guy of his stature and his greatness, hopefully he spends his entire career here and goes into Monument Park and into the Hall of Fame as a Yankee."

The Yankees held a press conference on December 21 to officially announce Judge's contract. As he welcomed the superstar back, Steinbrenner revealed that Judge would become the 16th captain in franchise history.

"Getting a chance to be the captain of the Yankees now, that goes without saying what an honor that is," Judge said. "I looked back at the list—Thurman Munson, Lou Gehrig, Ron Guidry, Willie Randolph, Derek Jeter, Don Mattingly. That's a pretty good list right there, not only great baseball players but great ambassadors of the game and great ambassadors of the New York Yankees. This is an incredible honor that I don't take lightly."

PART 4

THE GAME-WINNERS

The Shot Heard 'Round the Bronx

IT WASN'T THE "SHOT HEARD 'ROUND THE WORLD," BUT FOR Chris Chambliss and the Yankees, it was the shot that sent them to the World Series.

Chambliss' game-winning home run to lead off the bottom of the ninth inning of Game 5 in the 1976 American League Championship Series against the Kansas City Royals lifted the Yankees to the Fall Classic for the first time since 1964.

That 12-year drought probably felt significantly longer for the Yankees and their fans given the success the franchise had experienced; ever since making their first World Series in 1921, the Yankees had won 29 American League pennants and 20 world championships, never going more than three years without playing for the title.

While the first 29 AL pennants were the reward for having the best record in the AL, the 1976 season marked the first AL East title for the Yankees since Major League Baseball instituted divisional play in 1969.

The Royals and Yankees split the first two games in Kansas City, sending the teams back to the Bronx for the remainder of the best-of-five series. Chambliss homered and drove in three runs in a Game 3 win, leaving the Yankees one victory from the pennant. But the Royals slugged their way to a win in Game 4, forcing a winner-take-all Game 5 at Yankee Stadium.

The Yankees held a 6–3 lead in the eighth when George Brett—New York's biggest nemesis at the time—hit a three-run home run to tie the game. The ballpark had been raucous with anticipation of a pennant, but the mood of the crowd changed as Brett's blast cleared the fence.

"For us, that was just, 'Here we go again,'" Chambliss told the *New York Daily News* on the 40th anniversary of the game. "These things happened all year long. We went back and forth. It did quiet the Stadium, though. We had the lead and this great hitter bombs one and ties it. That quieted everybody down. But coming back up in the ninth got them excited again."

Many in the sellout crowd of 56,821 began throwing things on the field, causing a delay. Chambliss was set to lead off the home half of the ninth, so he waited for the field to be cleared by the grounds crew before stepping to the plate.

Royals right-hander Mark Littell, on the other hand, fired some warmup pitches to keep his arm loose. Littell had retired all five Yankees he had faced after entering the game with one out in the seventh, but the delay couldn't have helped the 23-year-old pitcher.

"It was really cold that night; Littell had to be cold," Chambliss said. "He was trying to throw pitches to keep warm."

"The way that the momentum and flow of the game just broke up, I felt good about Chris being up there," Willie Randolph said. "Out of all the guys on that team, Chris was Mr. Clutch. He would have some huge RBIs. He wasn't a power hitter, but he always came up with the big RBI."

In fact, Chambliss' 96 runs batted in that season ranked fourth in the AL, as he made the only All-Star team of his 17-year career. Chambliss, who earned 1971 AL Rookie of the Year honors with Cleveland, also had his best MVP finish in 1976, finishing fifth in AL voting.

The underappreciated first baseman finished that season with 17 home runs and a .293 batting average, setting career highs in hits (188), homers, and RBI in his sixth major league season.

"He didn't have an oversized personality, so he wasn't the guy that the press gravitated to after games for his insight," said Marty Appel, who was the Yankees' public relations director at the time. "He was a well-mannered, quiet guy who went about his own business. There would be rumblings from Steinbrenner like, 'Why do we have our cleanup guy hitting 17 home runs? We can do better than that.'"

Chambliss might not have been the most obvious candidate to come through with the pennant-winning home run, but as it turned out, his game-winning blast on July 25 against the Boston Red Sox in the Bronx could have been a sign of things to come.

The Yankees trailed the Red Sox by two runs with two out and two runners on base in the ninth, and with Chambliss coming to the plate, Boston manager Don Zimmer—yes, that Don Zimmer—brought in left-hander Tom House, who had held Chambliss 0-for-8 in his career.

Chambliss jumped on the first pitch from House and suddenly he was 1-for-9, depositing it over the fence for a three-run home run. The Yankees won the game 6–5, sending the 49,723 fans into a tizzy. The crowd continued to scream long after Chambliss had headed for the home clubhouse, prompting him to return for a rare curtain call.

"He came out of the dugout for a curtain call, which the fans had sort of demanded from the cheering," Appel said. "That was the first time that happened since Roger Maris, which led to what we have today, where it's much more common. That was something that started right there at that moment."

Less than three months later, Chambliss would once again step up to the plate at Yankee Stadium with an opportunity to do something special.

"The place was rocking, the stands were shaking; it was old-school Yankee Stadium baseball," Randolph said. "The place was going nuts and we were playing one of our hated rivals, so you could cut the tension with a knife. You had the announcement about people throwing stuff on the field, the grounds crew was picking everything up, but Chris stepped up there, nonchalant and cool as a cucumber.

"First pitch—bam! Then all hell broke loose."

Chambliss ambushed Littell on his first offering, driving it deep to right-center field. The crowd of 56,821 went bananas as the ball cleared the wall, many of them rushing onto the field to celebrate with their pinstriped heroes.

"I swung and hit it over the fence," Chambliss said. "I wasn't really trying to hit a homer—I never had success trying to hit a home run. I was just trying for a good swing."

"The at-bat was like slow-motion," Randolph said. "He took one swing and we were going to the World Series."

Chambliss rounded first base without any issues, but as he reached second base, the fans had made their way onto the infield. Chambliss was tripped up after he rounded second, getting back to his feet quickly as he realized a mob was rapidly closing in on the field.

"I didn't think I was going to get around the bases," Chambliss told reporters that night. "I was punching and struggling and people were trying to drag me down and rip my clothes off. My only thought was to get around. I knew I had to touch all the bases."

Fans swarmed Chambliss, some of whom tried to steal the batting helmet right off of his head. As he headed toward third base—or at least the area where third base had been before it was taken out of the ground—Chambliss took off his helmet and tucked it in his arm like a football.

And to further that analogy, he had a blocker in front of him, too.

"As all the people are coming on the field, and as Chris was rounding first base, I was thinking that if Chris didn't touch home plate, it wouldn't count," Randolph said. "I just had this crazy thought that I had to get out there and make some interference so he could get around the bases. I was out there knocking people over like I was a pulling guard."

Chambliss also knocked some fans over, though who could blame him? The crowd had gotten completely out of control.

"Someone grabbed my hat—and took a little of my afro with it—so I went after the guy," Randolph said. "I was finally like, 'What are you doing? Get off the field!' Just trying to get through the crowd to get back was scary; it was really terrifying. Reggie [Jackson] was knocking people over, [Graig] Nettles was whacking people with a bat. I don't know why, but my dad ran down to the to the field and jumped into the dugout. When I got to the dugout, I saw a cop had my dad in a headlock and was choking him. I was like, 'That's my dad! Let him go!' I grabbed my father and we ran down the tunnel."

Tucked away safely in the triumphant Yankees clubhouse, Chambliss was taking part in the celebration when somebody told him he never touched home plate. Chambliss threw on a jacket and was escorted to the field by a pair of security guards, only there was no plate to touch. It, like almost everything else on the field that night, had been lifted by the fans after they invaded the field.

"There was nothing there but the outline of the plate," Chambliss told the *New York Daily News*. "I put my foot on that and we went back inside. I heard rumors that the umpires saw it, but they had to be gone by then. I was later told by some of the umpires that, under those circumstances, they wouldn't have reversed it because of all of that. I know they came up with a rule later."

That would be Rule 4.09 (b), which allows umpires to award a run to a base runner who has not touched home plate "if fans rush onto the field and physically prevent the runner from touching home plate or the batter from touching first base." It is popularly known as the "Chris Chambliss Rule."

After the game, Chambliss tried to reflect on his historic hit, but the reality of the situation hadn't yet sunk in.

"Now I know how Bobby Thomson felt," Chambliss told reporters. "I didn't realize what had happened until I saw the fans coming from all over the place and the guys coming out of the dugout. It still hasn't hit me yet. I think it will be a couple of days, maybe until I see it on television, before it really hits me."

Manager Billy Martin had no such trouble expressing his exhilaration.

"When Chris hit that home run in the ninth, I don't think I've ever been happier or prouder in my entire life, even when I got the hit to win the 1953 World Series for the Yankees," Martin said. "I just started jumping up and down. I didn't know what to do. I waited for the ball to clear the fence—I never take anything for granted—and then I saw people flying all around me.

"To me, personally seeing [the pennant] come back to New York means more than anything I've done in my career. Now I think I know how Casey Stengel felt back then."

Chambliss joined Bill Mazeroski, whose home run in Game 7 of the 1960 World Series lifted the Pittsburgh Pirates past the Yankees, as the only players to end a series with a home run at that point in history.

Through the 2021 postseason, there had been 12 series that ended with a walk-off home run, though only the Yankees' Aaron Boone (2003 ALCS versus the Red Sox), the Blue Jays' Edwin Encarnacion (2016 AL wild card game versus the Orioles), and the Dodgers' Chris Taylor (2021 NL wild card game versus the Cardinals) have accomplished the feat the way Chambliss did—in a winner-take-all postseason game.

In case you're wondering, the term "walk-off" was not introduced into the baseball lexicon until April 1988, when reliever Dennis Eckersley used it during a postgame interview with the *San Francisco Chronicle*. The future Hall of Famer, who would give up one of the most famous game-ending home runs to Kirk Gibson in the World Series just six months later, used the term "walk-off piece" to describe the dejected pitcher walking off the mound after giving up the game, not the winning team walking off with a victory.

Thomson's "Shot Heard 'Round the World" did send the Giants to the World Series, but back in 1951, there was no such thing as "postseason games" other than the World Series, so the playoff between the Giants and Dodgers is not considered part of that list.

"Why was Chambliss' home run different than Bobby Thomson, except that was Giants versus Dodgers?" Appel said. "It accomplished the same thing in the same sort of dramatic moment as Thomson's; I think it should be mentioned in the same breath. It was Yankees–Royals, and it took them into the World Series just as Thomson's took the Giants into the World Series. That home run should be in the same sentence with Bobby Thomson, but it isn't."

Fenway Frenzy

Bucky Dent's middle name is Earl. At least it was until October 2, 1978.

That's when his name underwent a transformation, at least in the New England region. With one legendary swing at Fenway Park, Dent became a key figure—perhaps *the* key figure—in a rivalry described by many as the best and most heated in all of professional sports.

The story of Dent's famous—or infamous, depending on your baseball allegiances—home run starts about 18 months before he launched that ball deep into the Boston sky.

Dent had reported to spring training with the Chicago White Sox in 1977, preparing for his fourth full big-league season on the South Side. A sure-handed shortstop with a bat good enough to keep him in the everyday lineup, Dent had finished second in American League Rookie of the Year voting in 1974, then made his first All-Star team the following year.

During the first week of camp in 1977, Dent received a phone call from his friend Joe Illigasch, who was a producer on *60 Minutes*, the popular CBS news program.

"Joe said, 'Hey, we're doing a story on George Steinbrenner,'" Dent said. "Stay home tonight, because he's meeting with Bill Veeck and they're going to be talking about a trade for you.' I said, 'Oh my God, that's awesome!'"

Dent had been a Yankees fan while growing up in Hialeah, Florida, just 25 miles from the team's spring training site. He was drafted by the St. Louis Cardinals in the ninth round in 1969, but chose to attend Miami Dade College.

The Cardinals selected him again with the No. 6 pick in the secondary phase of the January 1970 draft—baseball had two drafts each year at the time, including a "secondary phase" in which players who did not sign from the previous draft were eligible—but he spurned St. Louis for a second time.

Five months later, the White Sox took Dent with the sixth pick in the secondary phase of the June draft, signing the shortstop. Dent worked his way through Chicago's system and made his major league debut on June 1, 1973, but he appeared in just 40 games that season, becoming the team's starting shortstop in 1974.

But now he had a chance to go play for the Yankees, who had been to the World Series in 1976 and looked to be in position to contend once again.

At least that's what Illigasch had heard; as the weeks passed, no trade had taken place. Spring training was coming to its conclusion, leaving Dent to prepare for another season in Chicago.

On the final day of camp, Dent's phone rang.

"I picked it up and I heard this voice in a crowd: 'I'm George Steinbrenner. I have a trade that will bring you to the New York

Yankees if you'll sign a contract,'" Dent said. "My heart started pounding. Nick Buoniconti, the Dolphins linebacker, was my agent at the time, so I told Mr. Steinbrenner I would call him back and I called Nick, I said, 'Make this trade happen; I want to go to New York.' He called back about 10 minutes later and said I had been traded to New York. I was ecstatic."

Dent signed a three-year contract with the Yankees that paid him $200,000 per season, prompting the *New York Times* to note that the Bombers "had added another expensive star to their glittering cast" with the trade.

Dent joined the Yankees in New York for the season opener, walking into a clubhouse filled with a number of outsized personalities, including manager Billy Martin, captain Thurman Munson, and new free-agent acquisition Reggie Jackson. The 25-year-old Dent felt pressure to perform for his new club, but given the headlines that encapsulated the Yankees that summer, he mostly blended into the background.

"When I got there, it was the year of Summer of Sam, the blackouts, all the chaos," Dent said. "I was just trying to fit in. I just wanted to win."

Dent hit .247 with eight home runs—his career high—and 49 RBI, batting ninth in the Yankees' powerful lineup. The Yankees had their ups and downs during that chaotic summer, but New York took over first place for good in the AL East in late August, then beat the Kansas City Royals in the AL Championship Series to earn their second straight trip to the World Series.

The Yankees beat the Dodgers in three of the first five games of the World Series, leaving New York one victory from a title with the next two games slated to take place in the Bronx.

Game 6 started off precariously for Dent, whose first-inning error opened the door for the Dodgers to take a lead on Steve

Garvey's two-run triple. Chris Chambliss bailed out Dent with a two-run homer in the second inning, but the real show had not yet begun.

Reggie Smith homered in the third inning to give the Dodgers a 3–2 lead, though he would ultimately be the least significant Reggie in the game. Jackson put the Yankees ahead in the fourth with a two-run homer against Burt Hooten, then took Elias Sosa deep in the sixth, belting another two-run homer on the first pitch.

Jackson led off the eighth with a solo blast off Charlie Hough, his third home run in as many pitches.

"Reggie hit the first home run, then another," Dent said. "The last one he hit, oh my God, the Stadium was just electric. I knew we were seeing something really special."

While the Dodgers had cycled through four pitchers—none of whom could figure out how to pitch to Jackson—Yankees starter Mike Torrez came back out for the ninth with a five-run lead, looking to lock down the championship.

The Dodgers tried to mount a rally, but Torrez retired Lee Lacy to end the game, sealing the Yankees' first World Series title in 15 years.

"There were a lot of high expectations to win that year, so to actually do it was just really awesome," Dent said. "I still get flashbacks of standing at short waiting for the last out, wondering if I would have to run for my life because people ran on the field back in those days. Was I going to jump on Torrez or run for my life? It was the greatest feeling. It's something you wait for your whole life."

Kids do dream of winning the World Series, but when they're in their backyard playing Wiffle ball, that fantasy rarely involves standing at shortstop waiting for the final out. Dent's fantasy scenario during his youth was to be Mickey Mantle, stepping to the plate in the ninth inning with two outs and the bases loaded.

That wasn't the precise setting when Dent forever etched his name into baseball lore, but it turned out to be pretty damn close.

The 1978 Yankees entered the season with their sights set on back-to-back championships, but the Red Sox had a stellar first half, building a double-digit lead in the AL East. On July 19, Boston led the second-place Milwaukee Brewers by nine games, while the fourth-place Yankees were an afterthought, sitting 14 games behind the Sox.

New York went on a nice run beginning in mid-August, slicing Boston's lead down to 6½ games by the time the calendar flipped to September. By September 13, the Yankees had erased the lead altogether, taking over sole possession of first place, carrying that lead into the final weekend of the regular season.

Clinging to a one-game lead, the Yankees hosted Cleveland that weekend, while the Red Sox had a three-game set with the Toronto Blue Jays at Fenway Park.

The Yankees won the first two games against Cleveland, while the Red Sox held serve with a pair of victories over the Blue Jays. New York suffered a different type of loss in the Friday-night game, as Willie Randolph suffered a hamstring injury while running to first base.

Needing either a win or a Red Sox loss on the final day of the season to clinch the division, the Yankees found themselves on the wrong side of both results. The teams finished the season with identical 99–63 records, setting up a winner-take-all playoff game the next day; a coin toss determined it would take place at Fenway Park.

"Leading up to that moment, just the day, how big of a game that was, you could feel the electricity in the crowd," Dent said.

"We were always very loose, but there was more of a serious vibe to that day. That game was the most nerve-wracking game I ever played in."

Carl Yastrzemski took Ron Guidry deep to lead off the second inning, getting the Red Sox on the board. Guidry and Torrez—the same pitcher who hurled a complete game in the Yankees' 1977 World Series clincher—traded zeros on the scoreboard after that through the fifth, but Jim Rice singled in a run in the sixth, doubling Boston's lead to 2–0.

Torrez was in total control through the first six innings, limiting the Yankees to just two hits. The game was still there for the taking, but the right-hander was making quick work of the Yankees inning after inning. To borrow a phrase from the great Yogi Berra, it was getting late early for New York.

"I just tried to keep the game close and wait for somebody to do something to help us," Guidry said. "I'm in the dugout and we're losing 2–0, but I'm thinking, 'If we can't score any runs, we're not going to win anyway.'"

Chris Chambliss and Roy White hit one-out singles in the seventh, putting the tying runs on base. Jim Spencer pinch-hit for Brian Doyle, who had started at second base in place of the injured Randolph, but he flied out to left.

Up stepped Dent, who hadn't exactly been tearing the cover off the ball of late; he entered the game with seven hits in his previous 54 at-bats—a meager .130 average—while driving in only two runs during that 19-game stretch. Dent had hit a mere five home runs in 122 games that season—including only one since the All-Star break—so as he walked toward the plate, hitting one out was the last thing on his mind.

Dent took the first pitch for a ball, then fouled Torrez's second offering off his left foot, sending a shooting pain through his leg. Trainer Gene Monahan emerged from the dugout to check on Dent, spraying the area with a numbing agent to help ease the pain.

"We didn't have any more infielders; we only had 24 guys because Willie was hurt and we had just pinch-hit for Doyle," Dent said. "I was staying in there; I didn't care."

As Dent prepared to step back into the box, a bat boy stopped him and handed him a new bat. Mickey Rivers had noticed a chip in Dent's lumber from the on-deck circle, so he handed his bat to the bat boy and had him bring it to Dent, who was still shaking off the pain of the foul ball.

Choking up on the bat as was his custom, Dent waited for Torrez to deliver the 1-1 pitch. The right-hander left a fastball over the plate and Dent took a big hack, sending a towering fly ball to left field.

Watching from his seat in the dugout, Guidry wasn't sure if the ball would clear the 37-foot-high Green Monster, but with the base runners going on contact, the game would likely be tied.

"Then the ball goes out," Guidry said. "Now all of a sudden we're winning."

Even Dent wasn't certain the ball was going to leave the yard, but the crowd's reaction was all the evidence he needed.

"I didn't know if it was going to be high enough to get out," Dent said. "Rounding first base and hearing how quiet Fenway was other than a sprinkling of Yankees fans, then I knew."

The Fenway faithful were stunned. The sellout crowd fell silent, watching in disbelief as Dent rounded the bases.

"Bucky was a clutch player, but nobody expected him to be the one to go deep at Fenway Park in that situation; everybody was a little surprised," Randolph said. "When that ball went over the wall, you could hear a small cluster of people in the family section, you could hear George and a few of the front-office people by the dugout, but that was it. It was the most deafening silence I had ever heard in my life. That place just went totally silent; it was eerie."

The Yankees held a one-run lead, but at Fenway Park, that wasn't a cause for celebration. Not yet, anyway.

Moments after Dent's homer, Rivers drew a walk and stole second base, scoring on Thurman Munson's double to make it 4–2. The Red Sox still had three turns at bat to get back into the game, but after Guidry gave up a one-out hit in the bottom of the seventh, manager Bob Lemon called closer Rich "Goose" Gossage into the game.

Gossage got through the seventh unscathed, then Jackson blasted a solo home run against Bob Stanley, who had relieved Torrez following the Rivers walk in the seventh. The Yankees now led by three runs and had their star closer on the mound needing only six more outs.

"It got really intense as the game went on," Dent said. "Gossage came in in the seventh inning and he started to struggle a little bit."

Four of Boston's first five batters in the eighth had hits, including RBI singles by Yastrzemski and Fred Lynn that trimmed the Yankees' lead to one. With runners at first and second and only one out, Gossage settled himself and got the next two batters, holding the one-run lead.

The Red Sox were due to send their 9-1-2 hitters up in the ninth; if any of them was to reach base, that would mean giving Jim Rice a chance to do damage with Yastzremski hitting right behind him.

Pinch-hitter Dwight Evans flied out to lead off the inning, but Gossage walked Rick Burleson, then Jerry Remy singled to right field, where Piniella made a great play that prevented Burleson from going to third base.

"That was the play of the game, I thought, because Rice hit a long fly ball that would have been a sacrifice fly and tied the game," Dent said. "The tension was high in the last three innings as the game started to build. We were down, we were up, then they started to come back."

Instead, Rice's fly ball advanced Burleson to third base, leaving runners at the corners with two outs.

"The last play of the game, Goose versus Yastrzemski; it came down to our guy against their guy," Dent said. "It's still vivid in my mind. He threw a fastball, but Goose had a knack of reaching back a little bit more and getting a little extra. Four feet from the plate, it just exploded and Yastrzemski popped the ball up to third base. You could just feel the wind go out of the ballpark after Nettles caught it."

The Yankees had won the AL East, giving them a shot at repeating as World Series champs. Dent's unlikely home run made him a household scourge all over New England, where Earl was no longer his middle name.

"It was like my badge of honor with them, being named Bucky F'n Dent," he said. "Going there and hearing people call me that, I always got a chuckle out of it. I still get it to this day."

Dent's home run was instantly a part of Yankees lore, joining a list of clutch hits that included Jackson's three-homer game in the 1977 World Series, Chambliss' pennant-winning blast in 1976, Roger Maris' 61st home run in 1961, Mickey Mantle's 500th homer, and Babe Ruth's famed called shot in the 1932 World Series.

"They still could have lost the game, and the home run would barely be a footnote," said Marty Appel, a longtime Yankees public relations director and author of *Pinstripe Empire*. "The fact that they won the game defined the enormity of that home run. You certainly didn't realize it that very day at that very moment."

Dent knew the home run's significance in terms of getting to the postseason, where the Yankees disposed of the Royals in the ALCS before beating the Dodgers in another six-game World Series. Dent hit .417 (10-for-24) with seven RBI in the series, earning MVP honors.

"You dream as a kid; I wanted to be a Yankee, I wanted to win a championship," Dent said. "I wasn't thinking about being the Most Valuable Player, but when it happens, you're like, 'Wow.' All those things in the backyard when I was 10, they all came true. It was special. To be named MVP was really an honor and a special thing."

Illigasch, Dent's friend who had informed him 20 months earlier that the Yankees were trying to acquire him, called to congratulate him on his incredible October run. Illigasch told Dent to prepare for a new level of fame, a concept Dent hadn't even considered.

"Joe told me, 'Bucky, that that home run is going to change your life.' I was like, 'What are you talking about?' He said, 'I'm telling you; it's going to change your life.'"

The impact was immediate; Dent was represented by the William Morris Agency, opening doors to the world of show business. The fruits of his labor came fast and furious: commercials for American Motors and Gucci, endorsements for Adidas and an acne medicine, a gum brand bearing his name, a ride on a float in the Macy's Thanksgiving Day parade, appearances on myriad television shows, and, of course, a role in the made-for-TV movie *The Dallas Cowboys Cheerleaders*.

"I didn't know what Joe meant at the beginning," Dent said. "But here we are 40 years later, and he was right. It did change my life."

The King's Coronation

To get an idea of Jim Leyritz's mindset in the biggest moments on the biggest stages, you must travel back to his days growing up as a kid in Cincinnati.

Leyritz spent his formative years as a fan of the "Big Red Machine," the star-studded Cincinnati team from the early to mid-1970s that ruled the baseball world. He and his friend Thom Brennaman—whose father, Marty, was the Reds' radio voice—would make annual trips to spring training, where they would have an opportunity to be bat boys a handful of times each spring.

On one of those occasions, Leyritz found himself alone with Pete Rose, giving the 12-year-old a chance to pick the brain of one of the game's most successful hitters. Leyritz posed a simple question to Rose, looking for the secret to the All-Star's success: *Why are you so good?*

"I treat every at-bat like it's the most important at-bat, whether it's the first at-bat in spring training or the last at-bat in the World Series," Rose told Leyritz. "If I take the first at-bat, even in practice, and I make it like it's going to be my last one, no matter what the situation I'm in, I won't feel that extra pressure."

Decades later, Rose's answer still resonates with Leyritz. From his days in high school ball through his time playing for the University of Kentucky, that advice stuck with him, giving him a consistent approach every time he stepped to the plate.

In 1985, the Yankees and Royals each offered Leyritz $8,000 to sign as an undrafted free agent. He chose the Yankees on the advice of his father, who believed his son's path to the majors would be quicker with New York than with Kansas City, a club that went on to win the World Series that year.

Leyritz spent five years making his way through the Yankees' farm system, always believing he was ready to advance to the next level before the team was ready to promote him.

"You could say a lot of things about Jim, but the one thing that you could definitely say about him is that he had complete confidence in his ability to hit the ball," said Bernie Williams, a teammate and roommate of Leyritz's in the minors. "He believed he was better than anyone else, and that confidence helped him on the field."

Initially signed as a catcher, Leyritz was asked to move around the diamond, seeing time at first base, at third base, and in the outfield. If that versatility was going to help him reach the big leagues, he was happy to be a jack of all trades.

On the final day of camp in 1990, Leyritz was sent back to the minors by manager Bucky Dent; Leyritz believed it was personal, dating back to a run-in the two had while Dent managed him in Single A.

Dent was fired on June 6, just 49 games into what had quickly become a lost season for the Yankees. Two days later, Leyritz made his major league debut, delivering a game-tying, pinch-hit single against the Baltimore Orioles at Memorial Stadium. By the end of 1991, Leyritz's days in the minors were behind him. With captain Don Mattingly leading the charge, Leyritz and fellow youngsters Williams, Kevin Maas, Roberto Kelly, and Hensley Meulens were lined up to be the homegrown core the Yankees hoped would return them to relevance following a pair of losing seasons, a decade without an American League pennant, and 13 years without a championship.

When Buck Showalter took over as the Yankees' manager, Leyritz was excited. He had played for Showalter in the minors and believed he would have an everyday job, but the manager had other ideas. Leyritz's versatility in the field made him an ideal bench player, relegating him to that role during the 1993–94 seasons.

"It was kind of neat to see the transition, but after being with Buck for three or four years in the minors, and now a couple years in the big leagues, sometimes relationships sour a little bit," Leyritz said. "He told me, 'Jimmy, you're more important to me on the bench than you are starting because you can come in the game and hit late, which most young kids can't do.' But I wasn't a young kid; I was 29, 30 years old. I wasn't happy about not being able to play on a regular basis because I was considered more important on the bench for the late innings."

Leyritz assumed backup catching duties in 1994, also getting a handful of at-bats at first base and as the designated hitter. He hit 17 home runs in 249 at-bats, furthering his belief that he should be playing every day.

"He had a lot of belief in himself," Paul O'Neill said.

The Yankees had turned a corner in 1994, posting the best record in the American League before the players went on strike. Expectations were high for the 1995 season, though Leyritz once again found himself as a bench player, backing up starting catcher Mike Stanley.

The role may have been wearing thin for Leyritz, whose offense regressed in 1995. He had little doubt that he would thrive if he were given consistent at-bats, but Showalter liked him in the backup catcher/bench spot. Leyritz had developed a rapport with rookie left-hander Andy Pettitte, catching the majority of his starts during the second half of the season, so when the Yankees earned the AL wild card spot and returned to the postseason for the first time since 1981, Leyritz was behind the plate for Pettitte's Game 2 start against the Seattle Mariners at Yankee Stadium.

Pettitte allowed four runs over seven innings, departing with the Mariners holding a 4–3 lead. The Yankees tied it up in the bottom of the seventh, and after the game moved to extra innings, the teams traded runs in the 12th, sending the game to the 13th.

Leyritz had gotten on base twice in the game, getting hit by a pitch in the sixth and reaching on an error in the eighth. His other four trips to the plate had produced very little, including a 13th-inning at-bat with Mattingly at second base and a chance to win the game. Leyritz hit a weak grounder back to the mound, where Tim Belcher fielded it with ease, holding Mattingly at second base before getting the out at first base.

Disgusted with himself, Leyritz—now 0-for-5 in the game—returned to the dugout and threw a tantrum, breaking his bat out of frustration.

"David Cone was standing at the top of the stairs watching me," Leyritz said. "He said, 'Dude, that's really impressive. You have that much energy after catching this many innings? Don't give up, man. You'll get another chance.'"

With the game still tied in the 15th and Leyritz due up third in the inning for the Yankees, Showalter walked over to the bat rack as Leyritz began to prepare for his at-bat.

"Jimmy, this is your last at-bat," the manager said to Leyritz. "Mike Stanley is going in to catch. Make it count."

Mattingly grounded out to start the inning, then Pat Kelly drew a walk against Belcher, putting the winning run at first base. Leyritz stepped up for what he assumed would be his final shot for the night, determined to do what his manager said: make it count.

Belcher fell behind with three straight balls, then fired a strike. The right-hander came back with another fastball that caught too much of the plate, allowing Leyritz to drive it to the opposite field for a two-run homer. Five hours and 13 minutes after the game had started, the Yankees were walking off the field with a 2–0 lead in the best-of-five series, needing just one win in three games at Seattle's Kingdome to advance to the ALCS.

"After we celebrated and piled on at home plate, I went up to Buck, gave him a hug, and said, 'Did I make it count, Skip?'" Leyritz said. "That was a great moment."

Incredibly, it wasn't the biggest home run Leyritz would hit during his time with the Yankees.

The Yankees went on to lose that series in Seattle, a stunning defeat that sparked an offseason of change. Showalter was out as manager, replaced by veteran skipper Joe Torre. That was good news for Leyritz, who had fallen out of favor with Showalter despite his memorable home run.

Torre planned to use Leyritz as Pettitte's exclusive personal catcher, also vowing to get him more at-bats by using him to fill in all around the diamond. It wasn't the everyday job Leyritz had been longing for all those years, but after getting his first taste of the postseason in 1995, Leyritz believed the Yankees were on the verge of something special.

For the fourth consecutive year, Leyritz finished the regular season with roughly 300 at-bats, and although his offensive totals were average at best, he and Pettitte formed a stellar battery. The young lefty went 21–8, finishing second in the AL Cy Young vote, throwing to Leyritz in 175⅓ of his 221 innings that season.

The Yankees didn't settle for the wild card as they had the prior season; Torre's troops captured the AL East title with a 92–70 record, the franchise's first division crown since 1980.

Predictably, Leyritz's postseason playing time was tied directly to Pettitte, giving the catcher the nod in Game 2 of the AL Division Series against the Texas Rangers, then Games 1 and 5 of the AL Championship Series against the Baltimore Orioles. Leyritz's leadoff homer in the third inning of Game 5 sparked a six-run frame for the Yankees, who held on to close the Orioles out in five games, delivering New York's first pennant since 1981.

Pettitte was blasted by the Atlanta Braves in Game 1 of the World Series, hit for seven runs in just 2⅓ innings. Some believed the extra rest—the Yankees hadn't played a game in seven days—hindered Pettitte, while others believed the southpaw might have been tipping his pitches.

Torre laid some of the blame on Leyritz, charging the catcher with falling in love with Pettitte's cutter rather than using his entire arsenal of pitches. After the Yankees lost Game 2 in the Bronx, Torre was toying with the idea of starting Joe Girardi behind the plate in Game 5—assuming the Yankees were able to extend the series that far with the next two games set to be played at Atlanta's Turner Field.

The Yankees won Game 3 behind a strong start by David Cone and a big night at the plate by Bernie Williams. Torre handed the ball to Kenny Rogers for Game 4, hoping the left-hander could churn out five or six good innings before handing a lead to the Yankees' rock-solid bullpen.

"Kenny goes out there and shits the bed in the first couple innings and we're down 6–0," Leyritz said. "I remember being on the bench with Pat Kelly and telling him, 'Thank God we didn't get swept.'"

Leyritz retreated to the clubhouse to lift weights, unaware that Torre had decided not to start him in Game 5. But with these games being played under National League rules in Atlanta, Leyritz was likely to get into the game at some point, so he was summoned back to the dugout.

Three runs in the sixth inning drove Braves starter Denny Neagle from the game, but the Yankees were unable to pull any closer despite Torre using O'Neill and Tino Martinez (who was traded from the Mariners to the Yankees after the 1995 season) as pinch-hitters in the inning.

O'Neill had pinch-hit for Girardi, so Leyritz took over catching duties in the bottom of the sixth. The Yankees went down meekly in the seventh, moving the Braves six outs away from a commanding three-games-to-one lead.

Atlanta manager Bobby Cox called on Mark Wohlers, his All-Star closer, to record those final six outs. Leyritz was due up fourth in the inning, but first he had to find a piece of lumber to use against the hard-throwing righty.

"Darryl Strawberry had a brand-new box of Mizunos next to the bat rack," Leyritz said. "I said to Straw, 'I've only got two bats left and I'm facing [John] Smoltz tomorrow; please let me borrow one of your bats. I don't want to break one of mine.'"

Strawberry gave Leyritz one of his bats, then followed Charlie Hayes' leadoff single with a hit of his own. Mariano Duncan grounded into a fielder's choice, putting runners at the corners with one out for Leyritz, who had asked bench coach Don Zimmer for a quick scouting report on Wohlers.

"Zim said, 'Jimmy, he throws 100 miles an hour; just get it in play,'" Leyritz said. "I didn't read a lot of the reports and I didn't really care about all the details; all I wanted to know was how hard the guy threw and what his pitches were. I didn't really know what pitches he had; I just knew he threw 100 miles an hour."

Leyritz saw that heat Zimmer had described on Wohlers' first pitch, a 98-mph fastball that he swung through. Wohlers followed with a pair of high sliders, then Leyritz fouled off a 99-mph fastball to even the count at 2-2.

"I said to myself, 'OK, you know he's going to throw a slider here.' Sure enough, 2-2 he threw a slider and I reached out and barely fouled it off," Leyritz said.

"As a catcher I'm thinking, 'OK, now you go back in with that 100-mph fastball.' Even Tim McCarver on the broadcast said, 'I think Wohlers is going to the slider too much.'"

Wohlers tried his luck with yet another slider, but this 86-mph offering hung over the plate just long enough for Leyritz to put a good swing on it. The ball sailed to left-center field, clearing the wall where left fielder Andruw Jones had done his best Spider-Man impersonation, scaling his way to the top of the 12-foot fence.

"I'm like, 'There's no way this guy is going to throw me another slider,' so I backed off the plate about a half-inch, and thought, 'OK, if he throws a fastball in, just take it because it's going to be a ball; just look out over the plate." Sure enough, he threw that hanging slider, and because I was looking out over the plate, even though I didn't crush it, I knew when I hit it that it was gone because it was in Atlanta, which was considered a launching pad at the time."

The game was tied 6–6, but the Yankees hadn't won anything yet. They still trailed in the series, and although Leyritz had come through with some late-inning heroics for a second straight October, he and his teammates still had the bitter taste of defeat in their mouths from the previous year in Seattle.

"As I was rounding second base, all I could think about was, 'This home run will mean nothing like the '95 one did,'" Leyritz said. "Even though it's a great moment, it will not be remembered for anything unless we win the series.'"

"What a great at-bat," Martinez said. "You're facing a guy that throws 100 mph, one of the best closers in the game, and he hangs a slider of all pitches and he hits it out of the ballpark."

As he crossed the plate, Leyritz looked toward the field seats where Braves owner Ted Turner and his famous wife Jane Fonda had been celebrating just moments earlier.

"Their heads were in their chest," Leyritz said. "I'm like, 'Perfect.'"

The Yankees scored twice against Steve Avery in the top of the 10th, then Graeme Lloyd and John Wetteland combined for a scoreless bottom of the inning, evening the series at two games apiece to ensure no less than a Game 6 back in the Bronx.

"Jimmy isn't cocky, but he had this arrogance about him when he would go to the plate and twirl his bat; he was up there knowing that he has a good chance to get a base hit and hit the ball hard," Martinez said. "Those moments never fazed him; the home run off of Wohlers that year really turned the whole series around and jumpstarted us to the '96 World Series championship. He always had that swagger; I played against him in Double A and he had that same aura about him."

The thrilling Game 4 victory did more than provide Leyritz with another career highlight; it forced Torre to change his mind about starting him behind the plate to catch Pettitte in Game 5.

"When he hit the home run in Game 4, I said 'You're catching tomorrow. I wasn't going to catch you, but after hitting the home run, I have no choice. I don't want you falling in love with that cutter. He has other stuff he needs to use,'" Torre said. "He went out and called a good game and Andy pitched a gem."

Indeed, he did. Pettitte threw 8⅓ scoreless innings, getting the better of future Hall of Famer John Smoltz in a pitching duel reminiscent of Smoltz's classic Game 7 showdown with Jack Morris and the Minnesota Twins five years earlier.

The series returned to New York for Game 6, where the Yankees finished off the Braves with a 3–2 win to clinch their first World Series championship in 18 years. Wetteland saved all four victories and was named World Series Most Valuable Player, but there was little question that Leyritz's clutch home run was the Yankees' most valuable play.

"You could argue that was the play of the series," Girardi said. "Jimmy really had a knack for that. Jimmy exuded confidence, and other people felt the confidence because of him. Mariano Duncan had the saying, 'We play today, we win today.' Jimmy Leyritz was like that, too."

With young catching prospect Jorge Posada ready to graduate to the big-league team to back up Girardi, the Yankees traded Leyritz to the Anaheim Angels six weeks after the World Series. He was dealt to the Texas Rangers prior to the trade deadline that July, then to the Boston Red Sox after the 1997 season.

The Red Sox traded him to the San Diego Padres in June 1998, the very team that opposed the Yankees in the World Series that fall. Leyritz—who hit three home runs against the Houston Astros in the NL Division Series and another in the NL Championship Series against the Braves—went 0-for-10 in the series as the Yankees swept San Diego, completing one of the greatest seasons in baseball history.

San Diego was talking with Boston about a deal to send Leyritz back to the Red Sox the following July, but once word of that potential deal made its way to George Steinbrenner, The Boss stepped in and reacquired the catcher at the trade deadline.

Now 35 years old, Leyritz didn't have the same pop in his bat that he had earlier in his career, leading to some good-natured razzing from his teammates on a regular basis.

"Jeter, Knoblauch and all those guys would make fun of me because I couldn't hit a ball out during batting practice," Leyritz said. "I kept telling them, 'Guys, don't worry; when it counts, I'll hit a home run.' Sure enough, my last at-bat in the '99 World Series, I hit a home run in the eighth inning. Jeter was like, 'You've got to be kidding me!' I said, 'I told you when it counted, I would hit a home run!' That became the last home run of the century."

Leyritz retired in 2000, finishing his career with 90 home runs and 387 RBI in 903 regular season games. The postseason was a different story for Leyritz, who homered eight times in 28 games, collecting a pair of World Series rings in the process.

"Your mind rules your body; he wills himself in those spots," Torre said. "He certainly was unlike most other players where he just oozed all that confidence and let you know about it."

Two of those homers will forever be remembered among the greatest in Yankees history, which is saying something given the franchise's track record of memorable moments. Which one does Leyritz treasure most? His answer might surprise you.

"Even though the '96 home run wound up being bigger than any home run I ever hit as far as that what it did for the franchise," Leyritz said, "For a personal moment, that walk-off at Yankee Stadium after catching all 15 innings of a playoff game is still my fondest memory."

Home Runs
and Healing

Smoke could still be seen wafting above downtown Manhattan, the smoldering ruins from the terrorist attack at the World Trade Center seven weeks earlier.

It was October 30, 2001. The Yankees were back in the World Series for the fourth consecutive year and the fifth time in six seasons, but this autumn was unlike any other. The horrific events of September 11 still felt fresh to all Americans, but for New Yorkers, it was personal.

Loved ones were still holding out hope that missing family and friends might be found, while those who had lost people during the attacks dealt with their grief daily, wondering when—or if—life would ever be the same.

October had been a cause for celebration in New York over the previous five years, at least for the faction of the city's baseball's fans who bled pinstripes. This year, however, baseball was a secondary thought for most New Yorkers, many of whom were finding it difficult to move on with their normal lives following 9/11.

In most years, the Yankees gave fans outside of New York a common enemy. Rooting against the Bronx Bombers was an annual rite of passage for fans from Boston to Los Angeles, all of whom had seemingly grown tired of New York's string of success.

For one fall, at least, that changed.

America rallied around New York after 9/11, astonished by the tireless work of the city's police, firefighters, and other first responders in the wake of the tragedy. As the Yankees worked their way through the postseason, something crazy happened: fans around the country were cheering for Joe Torre's team, uniting in their support for a team representing a city that had gone through unspeakable heartbreak.

"All of a sudden we were not the hated Yankees, but almost like America's Team," Paul O'Neill said. "America was pulling for New York, which was weird."

The Yankees had fought their way back against the Oakland Athletics after losing the first two games at Yankee Stadium in the AL Division Series, winning both games at the Coliseum. Game 3, of course, featured Derek Jeter's memorable flip play, then Bernie Williams drove in five runs in a lopsided Game 4 win, sending the series back to the Bronx for a winner-take-all Game 5.

"To play in the playoffs there, there was a feeling that the world was getting going again," said former Oakland slugger Jason Giambi, who would wind up signing with the Yankees after that season. "It was like, 'Here we go—Yankees baseball.

After such a horrific event, to try to get some normalcy, it felt really surreal."

Roger Clemens wasn't great in Game 5, but the bullpen backed him up with 4⅔ scoreless innings, locking down a 5–3 win that sent the Yankees back to the ALCS. There was no such close call in that series, as the Yankees disposed of the 116-win Seattle Mariners in five games, wrapping up another AL pennant.

The Yankees were back in the World Series, trying to become just the third team in major league history to win four straight championships. The 1936–39 Yankees had accomplished the feat with Lou Gehrig and Joe DiMaggio, while the 1949–53 squad won five consecutive titles while making the transition from DiMaggio to Mickey Mantle.

Torre's Yankees had thrust themselves into the conversation about the greatest teams of all time, and a fourth straight championship would strengthen their case. The Arizona Diamondbacks were all that stood in their way, but with co-aces Randy Johnson and Curt Schilling leading the way, winning another World Series was going to be a tall task.

Schilling and Johnson were dominant in the first two games at Bank One Ballpark in Phoenix, as the Diamondbacks outscored the Yankees 13–1. Schilling struck out eight batters over seven innings of one-run ball in Game 1, then Johnson twirled a masterpiece in Game 2, throwing a three-hit shutout, fanning 11 Yankees.

The Yankees were down, but not out. The three games coming up in the Bronx promised to be as emotional as any in recent history, the city coming together a few more times to try willing the home team to victory.

But before Clemens threw the first pitch in Game 3, President George W. Bush had one of his own to deliver.

Bush was in attendance to throw the ceremonial first pitch, a sign to the country and the world that the United States was bouncing back strong from the terror attacks. Wearing a bulletproof vest beneath an FDNY pullover, Bush strolled to the mound, gave a thumbs-up to the sellout crowd, then thought about the advice Derek Jeter had just offered him in the tunnel as he warmed up his arm.

"Don't bounce it," Jeter told Bush after suggesting he throw the pitch from the rubber. "They'll boo you."

Bush fired a strike to catcher Todd Greene, causing Yankee Stadium to erupt. Regardless of what was about to happen in the game, it felt as though the highlight of the night was already in the books.

"I had never felt what I felt before when I walked out of that dugout," Bush later said. "I felt the raw emotion of the Yankee fans."

Clemens took care of business, striking out nine Arizona batters over seven innings of one-run ball. Mariano Rivera breezed through the final two frames, sealing a 2–1 victory that pulled the Yankees back into the series.

The sight of Schilling on the mound in Game 4 was a scary one for the Yankees, which was apropos given that it was being played on Halloween night. Working on three days' rest, Schilling practically replicated his Game 1 pitching line: seven innings, three hits, one run, nine strikeouts.

Orlando "El Duque" Hernandez had done his part to match Schilling on the mound, giving up one run over 6⅓ innings. But Mike Stanton, who had induced a key double play to end the seventh, combined with Ramiro Mendoza to allow two runs in the top of the eighth, taking some air out of the Bronx crowd.

Arizona handed a two-run lead to its closer, Byung-Hyun Kim, who was being asked to get the final six outs. The first three were effortless; the side-arming Kim struck out the side in the eighth, catching Shane Spencer looking at strike three before blowing away both Scott Brosius and Alfonso Soriano.

If the Yankees were going to tie the best-of-seven series at two games apiece, they had three outs remaining to make something happen. Jeter tried to bunt his way on, but third baseman Matt Williams threw him out. O'Neill stroked a single to left field, giving the Yankees the base runner they needed to bring the tying run to the plate.

Kim struck out Williams, leaving Arizona one out away from a commanding 3–1 lead in the best-of-seven series. The Fox cameras caught general manager Brian Cashman watching anxiously from his box, his arms crossed as he waited for a miracle.

It didn't take long for the miracle to happen.

Tino Martinez jumped on Kim's first pitch, drilling it deep into the Bronx night. As the ball cleared the wall in right-center field, the 55,863 fans lost their collective minds. Bush's ceremonial first pitch the night before was emotional and inspirational, but this was the type of moment New Yorkers had been waiting for.

"I was up there basically trying to have a good at-bat and hit the ball hard," Martinez said. "To hit a home run to tie the game with two outs in the bottom of the ninth inning when you're about to go down 3–1 to the Diamondbacks, it was one of the most exciting moments of my career. Not just hitting it, but seeing the fans' reaction after that, which lasted until the end of the game. Those are the things you dream of as a kid."

As the game moved to the 10th inning, Torre called on Mariano Rivera to take over, as there would be no save situation that night. Rivera retired the Diamondbacks on three ground balls, sending the Yankees back to the plate.

Kim had already thrown 45 pitches over two innings, but Arizona manager Bob Brenly sent him back to the mound for the 10th. Brosius and Soriano both flied out, turning over the lineup for Jeter, the Yankees' leadoff hitter.

Jeter fouled off the first pitch he saw as the clock struck midnight, officially marking the end of October. For the first time ever, the World Series was being played in November.

"ATTENTION FANS" the stadium scoreboard read. "WELCOME TO NOVEMBER BASEBALL."

Some fans with foresight had brought signs reading "Mr. November," hoping to give that nickname to that night's hero.

Jeter quickly fell behind 0–2 against Kim, but the Yankees shortstop wouldn't go down quietly. He took a ball, fouled off a pair of pitches, then took two more balls to work the count full. Jeter sliced Kim's first 3–2 pitch down the right-field line, but it landed in the seats in foul territory.

Kim's ninth pitch hung over the plate long enough for Jeter to put his signature inside-out swing on the ball, lining it to right field. This one stayed fair, sneaking over the stadium's short porch. Mr. November was born.

"We had been experiencing moments like those since 1996," Williams said. "Every time that we needed a big hit or a big situation would happen, we would seem to get the benefit of the doubt with the baseball gods."

The Yankees had evened the series, and even though they would have to go back to the desert to win the series, they still had another game to play in the Bronx.

Unlike Schilling, Johnson didn't come back to pitch on short rest, so the Yankees found themselves matched up against right-hander Miguel Batista. New York countered with Mike Mussina, who had lasted just three innings in his World Series debut back in Game 1.

Mussina atoned for his Game 1 clunker, holding Arizona to two runs over eight innings. He struck out 10 in his 125-pitch effort, giving the Yankees everything he had in the pivotal game.

Batista didn't have the intimidation factor that Schilling and Johnson brought to the mound, but the 30-year-old pitched a brilliant game, blanking the Yankees over 7⅔ innings. Greg Swindell recorded the final out in the eighth, sending the game to the ninth with the Diamondbacks clinging to a two-run lead.

The Yankees had authored a memorable ending one night earlier, and while there was still one final chance for the offense to pull another rabbit out of its hat, something else dawned on the 56,018 fans in attendance as the home team took the field for the top of the ninth inning.

Paul O'Neill was about to play his final inning in the Bronx.

The popular right fielder, nicknamed "The Warrior" by George Steinbrenner, had intimated that 2001 would be his final season. Game 5 would not be the final game of his career, but the series was shifting back to Bank One Ballpark for Game 6, so O'Neill's time in the home pinstripes was coming to a close.

After Ramiro Mendoza delivered his first pitch to Steve Finley to open the ninth, a pocket of the Yankee Stadium fans began chanting O'Neill's name.

"PAUL O-NEILL! PAUL O-NEILL!"

Seconds later, the entire sellout crowd had joined in, saluting the longtime Yankee as he stood in right field. O'Neill tried to remain focused on the game—as they had shown in Game 4, a two-run lead was not too much to overcome—but it was visible that the chanting was having an effect on the 38-year-old.

The chant was interrupted by a foul ball, but as soon as Mendoza toed the rubber for the next pitch, it began again. This exercise continued throughout the inning, the fans wanting to shower the veteran with love one final time.

After Mendoza induced an inning-ending double play, O'Neill—trying his hardest to keep a stoic face as the fans continued to shout his name—began jogging off the field. He looked into the stands as he approached the dugout, doing everything in his power to keep his composure.

As he approached the dugout, O'Neill tipped his cap to the crowd, acknowledging the fans that had embraced him for nearly a decade.

"It was the right thing to do," O'Neill told reporters after the game. "I was saying thanks, obviously."

The O'Neill salute would be a forever moment in Yankees lore, but there was still the unresolved matter of Game 5. The Diamondbacks carried a 2–0 lead into the bottom of the ninth, but as the Yankees had shown one night earlier, the game was far from over.

During the top of the ninth, Fox had run a poll asking fans, "If you were Bob Brenly, would you bring in Kim for the 9th?" Of those that voted, 57 percent said they would not have utilized the closer again after his 62-pitch disappointment in Game 4.

With Jorge Posada, Shane Spencer, and Chuck Knoblauch due up for the Yankees, Brenly called on Kim to get the final three outs, wanting to give the pitcher a mulligan following his Game 4 meltdown.

Posada led off with a double, once again giving the Yankees an opportunity to bring the tying run to the plate. Spencer grounded out and Knoblauch struck out, leaving New York one out away from a 3–2 deficit in the series and a long flight to Phoenix ahead of them.

The Yankees were a collective 1-for-24 with runners in scoring position in the World Series, wasting one opportunity after another. Martinez had made his swing count in this situation in Game 4, but the thought of Brosius—who was hitting .132 in the postseason, was just 2-for-16 in the series and had gone 0-for-2 against Kim the previous night—replicating the feat seemed virtually impossible.

Or was it?

"The night before, Brosius hit a line drive foul off of Kim when he faced him; he made an out, but I knew he hit the ball hard," Torre said of Brosius, the Yankees' World Series MVP in 1998. "Brosius was one of those sleeping giants; he would come up with huge hits for us like he did in '98. He was a good pressure player."

Brosius took Kim's first pitch for a ball, then turned on the next offering, driving it deep to left field. He knew it was gone from the moment it left his bat, immediately raising his arm as he watched the ball sail into the seats.

"Here we are, down by two runs again," Martinez said. "I was sitting in the dugout by Bernie and when Scott hit it, it was a bomb, so we knew right away it was gone. When he hit it, Bernie and I looked at each other and our jaws just dropped. That was unbelievable."

"We had moments like that all the time; for it to happen back to back, that was a little bit more surprising," Williams said. "That could have happened once and it would have defined the series. To have it happen on consecutive nights, it was just remarkable."

The entire stadium shook as Brosius' ball cleared the fence, as delirious fans tried to process what had just happened. Nobody could believe what they had just witnessed, including Yankees radio voice Michael Kay.

"I never cheered in the booth; I'm not a homer or rooter when I do a game," Kay said. "Brosius hit the home run and I just freaked out. Not like over the air screaming like a college football analyst, but John [Sterling] and I both stood up, he's making his call, and I start punching him in the ribs over and over and over again. He didn't skip a beat; it was just so joyous that this was happening. If you ever listen to a tape of his call, you can hear his voice is kind of vibrating a little because I'm hitting him over and over again. It was one-of-a-kind amazing, and it came right after the Paul O'Neill chant. Everything about that World Series was wondrous and amazing."

Game 4 had been decided in the 10th inning on Jeter's "Mr. November" walk-off home run, but the sequel would take a little longer to conclude. Mariano Rivera and Mike Morgan traded a pair of scoreless innings apiece, then Sterling Hitchcock sat Arizona down in order in the top of the 12th.

Knoblauch led off the Yankees' 12th with a single, but there would be no further heroics by Brosius, who bunted the runner to second base. Alfonso Soriano, the Yankees' impressive rookie second baseman, followed with the biggest hit of his young career, lacing a single to right field that scored Knoblauch for the game-winner.

"The fever pitch noise of Yankee Stadium in Games 3, 4, and 5 were as loud as I've ever heard in my entire life," Martinez said. "The fans wanted it, we wanted it, and in many ways, America wanted it at that point for the first time ever."

Soriano's heroics capped a remarkable three days in the Bronx. Even two decades later, those who lived it still have trouble finding the words to describe those 72 hours.

"That wasn't just any three-game stretch; it's the World Series," Torre said. "It's in New York, and to have everything ratcheted up anyway and the emotions running high after 9/11, it was surreal. There's no other way to explain it. It was like an out-of-body experience, watching those games."

"Doing that with the backdrop of 9/11, having the opportunity to be there for those moments when the city really needed a boost from their sports teams, just to give them a reason to feel happy and to put a smile on their face, to start to get some sense of normalcy in that process, those home runs went a long way toward accomplishing that," Williams said. "The stadium was shaking up and down. The fact that we were able to give the city those moments is something I will never forget."

Two days later, the Diamondbacks torched Pettitte for six early runs, knocking him out of the game in the third inning of what would become a 15–2 Arizona win. This series, which had featured three lopsided games in Phoenix and three classics in the Bronx, was headed for a Game 7.

Clemens and Schilling battled each other zero for zero until Arizona right fielder Danny Bautista broke the scoreless tie with an RBI double in the sixth inning. The Yankees countered with a run in the seventh, with Martinez providing another clutch hit, this one an RBI single against Schilling that tied the game.

Soriano led off the eighth with a home run, a stunning blast against Schilling that left the Yankees six outs from a fourth straight championship.

"He hit that ball out of the ballpark and you felt like you were in the driver's seat," Torre said.

That's because Rivera came out of the bullpen to get the final six outs, something he had done time and time again during New York's dynastic run. The future Hall of Famer tossed a scoreless eighth, but the ninth proved to be a different story.

A single and a throwing error by Rivera put the winning run on base. One out later, Tony Womack delivered a game-tying double to right field, snapping Rivera's postseason streak of 23 straight successful save opportunities that dated back to the start of the 1998 playoffs.

Rivera hit Craig Counsell with a pitch to load the bases, setting up Luis Gonzalez's walk-off bloop single over Jeter's head. The Yankees had lost the World Series in stunning fashion, which shouldn't have been a shock to anybody who had watched these two teams do battle for more than a week.

"You didn't expect it to happen, but sometimes you just expect *something* is going to happen," Mussina said. "We're going to hit home runs off the same guy two days in a row to win the game? No, but that's the way it worked out. You can't even put a bat on the ball all series, then all of a sudden you hit two homers to tie the games? Then the best closer in the game gets beat in Game 7. It's a crazy game."

The Yankees were left to cope with an unfamiliar feeling. They hadn't lost a postseason series since 1997, ending a miraculous run that resulted in three consecutive trips down the Canyon of Heroes.

Yet despite the Game 7 loss, the memories from that World Series evoke plenty of positive memories—and goosebumps—for those who witnessed it up close.

"That's one World Series that you see the Yankees lost, but it almost felt like they won," Kay said. "I always say if you get one 'forever game' in a World Series, you've got a great World Series. If you have two, it's off the charts. There were three, even if you're not counting Game 3 with the president's pitch. With Games 4, 5, and 7, you could make the case that the 2001 World Series is one of the most dramatic World Series that was ever played. It almost seemed like bad fiction, but it happened."

O'Neill followed through on his plan to retire after the season, while Brosius made a surprising announcement that he, too, was hanging up his spikes. Knoblauch and Martinez departed as free agents, so while a good portion of the team's championship core remained, it was clear that the run for this group that had experienced so much success together was over.

"I don't know if it's because I knew I was retiring at the end of it, but my memories of Games 3, 4, and 5 and what was going on in New York City after 9/11, those are the memories I have of that World Series," O'Neill said. "They're more important to me than whether we won or lost, and I don't think I can say that about any other World Series that we were in. Sure, there was disappointment, but in the grand scheme of things, we were getting through something much bigger at the time in the country."

HISTORIC HOMER

The Yankees had won 11 World Series titles prior to 1949, with legendary figures such as Babe Ruth, Lou Gehrig, and Joe DiMaggio accomplishing astonishing feats for the Bronx Bombers.

None of them had ever hit a game-ending home run in the World Series. In fact, until Tommy Henrich took Dodgers right-hander Don Newcombe deep in the bottom of the ninth in Game 1 of the 1949 Fall Classic, nobody in baseball history had ever ended a World Series game by parking one in the seats.

The *New York Times*' John Drebinger wrote that for the first eight and a half innings, "scarcely a wheel turned or a soul in a gathering of 66,224 onlookers so much as dared to draw a deep breath" as Newcombe and Allie Reynolds engaged in a scoreless duel.

Broadcaster Mel Allen had tabbed Henrich with the nickname "Old Reliable" after a train of the same name that ran from Ohio to Alabama, which was renowned for always being on time.

THE FRANCHISE: NEW YORK YANKEES

Living up to that moniker, Henrich took two balls from Newcombe to start the ninth, then hammered a 2–0 hanging curveball into the right-field stands for a 1–0 Yankees victory.

"They call him 'Old Reliable' and they're not joking," broadcaster Red Barber said after watching Henrich round the bases. "With the startling suddenness of a pistol shot, the denouement—the climax—was reached."

"In the twinkling of an eye and long before the white pellet vanished deep into the lower right-field stand most everyone in the arena knew it was over," Drebinger wrote in the *Times*.

Henrich had never been the biggest star on the Yankees, a spot reserved for DiMaggio during Henrich's years in pinstripes. But the right fielder had a knack for coming through when it mattered, earning a reputation as one of the most fundamentally sound players in the game.

"He isn't one of the game's glamour boys," Arthur Daley wrote in the *New York Times* in May 1947. "He's just a coldly efficient workman who does everything remarkably well. He can field with the best of them, throw better than most and hit the big blow when it's vitally necessary, a ball player's ball player in every sense of the word."

Henrich made his first All-Star team in 1942, then missed the next three seasons while serving in the Coast Guard during World War II, but he returned in 1946, playing five more seasons with the Yankees. Henrich made the All-Star team each year from 1947 to '50, helping the Yankees to World Series titles in 1947 and 1949, giving him four championship rings in his 11 seasons.

He finished his career with a .282 batting average, 183 home runs, and 795 RBI in 1,284 regular season games, adding four more home runs in four World Series appearances.

"He was extremely good in big games, games that meant something," former teammate Dr. Bobby Brown told the Associated Press after Henrich died in 2009. "If we were ahead 10−1 or 10−2, he was just average. If we were behind 10−1 or 10−2, same thing. But get him in a big game and he was terrific."

Since Henrich's historic blast, only three other Yankees have hit walk-off home runs in the World Series: Mickey Mantle (1964 Game 3), Chad Curtis (1999 Game 3), and Derek Jeter (2001 Game 4).

Seventh Heaven

AN EXHILARATING HIGH. A DEVASTATING LOW.

Those six words represent Aaron Boone's brief playing career with the Yankees.

Yet less than 48 hours before the Reds traded him to the Yankees in a trade deadline deal, Boone believed he would be finishing out the 2003 season with Cincinnati, the only big-league franchise he had played for during his first six-plus years in the majors.

But as the deadline approached, chaos broke out within the Reds organization. General manager Jim Bowden and manager Bob Boone—Aaron's father—were fired on July 28. With a 46–58 record and Ken Griffey Jr. out for the season with an ankle injury, the Reds began to clean house. Closer Scott Williamson and slugger Jose Guillen were traded the day after the firings, and it looked like more players could be on their way out of town.

But Boone, who had just made the first All-Star team of his career, appeared to be one of the few assured to stay with the club after July 31. There was a sense among people inside the organization that trading Boone would be another public relations hit, and given the events of that week, that was the last thing the Reds needed.

Shortly after the firings took place, Boone met with some of the remaining front-office staff to discuss his future with the club.

"I said, 'If I'm going to be here, I want to be here for all the right reasons,'" Boone said. "They said, 'OK, we'll consider that.' Then I got put on the market a couple days before the trade deadline."

On July 30, Boone's agent, Adam Katz, told him that he would likely be dealt to the Dodgers, Mariners, or Yankees. When Boone awoke on the 31st, Katz informed him that Brian Cashman would be calling him momentarily. He was being traded to the Yankees for pitching prospects Brandon Claussen and Charlie Manning.

"It was a very emotional time," Boone said. "I had really strong ties in Cincinnati. I loved it there; I loved my teammates, I grew up in the organization, I had made my first All-Star team that year. I was very comfortable; I owned my first home there. I loved Cincinnati and loved playing there, but I also understood that I'm going to the Yankees and have a chance to win."

Cashman called Boone to welcome him to the Yankees, then asked him if he could meet the team in Oakland the next day for the start of a three-game series. Boone made the trip out west, where he was greeted by the Athletics' trio of Tim Hudson, Barry Zito, and Mark Mulder, who started the three games against New York. Boone went 2-for-11 in the series as the Yankees lost two of three.

"I joked with Cashman later on and said, 'I would have just met you in New York,'" Boone said.

Like myriad newcomers before him, Boone struggled during his first few weeks in pinstripes. He hit .125 with one RBI in his first 13 games, trying to get acclimated to his new surroundings while attempting to live up to the expectations of being an All-Star traded to a contender for the stretch run.

"You desperately want to ingratiate yourself and do well," Boone said. "I was a very streaky player; I could look like the best player on the field for a couple weeks, then look like I had never played the game for a couple weeks. You want to get out of the gates and do well; I was the trade acquisition at the deadline, so you want to show people why they went out and got you. There probably was a little bit of pressing going on."

On August 15, Boone belted a three-run home run in the ninth inning against Orioles closer Jorge Julio, lifting the Yankees to a much-needed comeback win. That hit seemed to relax Boone, who hit .302 with 12 RBI over his next 15 games, 11 of them Yankees wins.

The streakiness continued as he opened September the way he had opened August, going 2-for-19 against the Blue Jays and Red Sox, including two bad at-bats against Tim Wakefield, Boston's veteran knuckleballer. Despite Boone's hot-and-cold ways, Joe Torre remained firmly in his corner, sending him out to third base every day.

"I forget where we were, but I made an out and I came back to the dugout and said, 'Sorry, Skip. I'm better than this,'" Boone said. "He said, 'Don't ever apologize for the way you play the game.' That meant a lot to me."

Torre's faith was rewarded, as Boone heated up down the stretch. He hit .348 with five home runs and 18 RBI over the

Yankees' final 19 games, a 14–5 run for the club that locked up the American League East title.

The Yankees were headed to the postseason, a place Boone had never been since he broke into the majors in 1997. He scuffled in the AL Division Series, but the Yankees cruised past the Twins in four games.

That set up the showdown the baseball world had been waiting for: Yankees versus Red Sox in the AL Championship Series.

Boone had just three hits in 15 at-bats against Minnesota, and after an 0-for-6 start to the ALCS, he found himself out of the lineup for Game 3 as the series shifted to Fenway Park. His benching had less to do with his performance than the freakish success Enrique Wilson—a light-hitting utility infielder—had enjoyed against Pedro Martinez.

Wilson was 7-for-8 against the Boston ace that season, making him 10-for-20 against the three-time Cy Young Award winner. Torre planned to start Wilson at third base, and while Boone was ice cold at the plate, he didn't take it personally.

The two teams had split the first two games in the Bronx, then the Yankees won two of three in Boston, needing just one win at home to clinch the pennant. The Red Sox mounted a late-inning comeback in Game 6, forcing a winner-take-all contest with the biggest stakes possible.

For the winners, a trip to the World Series. For the losers, a long, cold winter of what-ifs and could've-beens.

"I had George in my ear all year long screaming at me about the Red Sox, the Red Sox, the Red Sox," Cashman said. "Everything was on the line."

With Martinez starting Game 7 for the Red Sox, Torre chose to bench Boone once again in favor of Wilson, who had gone 0-for-4 in Game 3. Boone had gone 2-for-3 with a walk in

Game 5, but an 0-for-4 in Game 6 didn't do much to persuade Torre to give him a shot against Martinez.

"When I found out I wasn't starting Game 7, I was disappointed, but mostly frustrated with myself for putting Joe in the position to make that decision," Boone said. "I wasn't swinging the bat well, which was frustrating. I certainly got it; this is Game 7—get over yourself right now. You have a chance to go to the World Series, so you need to lock it in and be prepared for any situation. I think I did that. I was ready to go, trying to be the best teammate I could be, prepared to go into the game for any situation that I might have been put into."

Boston jumped out to a quick lead with three runs against Roger Clemens in the second inning, two of them coming on a home run by Trot Nixon. Kevin Millar ambushed Clemens with a solo shot on the first pitch of the fourth, then the Yankees ace walked Nixon and gave up a single by Bill Mueller, putting runners at the corners with nobody out.

The Red Sox were threatening to break the game open, leaving Torre searching for an answer as he tried to apply a tourniquet to Boston's rally.

Enter Mike Mussina.

The right-hander had made 400 career starts without a relief appearance, but having started Game 4 in the series, he knew there was a chance the Yankees would need him to come out of the bullpen. Torre and pitching coach Mel Stottlemyre assured Mussina that they would give him ample time to warm up, using him to start a clean inning rather than bringing him in to clean up somebody else's mess.

Even the best-laid plans don't always come to fruition.

"That was the intention, but you get to the point where you panic a little bit when you get in trouble," Torre said. "You trust certain people."

Mussina had started warming up in the bullpen after Millar took Clemens deep, while left-hander Felix Heredia got up once Nixon drew his walk. Mussina assumed that Heredia would be called upon to face the switch-hitting Jason Varitek and left-handed-hitting Johnny Damon, but as Torre walked to the mound, he raised his right arm to signal for Mussina.

"They asked me to do something that I had never even bordered on trying to do," Mussina said. "I had to jog from the Yankee bullpen across the outfield to the infield in the middle of Yankee Stadium in the middle of Game 7 and we're getting beat at home. It's not like I walk in before the game starts like normal. It's 100 yards, and all I kept telling myself was, 'Don't trip and fall down jogging in here.' My heart rate had to be 140, because this is just not what I do."

Mussina told himself, "The guy on third is probably going to score, so let's just hold this to one run and see what happens." Varitek struck out, then Damon hit a ground ball to Jeter, who stepped on second base and fired to first for an inning-ending double play.

The Yankees had pulled the ultimate escape act thanks to Mussina, who stalked off the mound as the sellout crowd roared with approval.

Mussina came back out and threw a scoreless fifth, then Jason Giambi—who had been dropped to seventh in the batting order—got the Yankees on the board with a solo home run against Martinez in the bottom of the inning. Mussina returned for the sixth, retiring the side in order. He had thrown three scoreless innings of relief, restoring order to the Yankees' pitching staff in the process.

"He came up to me after I took him out of the game and said, 'I thought you were going to bring me in to start an inning?'" Torre said. "I said, 'Well, I guess I lied to you.' Then I said, 'This may give us a nice thought for next year; maybe we can use you as a swing guy.' He laughed and walked away."

Giambi launched another solo homer against Martinez in the seventh, slashing Boston's lead to 4–2. As Martinez's pitch count continued to rise, the Yankees were sensing a shift in momentum.

"They were about to put the game away and Moose comes in and does his thing, which was a little shot of adrenaline," Boone said. "Giambi hits the homer, then hits another; you're like, 'Ooh! Come on boys, let's hang around!' We kept having little things happen in the game that made it feel within reach."

David Wells entered the game with one out in the eighth, but future Hall of Famer David Ortiz gave him a rude welcome, crushing his first pitch for a home run.

"When Papi hit the home run, I remember how pissed off Boomer was, because we were all feeling the same thing: we were back in it, having these little victories," Boone said. "That home run took some air out of us. But we were still there."

Martinez had thrown 100 pitches through seven innings, but Red Sox manager Grady Little sent him back to the mound for the eighth. Lefty Alan Embree and righty Mike Timlin were getting loose in the bullpen, but Little had faith that his ace had something left in the tank.

Jeter hit a one-out double, then Bernie Williams drove him in with a base hit, cutting Boston's lead to two runs. Little came running out of the dugout, and with Hideki Matsui on deck, every person in the ballpark assumed Embree was coming in for the lefty-on-lefty matchup.

Little arrived at the mound and delivered some words to Martinez, then returned to the dugout without making a change. Martinez had thrown 115 pitches, but Little wasn't ready to take the ball out of his hands.

Martinez pumped in two quick strikes to Matsui, but his third offering caught too much of the plate. Matsui hammered it down the right field line, the ball bouncing into the stands for a ground-rule double. The Yankees had the tying runs in scoring position with one out.

Surely Martinez's night was over. Only it wasn't. Little left him in to face Jorge Posada.

"I definitely remember thinking he was getting tired and that we had a shot," Boone said. "When Grady left him in, I wasn't shocked. Maybe a little bit surprised, but it was Pedro Martinez."

Posada flared a 2-2 pitch to shallow center field, where three Red Sox fielders converged but were unable to catch it. Williams and Matsui scored to tie the game, while Posada wound up at second base, letting out a huge roar as he looked toward the Yankees dugout.

"It was unbelievable," Boone said. "We had these little things happen that kept us in the game, but once we tied it, now it's, 'We're winning this game.'"

Little climbed the dugout steps, still seemingly hesitant to remove Martinez. But that's what he did, calling on Embree to face Giambi, who flied out to center for the second out. In came Timlin, who intentionally walked Ruben Sierra.

Nobody realized it at the moment, but Torre's decision to send Boone into the game to pinch-run for Sierra turned out to be rather important.

The Yankees went on to load the bases, but Timlin retired Alfonso Soriano, preserving the tie score. Rivera and Timlin traded zeros in the ninth, then Rivera and Wakefield did the same in the 10th. The Yankees closer came back out for the 11th and sat down the Red Sox on 11 pitches, giving Rivera a season-high 48 pitches—the most he had thrown in a postseason game since he threw 49 in his playoff debut during the 1995 ALDS.

"He was just in command; very Mo-like, incredibly efficient, just buzzing his way through that lineup," Boone said. "It was so impressive. I remember hearing that that was going to be his last inning no matter what. I don't know if I believed that."

Boone was slated to lead off the bottom of the 11th against Wakefield. He hadn't swung a bat all night, but Boone felt what he called "an odd bit of confidence" as he prepared for his at-bat.

"I remember running off the field feeling like I'm going to do something," Boone said.

As he grabbed his bat and helmet, Boone received some advice from Torre.

"He was squeezing the sawdust out of the bat," Torre said. "The only thing I said to him was 'Just try to hit a single to right field; you may hit a home run to left, but just try to hit a single to right.' I can't tell you he ever heard me, though."

Initially, Boone had decided to take the first pitch, but as he walked toward the plate, he realized he was overthinking it. See the ball, hit the ball. Whether it was the first pitch or the sixth, get a good pitch to hit and put a good swing on it. It wasn't rocket science.

"The first one turned out to be pretty good," Boone said. "Fortunately, I was able to run into it."

Boone hit a high, towering blast to left field, raising his arm in the air as he watched the ball settle into the left-field seats. The Yankees were going to the World Series. All of Boone's frustration and anxiety of the past few weeks were a distant memory, instantly replaced by one of the great highlights in franchise history.

"It's a little bit of a blackout moment, honestly," Boone said. "I wish I could remember it more vividly. I do recall telling myself as I'm running around the bases, 'Drink this in. Drink this moment in.'"

Boone could barely speak as he was interviewed on the field by Fox's Curt Menefee on the field just minutes after his home run.

"Like Derek told me, the ghosts will show up eventually," Boone said. "They did, man. This is stupid."

The Yankees celebrated their pennant on the field, a mosh pit of pinstripes with plenty of hugs and more than a few tears. Boone was the hero of the moment, but seeing an emotional Rivera collapse on the mound, a joyous Mussina pumping his fist, or an elated Giambi bear-hugging anyone within reach, it was easy to remember how many great performances helped make this epic victory possible.

"It felt like it was going to be one of those special nights, for sure," Giambi said. "The way it all had gone, how we came back, you just knew something special was going to possible."

The celebration moved into the clubhouse, where the chilled champagne was awaiting the victors. Even Cashman, his top button undone and sleeves rolled up, got in on the action.

"It was just like a lightning strike; boom! Right off the bat, you knew was gone and it was, 'Oh my God, we're going to the World Series again!'" Cashman said. "You don't usually ever see me down celebrating, but I was in the clubhouse with champagne, spraying it everywhere because after being beaten down by The Boss all year long, it was me emotionally letting loose."

Ironically, one of Boone's most vivid memories from the aftermath is watching Mussina celebrate.

"I loved Moose as a teammate; very dry and smart, kind of funny in his way, cutting in his way," Boone said. "Just to see him that night, he was like a kid. I just enjoyed how much he was enjoying the celebration in the moment."

As magical as Game 7 was for the Yankees, the final chapter of the 2003 season didn't have a happy ending. The Florida Marlins beat the Yankees in six games, dealing Torre's club its second World Series defeat in three years.

"I just really thought we were destined to win because of how we got there," Mussina said.

Boone and the Yankees avoided arbitration after the season, agreeing to a one-year, $5.75 million contract for 2004. The Yankees had unfinished business to tend to, and Boone was excited to go through an entire year in pinstripes rather than being dropped into the middle of a pennant race the way it happened in 2003.

Exactly three months after his pennant-winning home run, Boone's world was turned upside down. It was a quiet Friday night in January, so when he got a call from his brother-in-law asking if he wanted to join him for a pickup basketball game at a local gym near his home in Newport Beach, Boone decided to go.

During the game, he was playing defense when a player on the other team saved a ball from going out of bounds, causing another player to crash into him. Boone fell to the court and knew immediately that he had injured his left knee. Tests revealed it was a torn ACL, ending his 2004 season before it ever had a chance to get started.

"I don't feel like I did anything reckless," Boone said. "Life happens. I don't have that regret of, 'Man, I screwed up.' I was going down there on a Friday night to get some exercise. I wasn't in there mixing it up by any means; it could have easily as happened exercising, so it wasn't overly hard to live with."

Less than a month later, the Yankees had traded for two-time AL Most Valuable Player Alex Rodriguez, who had agreed to move from shortstop to third base to join New York. Eleven days after the trade, Boone was released, paid approximately $917,000 of his contract, which the Yankees contended he had violated by playing basketball.

Boone went on to play for four more teams between 2005 and '09 before retiring as a player in early 2010, embarking on a successful run as a broadcaster. In December 2017, the Yankees hired Boone to be their manager, bringing him back to the Bronx nearly 15 years after he put his stamp on the franchise.

Nearly two decades later, Boone's recollections of the home run have come from the myriad replays he has seen of his legendary swing. Asked how many times he has seen the highlight, Boone paused.

"Today?" Boone deadpanned before laughing. "I've seen it a lot."

PART 5

THE ACQUISITIONS

Kansas City Heist

THE YANKEES HAD NO IDEA WHAT THEY WERE GETTING WHEN they acquired Roger Maris from the Kansas City Athletics in December 1959. Likewise, Maris was equally unaware of the impact the deal would have on his life.

Maris had been a solid player for the Athletics during his year-and-a-half stint in Kansas City, hitting 35 home runs and driving in 125 runs in 221 games while making his first All-Star team in 1959. He had been dealt to the Athletics in June 1958, just 14 months after making his major league debut with Cleveland.

Following the first pennantless season in five years for the Yankees, general manager George Weiss had been searching for a new right fielder after the 1959 season, talking with several National League clubs about potential trades. Arthur Daley of the *New York Times* wrote of Weiss' myriad failures to acquire a star, "the Bombers stopped shooting at the moon and decided to shoot fish in a barrel."

Weiss ultimately turned to Kansas City—a franchise that had made 14 deals with him over the previous four years—in an effort to obtain Maris, who had been given a stamp of approval by Athletics manager Harry Craft.

"Craft was managing Kansas City in 1959, and at one point Kraft goes over to Casey Stengel and says, 'You guys ought to get Maris; he's terrific,'" said Marty Appel, a former Yankees public relations director and author of *Pinstripe Empire.* "This is the manager of the A's suggesting they trade his best player!"

Kansas City had been known throughout baseball circles as the Yankees' "farm system," with some New York writers often referring to the club as the team's "country cousins."

When the Yankees traded Hank Bauer, Don Larsen, Norm Siebern, and Marv Throneberry to the Athletics for Maris, Joe DeMaestri, and Kent Hadley, the lede of the *New York Times'* story read, "The Yankees finally broke the trading barrier yesterday and no one need more than a single guess to name the party of the second part."

Bauer had been a key part of the Yankees' championship run, winning seven World Series rings between 1949 and '57. But the 37-year-old had been declining in recent years, while Larsen—best known for his perfect game in the 1956 World Series—had never lived up to the hype of his signature moment. Siebern, a 26-year-old left fielder/first baseman, was the biggest piece going back to Kansas City; he would later make three All-Star teams, but the deal worked out pretty well for the Yankees.

"For the Yankees, it was really good business; it's the way you're supposed to do it," Appel said. "They traded Hank Bauer for Roger Maris; same position, right field, but you're buying 10 years younger. Bauer for Maris is as perfect a trade as a team can make."

The Yankees had leaned on the Athletics time and time again for roster help, with Kansas City proving to be an all-too-willing partner.

"Kansas City traded everybody to the Yankees," Appel said. "There was an incestuous thing going on there."

The 25-year-old Maris was the best player in the trade and the answer to the Yankees' void in right field. He was a solid hitter with impeccable baserunning skills and excellent defensive prowess, but nobody believed New York had just acquired a future American League Most Valuable Player.

Yet in 1960, that's precisely what he was.

Maris had a breakout season after putting on the pinstripes, belting 39 home runs with a league-high 112 RBI in 1960 as the Yankees won 97 games and the AL pennant. Maris posted those numbers in just 136 games, while his celebrated teammate, Mickey Mantle, homered 40 times and drove in 94 runs while appearing in 17 more contests. Maris edged Mantle in the second-closest MVP vote of all time, 225 points to 222, though Baltimore's Brooks Robinson was the only player named on all 24 ballots.

The Yankees lost the World Series to the Pittsburgh Pirates in heartbreaking fashion when Bill Mazeroski hit a walk-off home run in Game 7.

Maris returned in 1961 under new manager Ralph Houk, who had replaced Stengel following the Yankees' World Series defeat. Maris started out slowly—he hit just one home run in April and had only three through May 16, when he finished play with a paltry .208 batting average.

Maris went on a tear after that; he smacked home runs in four straight games from May 17 to 21, finishing May with a

.325 average, nine home runs, and 13 RBI over the final nine games that month.

The power surge continued into June, as Maris belted 15 more home runs. Maris hit eight more homers in the first 13 games in July, giving him 35 in the Yankees' first 86 games. That put him on pace to challenge Babe Ruth's single-season record of 60, set in 1927. Mantle had 31 at the time, though he would hit six in his next six games, putting him ahead of Maris 37–36.

Right around that time, Commissioner Ford Frick—a former sportswriter who had ghostwritten Ruth's book in 1928—announced that unless a player hit 60 or more home runs in 154 games, Ruth's record would stand and the new mark would have "a distinctive mark in the record books." Frick never made mention of an asterisk, a concept first offered up by local sports columnist Dick Young.

"You can't break the 100-meter record in the 100-yard dash," Frick said, comparing the 162-game schedule of 1961 to the 154-game season Ruth played when he hit 60.

Yankees fans began openly rooting for Mantle to break the record, preferring the longtime Yankees hero to Maris, a relative newcomer in his second season in pinstripes.

"People hated me for it, especially the press," Maris was quoted as saying the following spring. "The Yankees played a part, too. Let's not kid anybody. The Yankees wanted Mickey Mantle, not me, to break the record."

Fans weren't the only ones pulling for Mantle to win the home run race.

"All the teammates were for Mickey to break the record," second baseman Bobby Richardson told the *Washington Post* in 1998. "Mickey was thought of as the 'true' Yankee. Roger had been traded in from Kansas City. I think Roger understood.

He was an unusual ballplayer. He didn't care about individual honors."

Maris began to lose hair from the stress of the situation, clearly upset by the negative attention being thrust in his direction with each home run he hit.

"It was very surprising, and the pressure was real; there were people saying he was undeserving, that Mantle was more deserving," Appel said. "He didn't get along well with the press, mostly after '61, but he brought that on himself because he was kind of a red-ass toward the press. After games, he would hide out in the training room, and he had a little plaster of paris hand giving the finger that he put on his stool in the clubhouse. The writers would come in and just see that plaster of paris finger."

Maris finished July with 40 home runs to Mantle's 39. On August 10, Mantle held a 43–41 lead, but Maris took the lead on August 15, never looking back. Mantle stalled at 54 home runs, hitting just one in his final 11 games as he battled a virus during the second half of September before missing the final three games with an abscess in his hip caused by an injection.

Maris entered September with 51 homers, hitting five in the first 10 games of the season's final month. He hit his 59th home run in the Yankees' 154th game, ending his shot of matching Ruth's record in the same number of games.

Six days later, Maris hit No. 60, leaving him three games to break Ruth's mark. For all the talk about 154 games versus 162, it should be noted that Maris' 60th homer came in his 684th plate appearance, five fewer than Ruth had needed 34 years earlier.

Maris entered the final game of the season stuck on 60, but Maris hit No. 61 with a fourth-inning blast into the right-field stands against Boston's Tracy Stallard, setting the record in front of just 23,154 fans at Yankee Stadium.

Maris finished the season with 61 home runs and 141 RBI, winning his second consecutive AL MVP award. Whereas Maris had beaten Mantle by three points in the 1960 MVP vote, this time his margin of victory was only four points, 202–198.

"The story for both of those MVPs was how Mickey lost by one vote each year, Appel said, noting that the difference between first- and second-place votes was five points. "If somebody had voted Mantle over Maris—just one person—it would have flipped it and Mantle would have retired with five MVPs."

The Yankees went on to win the 1961 World Series, though Maris hit just .105 with one home run in the five-game triumph over the Cincinnati Reds.

Maris followed up his 61-homer season with another solid effort, hitting 33 home runs with 100 RBI despite suffering a hand injury during spring training that never fully healed. Maris was named to the All-Star team for the fourth straight season, but his performance wasn't good enough in the eyes of some; United Press International voted Maris "Flop of the Year."

Injuries and inconsistency hampered Maris' next three seasons; he hit 23 homers while playing just 90 games in 1963, then swatted 26 home runs in 141 games in 1964. He was limited to only 46 games in 1965, then played most of 1966 with a misdiagnosed broken bone in his hand. Still, the Yankees reached the World Series in each of Maris' first five seasons in pinstripes, winning the championship in 1961 and '62.

Maris was traded to the St. Louis Cardinals in December 1966, revealing the following spring that had he not been dealt, his time with the Yankees would have ended one way or another.

"I never would have gone back to New York to play," Maris told the *New York Times* in March 1967. "I'd had it in New

York. They had to trade me, and it was the best thing that ever happened to me."

Maris' Cardinals beat the Boston Red Sox in the 1967 World Series, then returned to the Fall Classic in 1968, losing to the Detroit Tigers. Maris retired at the end of the 1968 season, hanging up his spikes at the age of 34. Cardinals owner Gussie Busch set Maris up with an Anheuser-Busch beer distributorship in Gainesville, Florida.

Maris' hard feelings toward the Yankees did not dissipate following his retirement, as he didn't return to Yankee Stadium for more than a decade after being traded to St. Louis.

The ice was finally broken after George Steinbrenner purchased the team in 1973, paving the way for a reunion. Steinbrenner and Maris first met in the spring of 1977, but Maris declined an invitation to take part in the Yankees' Old Timers' Game that year. In April 1978, Maris finally returned to the Stadium, appearing with former teammates Mantle, Yogi Berra, and Billy Martin to help raise the Yankees' 1977 World Series championship banner. The fans—who had no idea Maris would be making his return to the Bronx—showered him with affection, chanting his name after he was introduced.

"I know what he went through, I appreciate it," Reggie Jackson told the *New York Times* that day. "The press, the public, the pressure.... The agony of victory. That's what he went through. I was excited for him when he came back and heard the cheers."

Seven years later, at the 1984 Old Timers' Game, Maris' No. 9 was retired by the Yankees, who hung a plaque in Maris' honor in Monument Park.

Maris finished his career with 275 home runs, 850 RBI, and a .260 batting average over 12 seasons. He remained on the Hall of Fame ballot for the maximum 15 years of eligibility, but he never came close to garnering the necessary 75 percent of the vote for election, topping out at 43.1 percent in his final year on the ballot.

"Dad's Hall of Fame is having his number retired in Yankee Stadium up there with Babe Ruth and Gehrig and Mickey and DiMaggio," Maris' son, Randy, told the *New York Times* in 2011.

Maris may have reconciled his issues with the Yankees, but his feelings toward Frick for questioning the validity of his 61-homer season stayed with him for the rest of his life.

"By doing that, he was telling everybody, the sportswriters and the American public, 'Whatever Roger Maris does, we are not going to accept it,'" Maris told the *Chicago Tribune* in 1984. "Frick never did mention that when I hit No. 60, I had four fewer at-bats than Babe Ruth.

"It was hard for me. At least a lot of players can go one place and have peace of mind. But there wasn`t a park I went to that I wasn't booed. They even booed me in spring training. It didn't let up until after the Yankees traded me. All the record brought me was a headache."

Maris was diagnosed with non-Hodgkin lymphoma in late 1983. He died on December 14, 1985.

Mark McGwire of the Cardinals broke Maris' single-season home run record in 1998, hitting 70 home runs. Like Maris and Mantle 37 years earlier, McGwire engaged in a home run race with Chicago Cubs slugger Sammy Sosa, who finished the season with 66 homers.

McGwire and Sosa combined for five seasons with 63 or more homers between 1998 and 2001, but Barry Bonds of the Giants broke McGwire's record in 2001 with a 73-homer season. Maris' 61-homer mark from 1961 remains the AL record, while many still consider him the true single-season record holder as a result of suspected—or in the case of McGwire, admitted—steroid use by those who have eclipsed his mark.

"Maris was legendary because of what he had to overcome and because of whose record he broke," Appel said. "And even with the whole steroid era, he still holds the American League home run record. That's remarkable."

Shooting for a Star

George Steinbrenner wanted Reggie Jackson in pinstripes. It was that simple.

The Yankees had returned to prominence under Steinbrenner's watch in 1976, winning their first American League pennant in 12 years, but after watching his club get swept by the Cincinnati Reds in the World Series, The Boss decided Jackson was the missing piece.

The Montreal Expos, San Diego Padres, and New York Mets took their shot, but by the end of November 1976, Jackson had signed a five-year deal worth nearly $3 million to join the defending AL champions.

"It was like trying to hustle a girl in a bar," Jackson told the *New York Times* of Steinbrenner's recruiting efforts. "Some clubs offered several hundred thousand dollars more, possibly seven figures more. But the reason I'm a Yankee is that George Steinbrenner outhustled everybody else."

Thurman Munson, the gritty captain whose personality was the polar opposite of Jackson's, had urged Steinbrenner to sign the outspoken and egotistical outfielder who had already won three World Series rings with the Oakland Athletics and been named Most Valuable Player of the 1973 Fall Classic.

"Go get the big man," Munson told Steinbrenner, according to the *Times*. "He's the only guy in baseball who can carry a club for a month."

So that's what Steinbrenner did, wining and dining Jackson in New York City in an attempt to sell the slugger on a future in the Bronx.

"He brought them a genuine cleanup hitter, which they didn't have in Chris Chambliss," said Marty Appel, a longtime Yankees public relations director and author of *Pinstripe Empire*. "That's why George wanted him so badly."

Steinbrenner also wanted a star who would put fannies in the seats, something Jackson had proved capable of doing during the first decade of his career.

"I didn't come to New York to be a star," Jackson famously said. "I brought my star with me."

Although he clashed with Munson and manager Billy Martin early on, Jackson's impact was immediate. He hit 32 home runs and drove in 110 runs in 1977, making the first of five consecutive All-Star teams as a Yankee.

"Reggie had a presence in the clubhouse; you never knew what he was going to do," Bucky Dent said. "He might hit one 500 feet, so he was one of those guys that when he went to the plate, you stopped to watch him."

It didn't help that Jackson popped off during an early-season interview with *Sport Magazine*, uttering his infamous "straw that stirs the drink" comment, one which rankled many players, including Munson.

"He was never really liked by his own teammates, but they recognized the fact that he was a winner and a guy that was going to get big hits for them," said longtime *New York Daily News* baseball writer Bill Madden. "Essentially, he was the missing ingredient from '76. There was a grudging respect for Reggie, but he was never really embraced by the rest of the team."

As disruptive as Jackson could be, the extracurricular noise took a back seat to his performance, allowing the Yankees to succeed despite the black cloud of controversy that consistently swirled above the Bronx.

"We needed Reggie," said Willie Randolph, who was in his second year with the Yankees. "He had all the bravado, he had a reputation coming in; Reggie was a big star, so there was some jealousy and envy. He had a big mouth, and he was always talking, he was a good-looking guy, a flashy guy; a lot of guys didn't like that about Reggie. He wasn't afraid to tell you how it was and how he felt about things.

"He had a cockiness and brashness about him. He would compete as well as anybody. Back then we didn't call it swag, but he had a little swag that maybe we kind of needed in a way."

The Yankees returned to the World Series in 1977, a series that would come to define Jackson's time in New York. After hitting home runs in Games 4 and 5 in Los Angeles, Jackson was a one-man wrecking crew in Game 6, putting on one of the most legendary displays in World Series history with home runs on three consecutive swings.

The Yankees finished off the Dodgers that night and Jackson was named series MVP, becoming the first player in history to earn that honor with two different clubs.

"What he did in the World Series, I had a ringside seat for it; you can't even write that in a Hollywood script," Randolph said. "Reggie's impact was unbelievable; I'm not saying he got us over the hump, but it was a big shot for us to bring him in at that time. Even with the Bronx Zoo stuff and the back pages, we were all able to focus at the right time. We didn't let that get in the way, and when it was time to play, we had each other's backs. We played together, we fought together, and we turned into a team that at the end of the day was as close as any team I've ever been on."

Jackson's legendary World Series had finally earned him the adulation of the New York fans, but the following spring, he expressed his dissatisfaction with the way his maiden season in pinstripes had played out prior to that magical night.

As Tony Kornheiser wrote in the *New York Times*:

> Most of his teammates—and his manager—had a dislike for him, and they showed it by leaving him virtually alone on one side of the clubhouse. They had won a pennant without him, and they treated his coining and all the attention he received from the news media like an invasion. The press quickly got on him for his terrible defensive play and his mediocre offensive play early in the season. The fans gave him a booing unheard of in New York since the days of Roger Maris. Until the final game of the World Series, Jackson was the villain.

"Is 'hell' the right word? Double it," Jackson told Kornheiser in March 1978. "Honest to God in heaven, I didn't think it would be like that. You think I'd have gone to the Yankees if I knew? Think a person wants to be disliked? I thought guys would say, 'Here's a man who played in the Series. He can help us. Let's go along with his program, because he's been there.'"

Fans showered Jackson with affection—and candy bars—at the home opener in 1978, the Yankees' first game in the Bronx since his three-homer effort in the World Series.

The Yankees had handed out the "Reggie Bar" to fans that day. When Jackson belted a three-run homer in the first inning against White Sox left-hander Wilbur Wood, fans showed their love by flinging the candy bar onto the field much as a hockey crowd would throw hats onto the ice after a player tallied his third goal in a game.

"I didn't want to get hit in the head," Jackson told reporters after the game. "But I knew it was a gesture of appreciation."

Jackson and the Yankees overcame a 14-game deficit against the Red Sox in 1978, beating Boston in a one-game playoff at Fenway Park before repeating as World Series champions later that month.

Munson's tragic death in August 1979 proved to be too much for the Yankees to overcome, creating a hole that impacted the club in subsequent years.

"We were never the same without him," Jackson told the *New York Post*. "We were good, but we weren't the same without him."

Midway through the 1980 season, Jackson expressed his desire to finish his career with the Yankees. His contract was set to expire at the end of the 1981 season, but Jackson—who had earned the nickname "Mr. October" thanks to his 1977 heroics—was not ready to leave New York, especially now that Martin was no longer in the manager's office.

"I've asked George Steinbrenner," Jackson told the *New York Times* in June 1980, "at his convenience, any time now through December, if we can sit down and get it out of the way before spring training starts next year. I don't want it to linger if I can help it. I don't want it to turn into a public thing. I'd like a four-year extension, but I'll listen to three years, and I'll listen to five years.

"I don't know where I fit in Yankee history yet. Right now, that's hard to say. Eventually it will depend on how many numbers I put up on the board, and it will depend how the team plays around me."

Prior to the 1981 season, the Yankees signed Dave Winfield to a 10-year contract, pairing the slugger with Jackson—who had helped recruit Winfield—in the middle of the lineup. Jackson's extension had never materialized, and though the Yankees returned to the World Series in 1981, they lost to the Dodgers.

"Reggie was different; I was happy to play with a guy who was the self-proclaimed 'straw that stirs the drink,'" Winfield said. "He had some fantastic feats of hitting. It's hard to say what he thought about me, but I think it struck him a little bit that a relatively unknown guy could come in and make more money. We hit next to each other in the batting order, and there's one point that I felt bad for him, because George Steinbrenner was attacking him for not playing well, saying they had to check his eyesight. I saw that weighing on him."

Jackson, who missed half of the 1981 World Series after suffering a calf injury during the ALCS, was allowed to depart as a free agent, signing a four-year contract with the California Angels that paid him nearly $1 million per season. The Yankees had pursued Jackson to some extent, but the club would not guarantee the 35-year-old a spot as an everyday outfielder, viewing him as a designated hitter-in-the-making.

"No matter what George would have offered, Reggie wouldn't have played the outfield in New York," Jackson's agent, Gary Walker, told the *New York Times*. "There is enough of the little boy left in Reggie that he wants to play the outfield regularly."

Jackson went on to play five seasons with the Angels before finishing his career in 1987 with one final season in Oakland. The 1973 AL MVP retired with 563 home runs, 1,702 RBI, and 2,584 hits, 14 All-Star appearances, five World Series championships, and a pair of World Series MVP awards. In 1993, Jackson was elected to the Baseball Hall of Fame in his first year of eligibility, garnering 93.6 percent of the vote.

Although he played just five of his 21 seasons in the Bronx, the Yankees retired Jackson's No. 44 less than two weeks after his induction in Cooperstown.

"People talk about tradition; I believe it started here," Jackson said as his number was unveiled in Monument Park. "Anywhere you go in the world, the greatest name in sports belongs to the Yankees. To be honored today is the culmination of my goals as a player."

THE FIRST BIG FISH

Free agency in baseball as we know it didn't come into play until 1976, but the sport had already seen a preview of what would become a landscape-altering phenomenon.

Jim "Catfish" Hunter, the reigning American League Cy Young Award winner, became a free agent after the 1974 season after Oakland Athletics owner Charles O. Finley failed to make certain payments required by his contract.

The *New York Times* referred to Hunter's free agency as "the most celebrated bidding war in

American sports history," so what other team would emerge as the winners of such a sweepstakes?

George Steinbrenner was in the midst of a two-year suspension following his conviction for making illegal political contributions, leaving the negotiating to general manager Gabe Paul.

Paul told the *Times* that before Steinbrenner stepped away from the Yankees, he had told the GM, "Any time you have an opportunity to buy the contract of a player for cash, I want you to go ahead whenever, in your judgment, it would be advantageous to the Yankees."

Adding a pitcher of Hunter's ilk certainly qualified, so Paul pursued the right-hander as soon as he hit the open market. Every team in the majors aside from the San Francisco Giants did the same, but the Yankees ultimately landed the ace, signing him on New Year's Eve to a five-year contract worth approximately $3.75 million.

"The publicity of the money that he got made him a national story," said Marty Appel, the Yankees' public relations director at the time. "The first day he was in spring training, Howard Cosell came down with a crew from ABC and they set up this whole thing where they hired a Brinks truck and Catfish got out of the truck in uniform."

The signing sent shockwaves throughout the game. If Hunter could land a contract of that nature as a free agent, players around the league could position themselves for similar opportunities if they were able to freely shop their services.

"It opened the eyes of all the other owners when they saw each other bidding wildly for this pitcher," said longtime *New York Daily News* baseball writer Bill Madden. "They realized that free agency was going to drastically change the salary structure of baseball."

In the middle of the 1976 season, the league and the players union collectively bargained a new Basic Agreement that gave players with six years of major league service time the right to become free agents. Hunter was the first player to cash in on the free market, but now he would certainly not be the last.

"It sent a message to all players that this is your true value on the marketplace," Appel said. "It inspired the labor bargaining that was to come within the next 12 months. The signing was so important in baseball history for just setting all of those things in motion."

Hunter threw 30 complete games in his first year with the Yankees, going 23–14 with a 2.58 ERA and 328 innings pitched in 39 starts. In 1976, Hunter helped lead New York to its first AL pennant since 1964, though they were swept by the Cincinnati Reds in the World Series.

That season, he joined Cy Young, Christy Mathewson, and Walter Johnson as the only pitchers in major league history to win 200 games by the age of 31.

Having thrown more than 625 innings during his first two years in pinstripes, Hunter began his decline during his third season. He contributed to the Yankees' championship teams in 1977 and 1978, then retired after the 1979 season.

"He was done," Appel said. "They were determined to get their money's worth upfront and in a hurry. Those 30 complete games in 1975 were kind of outrageous. You look back on it now and it's clear they were going to get everything they could out of him as fast as they could."

Hunter was inducted into the Baseball Hall of Fame in 1987. He died in 1999 at the age of 53, one year after being diagnosed with ALS, also known as Lou Gehrig's Disease.

25

Imperfect Fit

THE SAN DIEGO SLUGGER WAS READY FOR A CHANGE.

Eight years with the Padres had resulted in seven sub-.500 seasons, five managerial changes, and zero trips to the postseason. Dave Winfield was establishing himself as one of the best players in baseball, but the constant turnover in San Diego made him feel like a hamster running on a wheel. The team just wasn't going anywhere.

"It was time for me to play for a team that could win," Winfield said. "And at the same time, from a business standpoint, one that could pay me my value."

Winfield had been the No. 4 overall pick in the 1973 draft, signing with the Padres for $15,000 and a one-way ticket to the major leagues. The 21-year-old debuted on June 19, just two weeks after the draft, going 1-for-4 in a loss to the Houston Astros.

Winfield—who had also been drafted by the NBA's Atlanta Hawks and NFL's Minnesota Vikings—showed promising signs during his first four years with the Padres, but he broke out in 1977, hitting 25 home runs with 92 RBI in 157 games. Halfway through the season, Winfield and his agent, Al Frohman, negotiated a new four-year, $1.4 million contract; the following year, he became the first captain in the Padres' brief 10-year history.

But as he approached free agency at the end of the 1980 season, Winfield was the belle of the ball; a number of teams seemed to have their sights set on him, including the Yankees, the New York Mets, the Los Angeles Dodgers, and the Houston Astros.

Having turned down a seven-year, $5 million contract offer from the Padres, Winfield entered his name in the free-agent re-entry draft, a short-lived system that determined which teams could negotiate with which free agents. Under that system, a maximum of 13 teams were permitted to "draft" the right to negotiate with a free agent, with the selections based on the reverse order of standings. During the first four years of the system, only one player—Twins right-hander Dave Goltz—had been claimed by the maximum 13 teams before the first round was completed.

The Yankees, by virtue of their 103 wins in 1980, were set to pick in the 26th spot, leading some to wonder whether they would even have a shot at Winfield. Richard Moss, Winfield's attorney, reached out to teams Winfield had no interest in speaking with, encouraging them not to select the outfielder in the draft.

George Steinbrenner suspected that a number of teams were planning to throw their hats in the ring for Winfield for no other reason than to prevent the Yankees from doing so. He even tried to engage in trade talks with the Padres, attempting to work out a sign-and-trade deal, but Winfield had already filed to become a free agent.

A total of 10 teams selected Winfield in the draft, though the Yankees, Mets, and Cleveland were viewed as favorites. The *New York Times* reported that the Mets initially discussed an eight-year deal worth $12 million, but their formal offer didn't include aspects involving Winfield's charitable foundation, the first of its kind launched by an active athlete. Steinbrenner had included that in his pitch, which was very important to Winfield.

"George went after Winfield the way he went after Reggie," longtime *New York Daily News* baseball writer Bill Madden said. "He was going to get his man, no matter what it cost."

A little more than one month after the re-entry draft, Winfield and the Yankees agreed to a 10-year contract worth $16 million, though as the *Times* reported, the deal included cost-of-living raises that could raise the value north of $23 million.

"My agent and advisors had talked about it for months and months; we kind of understood where the environment was headed when it came to contracts and such," Winfield said. "When you talk about it enough, it becomes a reality. We were talking about 10 years and a lot of money for a number of months; it was still a big number back then, but people were aware that that's what I was going to ask for."

It wasn't just the largest contract in baseball history; it was the largest in North American team sports. Only Steinbrenner either hadn't studied the details of the contract or didn't understand them, so when he read about it in the *Times*, The Boss was livid. The two sides ultimately reached a compromise that brought the value of the contract down a few million dollars.

"George went ballistic," Madden said. "He thought that Frohman had deceived him. He never forgave Frohman, and Winfield was intensely loyal to Frohman. There were always these conflicts coming up until it really blew up."

It took some time for Winfield to adapt to life with the Yankees, from the media attention to the fans. The media presence was overwhelming compared to what he had experienced in San Diego, a market in which Winfield said he could count outlets covering a game "on one hand."

"There was no 24-hour news cycle, no social media, and really only one major newspaper," Winfield said. "There were very few opinions or anything else in San Diego."

The Yankees would draw big crowds everywhere they went, and unlike his time with the Padres, Winfield noticed crowds of fans mobbing the team's bus, the hotel, or anywhere else they went.

"We were kind of the rock star team of baseball," Winfield said. "Whether they loved you or hated you, they would show up to watch us play. They would hang around the hotel. When you played in San Diego, you never really worried about your uniform or your stuff. By the end of my first year with the Yankees, I would say, 'Man, where's my other set of pants?' or 'Where's my other jersey? Where's my other bat?' I didn't know people would be around there looking for that memorabilia and just abscond with it."

Winfield's teammates were impressed by his talent and work ethic. Bucky Dent played with Winfield during the first two years of his New York tenure, then managed the Yankees for parts of the final two years of the outfielder's contract.

"He could hit the ball as hard as anybody I had ever seen," Dent said. "He was big, he could run, he had a great arm; he was a tremendous athlete. He could do it all. He was fun to play with."

Winfield's imposing 6'6", 230-lb frame was not a common sight in the game in the early 1980s, which made his game even more impressive.

"I had never seen anybody play the way he did at that size," Willie Randolph said. "I had never seen a beautiful athlete like that; you never saw stuff like that back in those days. Dave did things on the field that you wouldn't believe."

Winfield was a true five-tool player. He had massive power but didn't consider himself a home-run hitter. Had he wanted to lead the league in homers, he probably could have, but Winfield took pride in his baserunning, his throwing arm, and his ability to hit the ball all over the field.

"I knew that I had five tools and I would work on them every day; that's the kind of player I was," Winfield said. "I knew that people didn't really know all of my abilities because they'd never seen me. When you played in the other league on the other coast in a different time zone, a lot of people hadn't seen much of me. They would stand there and watch to see how I played. I was confident; internally, I knew that I was going to be fine."

Winfield hit .294 with 13 home runs and 68 RBI in 105 games during the strike-shortened 1981 season, helping the Yankees return to the playoffs.

"He was going to lead this team to many pennants, which he had never done in San Diego," said Marty Appel, longtime Yankees public relations director and author of *Pinstripe Empire*. "That was the expectation, that he was the kind of guy that could carry the team like Reggie did."

Winfield had a solid first-round performance against the Milwaukee Brewers, batting .350 (7-for-20), though he didn't drive in a run during the Yankees' five-game victory. Despite Winfield's 2-for-13 (.154) ALCS, in which he had two RBI, the Yankees swept the Oakland Athletics in three games to advance to the World Series, where they faced the Dodgers.

"I was excited to be to playing in a place and with people where the expectations were to win," Winfield said. "And they had been so close [over the previous two years], I felt that by adding my presence and contributions, that we could do it again. I was confident in that."

But Winfield struggled badly in his first trip to the Fall Classic, going 1-for-22, an .045 average. Winfield's lone hit came in the fifth inning of Game 5, a one-out single that would soon be followed by an inning-ending double play off the bat of Jackson. Yet Winfield signaled for the ball to be thrown to the Yankees dugout; did Winfield really want that memento from his first World Series hit after an 0-for-16 start?

"No, I didn't save the ball," Winfield told reporters after the game. "Some guys were kidding me before that at-bat about batting .000, so I said, 'When I get a hit, I'll ask for the ball.' So, when I did get a hit, I asked for it. I was just trying to lighten things up a little."

The Yankees fell in six games, then watched Jackson depart as a free agent after the season, signing a four-year deal worth about $4 million with the California Angels. Although Steinbrenner had criticized Winfield for his poor showing in the World Series, Winfield returned for 1982 with a positive outlook, believing the Yankees would return to the Fall Classic.

"I took it one year at a time, but I thought, 'OK, now we know how to do this. I know how to do this,'" Winfield said. "You can't anticipate beyond each year, because we had some aging guys and had to keep turning things over and adding new players into the mix."

With Jackson gone, the expectations for Winfield grew considerably. Prior to spring training in 1983, Steinbrenner commented at a dinner that you need to have a World Series ring to be considered a winner, a direct shot at Winfield. Jackson had helped deliver two such rings to The Boss in his first two years with the Yankees, but Winfield had started out 0-for-2.

"When I lost Reggie, it left a void," Steinbrenner was quoted as having said by the *New York Times*. "Dave Winfield is not the winner Reggie Jackson was. Until you wear one of these, you are not a winner. Winfield is almost there."

The Jackson shadow loomed large despite the fact that he was playing on the other side of the country.

"People got nasty early," Winfield told the *Times*. "They wanted me to pick up Reggie's home runs and mine, too. It was a rough proposition. People were a little upset early on. I don't know why they were mad at me. But it turned around. This year they'll forget about him to a large degree. They'll come out when he's playing, but the team is back to normality. They'll be rooting for us."

Just as he had in 1982, Winfield topped the 30-homer and 100-RBI marks in 1983, but once again, the Yankees missed the playoffs. Those two years also brought a new twist to the Steinbrenner–Winfield dynamic, as Winfield's foundation sued Steinbrenner twice, charging that the owner had not made the donations agreed upon in the player's contract.

"What distracted me from the very first year was the Steinbrenner relationship," Winfield said. "The very first year, he reneged on a couple of things in my contract and the way that my foundation was treated. It happened in the very first year, and it went on for 10 years. It was never really supportive, which made it difficult. It wasn't just about whether we won or lost; it was a lot of things away from the ballpark, things in court and a lot of other things.

"I was not a troublemaker. They could see what they were getting before I went to the Yankees. You would never think that I would be in as many battles with management as you saw. That was not me."

In 1984, Winfield and 23-year-old teammate Don Mattingly battled for the American League batting title; Winfield was hitting .370 to Mattingly's .330 at the All-Star break, but as the calendar turned to September, Winfield's lead had withered to .352–.349.

"The team really didn't do anything that year, so people just came to see Donnie and I," Winfield said. "Two guys who could really hit. There was never a rivalry; there just wasn't. We were teammates doing the best we could to help the team win. It just happened that there was that race going on that year."

It seemed everybody was rooting for Mattingly, from fans to teammates to Steinbrenner himself. Mattingly, who was in his first full season as the everyday first baseman, was thankful that his veteran teammate didn't take out any of his frustrations on him.

"I was the underdog, and everybody likes the underdog," Mattingly said. "It seemed like there were a lot of people wanting me to win—and The Boss, even, because of his run-ins with Dave. [Winfield] made it not awkward; he could have made me really uncomfortable, he could have treated me badly. I always had tons of respect for that, because it was really a lot harder on him than it was on me. I realized that later; I was the young kid, not making any money at the time, and he was the guy that had been there, signed a big free-agent contract."

"It was fascinating to see two of the best hitters in the game going at it," Randolph said. "That should have been really enjoyable, but it didn't always seem that way. It turned into a David and Goliath kind of scenario. It was awkward that they were on the same team. Within your own stadium, it almost felt like sides would be played there. It made it a little uncomfortable."

Winfield led Mattingly by two points—.341 to .339—heading into the final game of the season against the Detroit Tigers at Yankee Stadium. Asked before the game who he thought would emerge victorious, manager Yogi Berra said, "Both of them. I wish they would break even today."

Winfield was 1-for-4 with a walk in the finale, finishing at .340; Mattingly went 4-for-5, winning the batting crown with a .343 average. Mattingly singled past the second baseman in his final at-bat, then Winfield hit a fielder's choice to third, forcing Mattingly out at second. Berra removed Winfield for a pinch-runner, allowing the two stars to shake hands by first base before exiting to a standing ovation from the Bronx crowd.

"It was great the way they both walked off the field together to standing ovations," Randolph said. "That was really cool; I'm glad it ended like that."

"Mattingly was a homegrown guy that every Yankee fan loved," said longtime Yankees broadcaster Michael Kay, who also covered the team for both the *New York Post* and *New York Daily News*. "I think you'd be hard-pressed to find a Yankee fan that didn't love Mattingly, and for some reason because of that batting title battle, it seemed like Mattingly and Winfield were against each other. They weren't. They actually were great together."

Nearly 40 years later, Winfield seems like a man with a lot of thoughts on the situation, noting that "there was so much more going on behind the scenes" during the race.

"It wasn't just two guys playing baseball," Winfield said. "I didn't bring any of that up or make any excuses or anything like that. Had I come out on top in the batting race, they would have probably gotten some content or commentary from me about what I was going through that year. I didn't bring it up and I didn't use anything as an excuse or anything else, but it wasn't just a batting race."

Although Winfield declined to delve into any further details, he told Art Rust Jr.—a New York sports radio personality and author—that racism played a role in the way he and Mattingly were treated during the batting race.

"I've experienced racism in my life," Winfield told Rust Jr. in 1992. "It was all around me when I was on the Yankees and competing with Don Mattingly for the batting title. Here we both were, two guys on the same team, fighting one another for the same thing against a background of manipulative media and the perceptions of hundreds of thousands of fans that were created by that media. There was a vast difference in the amount of encouragement each of us got from the press and the public."

Winfield was holding up his end of the contract; he averaged 28 home runs and 108 RBI with a .288/.349/.503 slash line between 1982 and '86, making the AL All-Star team in each season. The Yankees were competitive, winning 90 games or more in three of those five years, but New York didn't reach the postseason in any of them, enraging Steinbrenner.

"He was never going to be the chosen one," Appel said of Winfield. "It's very much a shame."

In September 1985, as the Yankees' playoff hopes began to dwindle, Steinbrenner uttered a line to reporters that would come to define his relationship with Winfield: "Does anyone know where I can find Reggie Jackson? I let Mr. October get away, and I got Mr. May, Dave Winfield."

More than 15 years later, at a press conference following his election into the Baseball Hall of Fame, Winfield was asked about Steinbrenner's "Mr. May" comment.

"It was irreverent, it was off-color, it was improper, it doesn't fit," Winfield said in January 2001. "I always rejected it. It doesn't apply. It was an inappropriate remark at the time. I didn't appreciate it then."

Steinbrenner attempted to trade Winfield on several occasions, once to the Texas Rangers in 1984, then again in 1987 to the Detroit Tigers.

"San Diego was pretty low key, so I definitely wouldn't have thought at the end of my tenure that I would be the guy caught up in the middle of so much controversy—none of it created by me—or have as much tension or as many distractions as I had in New York," Winfield said. "It hardened me and toughened me. I'd think, 'Why is this going on?'"

The off-field issues with Steinbrenner didn't impact Winfield's performance on the field, as he continued to make All-Star teams in 1987 and '88. After tying the major league record for April with 29 RBI while hitting .398, Winfield poked fun at Steinbrenner for his infamous quote.

"The month is over," Winfield told the *Times.* "We go on to May, and you know about me and May."

Winfield and Steinbrenner were involved in further lawsuits against each other regarding the player's foundation; Winfield accused The Boss of failing to make his obligatory payments, while Steinbrenner countered with a claim that Winfield was misusing foundation funds for his personal gain rather than as a way to help children.

"He was phenomenal, but I don't think he was ever looked at that way because of the war that he got into with George Steinbrenner," Kay said. "You had an owner that wasn't in love with the player, they were always sniping each other and there were lawsuits and stuff like that. That took away from his greatness, because he was just an unbelievable player."

Steinbrenner tried to trade Winfield again in 1988, this time to the Houston Astros. Winfield vetoed the deal, which was his right as a 10-year veteran who had spent at least the past five with his current club.

"Dave didn't really enjoy it or was embraced like he should have been because of all the other stuff that went on away from the field with Steinbrenner," Randolph said. "It's unfortunate that that couldn't have been a happier marriage in a way."

Despite his issues with Steinbrenner, Winfield continued to be a strong presence in the Yankees clubhouse. By 1986, Mattingly had become arguably the best player in the game, but Winfield was a respected veteran who young players could look to as they embarked on their careers.

"Even at that late stage of his career, he was a guy that commanded a lot of respect and was an imposing presence in the dugout," said Bernie Williams, who spent time with Winfield during spring training before he reached the major leagues. "I was always in awe seeing him, taking batting practice with him. The way he carried himself in the clubhouse, he was one of the people I wanted to emulate."

Winfield missed the entire 1989 season following back surgery, ending his streak of 12 straight All-Star appearances. He opened the 1990 season with the Yankees, but the headlines surrounding Winfield had nothing to do with his return to the field.

In January 1990, Steinbrenner paid $40,000 to a man named Howie Spira, an admitted gambler who had claimed to have worked as a publicist for Winfield's foundation. In exchange, Spira was to provide Steinbrenner with dirt to use against

Winfield, part of what Spira said was a promise of $150,000 and a job at a Tampa-area hotel owned by Steinbrenner.

The payment became public news in March 1990, prompting Commissioner Fay Vincent to appoint attorney John Dowd—whose report the previous year had led to Pete Rose's banishment from baseball—to investigate the matter.

In May, the Yankees traded Winfield to the California Angels, one of seven teams the player had listed as an acceptable trade option as part of his contract. But Winfield argued that his 10-5 rights—the same clause he had used to veto a trade to Houston two years earlier—gave him the ability to nix the trade.

Five days later, Winfield agreed to the trade after the Angels gave him a contract extension that guaranteed him at least $2.45 million in 1991 and as much as $9.1 million over three years.

Less than three months after the news of Steinbrenner's payment to Spira broke, Vincent met with the owner to discuss Dowd's findings. The Boss "offered multiple and conflicting explanations of his decision to give $40,000 to Mr. Spira, ranging from charity to extortion"—only Vincent wasn't buying what Steinbrenner was selling.

Nearly two months later, Vincent had decided to suspend Steinbrenner for two years for his actions, which the commissioner had ruled were against "the best interests of baseball." But The Boss—who was trying to hold on to his other gig as vice president of the United States Olympic Committee—did not want the record to reflect a suspension.

"Vincent wanted to appease all the people that hated George," Madden said. "George was afraid of losing his position on the Olympic Committee if he was suspended from baseball, so Vincent told him if he didn't want to be suspended, they could put him on the permanent ineligible list."

Steinbrenner signed an agreement in which he was banned from running the Yankees on a day-to-day basis, though he would eventually be suspended by the USOC, as well. He was also forced to divest himself of a majority share in the Yankees, reducing his ownership stake from 55 percent to 49 percent.

Spira was convicted of trying to extort money from Steinbrenner, sentenced to two years in prison. He was also convicted on two unrelated counts, adding six months to his sentence.

Freed from the circus atmosphere in which he had lived for nearly a decade, Winfield made his debut with the Angels on May 17, 1990. The 38-year-old thrived in his new surroundings, hitting 19 home runs with 72 RBI in 112 games, earning Comeback Player of the Year honors from *The Sporting News*.

Winfield played for the Angels in 1991, then signed with the Toronto Blue Jays in 1992, finally winning that elusive World Series ring. He hit 26 home runs and drove in 108, belting what turned out to be the game-winning two-run double in the 11th inning of the Blue Jays' Game 6 clincher against the Atlanta Braves.

At 41, Winfield signed with the Minnesota Twins for the 1993 season, playing in his hometown until the players went on strike in August 1994. Minnesota traded him to Cleveland during the strike, but the season never resumed. Winfield signed back with Cleveland for the 1995 season, but a shoulder injury limited him to just 46 games. He was left off Cleveland's postseason roster, retiring at the end of the year.

"The last third of my career, those were the best years of my career and my baseball life," Winfield said. "Going to the Angels, getting out from under all of this; my 3,000th hit, Comeback Player of the Year, the World Series, securing my place in the Hall of Fame. Just being able to play baseball and to feel wanted for my leadership, my experience, all of that stuff—I didn't experience that for a decade. It got better."

Winfield and Steinbrenner—who was reinstated by Vincent in 1992—didn't speak for about a decade after Winfield left New York, but at some point, Steinbrenner recognized that his handling of the situation left much to be desired.

"All of that never should have happened," Steinbrenner told the *New York Times* in 1998. "Dave Winfield was one of the greatest athletes I've ever known. What part of it is me, I'll take the blame."

A couple years later, Steinbrenner and Winfield got together to talk things out.

"We talked and laid things out on the table that had never been said before," Winfield told reporters at the 2010 All-Star Game, just hours after Steinbrenner had died. "He apologized to me for the things that he did. It's almost like you see a curtain drawn back, a veil lifted, just a complete change. And our relationship changed from then on, and we got to know each other real well."

Winfield was inducted into the Baseball Hall of Fame in 2001, and while he and Steinbrenner had hashed things out by then, he chose to have a Padres logo adorn the cap on his plaque in Cooperstown. During his induction speech, Winfield surprised the audience with his words about The Boss.

"To George Steinbrenner, I want to thank you for bringing me to the Yankees," Winfield said. "I'm serious…. It's an experience that changed my life in a positive way. I'm glad time and clear minds have brought on a friendship we didn't have all along and I'm glad we have it today."

Seven years after his induction, Winfield took part in the final Old Timers' Day at the old Yankee Stadium in 2008, then returned for the last game at the House that Ruth Built in September.

"That was one of those one-of-a-kind experiences that kind of punctuates your career," Winfield said. "We crossed generations; decades of extraordinary players who contributed something to the organization. I was glad to be able to do that with the youngsters out there and the grizzled veterans. It was one of those special days in baseball for me."

26

The Warrior

Paul O'Neill was an Ohio kid in every sense of the word.

Born and raised in Columbus, O'Neill was selected in the fourth round of the 1981 draft by the Cincinnati Reds, the team of his youth. Cincinnati was less than two hours from Columbus, so when O'Neill reached the majors in 1985, it was a happy homecoming for the outfielder.

A World Series title in 1990 and an All-Star appearance in 1991 made O'Neill a popular figure in Cincinnati. There was no reason for him to believe the Reds would trade him, but less than three weeks after Jim Bowden took over as general manager in mid-October 1992, O'Neill came home to a stunning message on his answering machine.

He had been traded to the Yankees for Roberto Kelly, an athletic 28-year-old outfielder who had made his first All-Star team that season.

"I was basically the first move that Bowden made," O'Neill said. "When you grow up in the Midwest and you root for the Cincinnati Reds and you play for them and they trade you, initially you're disappointed because they're basically saying, 'We don't want you; you're not good enough to be here.'"

Yankees general manager Gene Michael called O'Neill that night, welcoming him to New York. The Yankees had scuffled through four straight losing seasons, but there was a sense that things were headed in the right direction under new manager Buck Showalter.

It also helped that George Steinbrenner had been banned from the day-to-day management of the team, allowing Michael and the rest of the front office to develop its young prospects rather than trading them away for big-name veterans, a common approach for the boisterous owner. One of those players was a young center fielder named Bernie Williams, who would now have a chance to play every day with Kelly no longer blocking his path.

"It didn't take long to understand that things were going to change a little bit in New York," O'Neill said. "Looking back, it was the perfect time to come there because the team hadn't won in a while, and they were starting to turn it around and bring in players."

The prospect of living in New York was overwhelming for O'Neill, whose only experiences there involved staying in midtown Manhattan during the Reds' trips to play the Mets at Shea Stadium. O'Neill was not a fan of the bustling city, but after his introductory press conference, he and his wife, Nevalee, looked at houses in nearby Westchester, a suburban option he didn't realize existed.

"I didn't know much about New York other than playing there as a visiting player," O'Neill said. "It was a totally different look than what I remembered from staying on 42nd Street."

The transition from the comforts of Cincinnati—and playing for a team that had won the World Series just two years earlier—was easier than O'Neill had expected. The Reds had stressed the need for O'Neill to hit for power, turning him into a pull-happy hitter. He belted a career-high 28 home runs in his All-Star 1991 season, but he hit just .256. In 1992, he hit just 14 home runs and his average dropped to .246, two figures that likely factored into Bowden's decision to move him prior to his age-30 season.

Ironically, the trade was panned by most New Yorkers. O'Neill was a career .259 hitter, seen by many as a less dynamic player than the younger Kelly. But Michael was attempting to balance the Yankees' lineup with another left-handed hitter, and O'Neill had the type of plate discipline the GM sought in a hitter.

"I always said we were too right-handed," Michael said at the time. "I feel this is a quality hitter and Yankee Stadium should be conducive to his hitting."

"He made me feel very comfortable," O'Neill said. "He knew a lot about me, and he made me feel like I was going to make a difference there. That in itself was important. I had gone through a time with Cincinnati where they wanted me to be a true home run hitter and pull everything; that wasn't my style, and it didn't help me. In New York, they wanted me to hit the way that I hit; as a left-handed hitter, I would be able to get some balls that I pulled out of the ballpark, but the left-field gap was also a great place to live."

For an Ohio kid who had spent his entire life in his home state, the move to the Yankees was an eye-opening experience. He grew up watching the Big Red Machine dominate the league, but the Yankees' history was so much bigger than he had realized from afar.

"My first spring training, I remember seeing Reggie Jackson and Yogi Berra; I was like, 'Wait a minute here, this is something different,'" said O'Neill, who clicked instantly with Don Mattingly, the team's captain. "The tradition, who the New York Yankees are, it hit me immediately."

With Danny Tartabull manning right field, the Yankees initially used O'Neill as a left fielder despite his stellar defensive reputation in right. By Memorial Day, O'Neill had supplanted Tartabull in right field as the Yankees began using the latter as their designated hitter.

"He was very instrumental, because he gave legitimacy to a position that really needed somebody to anchor it," Williams said. "Right field became sort of a no man's land until O'Neill came and really solidified himself in that position. He was very reliable as an All-Star-caliber outfielder; he took a lot of pride in throwing people out at second base when they tried to stretch out a double with that short porch in right field. He made it an art, fielding that ball on the bounce and firing a strike to second base. He became a weapon in the outfield."

O'Neill's first season in New York justified Michael's decision; he hit .311 with a .367 on-base percentage, swatting 20 home runs. The Yankees won 88 games, and although that wasn't good enough to reach the postseason for the first time since 1981, it was a big step in the right direction.

Steinbrenner had been reinstated in 1993, though Michael had convinced him to allow the club to develop the core of young players, believing they would serve as the backbone of the Yankees for years to come.

The Yankees appeared primed to break their 13-year playoff drought in 1994, posting an American League–best 70–43 record when the season was halted by a player strike, one that canceled the postseason and World Series. O'Neill was a big part of that success, winning the AL batting title with a .359 average while hitting 21 home runs in 103 games.

"There was no shifting on him because he was equally adept at pulling the ball when he saw that pitch inside or hitting it to the gap in left-center," Williams said. "He didn't care much about hitting home runs, but he could hit them when he wanted to. He was the perfect player with the perfect attitude to be a Yankee."

The Yankees finally returned to the postseason in 1995, winning the AL wild card with 79 wins in the 144-game strike-shortened season. O'Neill made his second consecutive All-Star team, finishing the year with a .300 average and 22 home runs in 127 games.

New York fell to the Seattle Mariners in a dramatic five-game series, but the foundation had been set for a winning culture. At least that was the perception, though Steinbrenner's decision to replace Showalter with Joe Torre caused some to wonder whether The Boss' decision-making would get in the way of the progress.

Torre proved to be the perfect fit for the Yankees, instilling a tranquil presence into an environment that can be far from calm. The Yankees won 92 games, claiming their first AL East title in 15 years. O'Neill hit .302 with 19 home runs, but the contributions from young players such as Derek Jeter, Andy Pettitte, and Mariano Rivera helped transform the Yankees from burgeoning contender to World Series champions.

"I started feeling we were competitive in 1994, the strike-shortened year; then we finally get to the playoffs in '95, which was a heartbreaker," O'Neill said. "In '96, we won the World Series and we felt like we were finally on the map—and it was only going to get better because Derek had just started his career."

O'Neill hit .324 in 1997, making his third All-Star team in four years. The Yankees returned to the postseason as the AL wild card, but they were stunned by Cleveland in the AL Division Series, costing them a chance at back-to-back championships.

When the Yankees opened the 1998 season with a 1–4 record, there was buzz that Torre's job was in jeopardy. While that may have seemed crazy to some, it was standard operating procedure in Steinbrenner's world—and the players knew it.

"I just loved being part of the intensity of winning," O'Neill said. "Mr. Steinbrenner would put together teams that continually contended. He always said that New York deserves a winner, so there was a feeling and a pressure every year that we were supposed to win."

Nobody knew it at the time, but the 1998 season would prove to be the greatest in Yankees history. New York won 114 games during the regular season, then cruised through the postseason for their second World Series title in three years. The Yankees made it back-to-back titles with another triumph in 1999, then completed the three-peat in 2000, beating the crosstown rival Mets in the World Series.

O'Neill's gritty 10-pitch walk in Game 1 of that Subway Series against closer Armando Benitez sparked a ninth-inning rally for the Yankees, who tied the game before winning it in 12 innings. The Yankees went on to win the series in five games, closing the 20th century in fitting fashion—with another parade down the Canyon of Heroes.

"The disappointment of '97, I'll never forget that feeling of losing to Cleveland," O'Neill said. "I'm not sure 1998–2000 happens without that, because there's a fear of losing again."

The 1999 World Series will always be bittersweet for O'Neill, whose father, Charles, died hours after the Yankees' Game 3 victory over the Atlanta Braves. The following morning, Nevalee called Torre and told him in no uncertain terms, "He needs to play tonight."

"Sometimes you don't know where somebody's head is when something like that happens, so I was pleased to get that phone call," Torre said. "That's a tough thing for a manager to try to figure out. When that game was over and we were all on the mound, we were hugging each other and he was crying his eyes out. Just bawling. It was quite powerful."

O'Neill had developed a reputation as the heart and soul of those Torre-era championship teams. He didn't have the star power of Jeter or the astonishing consistency of Rivera, but unlike many of his teammates, O'Neill routinely displayed the intensity and raw emotion that matched his approach on the field.

"He was hungry," Torre said. "You knew he wanted to win, and if he didn't get hits, he may come in and break things or whatever, but he was never mad at anybody but himself. Even if an umpire called him out on strikes, he may have said something to the umpire, but he was more mad at himself that he got to the point where one strike would get him out. It was always aimed at himself."

Well, not always. On more than one occasion, O'Neill aimed that anger at an unsuspecting dugout water cooler, seemingly unaware that he was in full view of television cameras.

"It's like I was a different person," O'Neill said. "When I look at those highlights, I'm like, 'What were you thinking?' People are wired differently. I didn't have a great way of getting out of the camera's eye, I guess, as I vented my frustration."

O'Neill's actions weren't meant to show anybody up. His desire for perfection engulfed him, so when he swung at a bad pitch or made an out, he took it personally.

"When you're doing something, it's your life," O'Neill said. "Baseball, everybody says it's fun and it's a game, but when it's your life, it's a little more than that. You live it every single day; you wake up in the morning thinking about the game, you go to bed at night thinking about what happened in the game. You're living not only a dream, but something that you try to be a perfectionist at. It's a very hard game going in looking for perfection."

Steinbrenner was so fond of O'Neill and his style of play that he referred to him as his "Warrior," a nickname that stuck— much to O'Neill's chagrin.

"He said that to somebody and I heard about it secondhand," O'Neill said. "I was almost embarrassed at the time. It's kind of corny, but now that I look back and it's all over, I appreciate that he felt I played hard."

The Yankees returned to the World Series in 2001, but their pursuit of a fourth consecutive title wasn't in the cards. O'Neill had let it be known that he planned to retire at the end of that season, prompting the Yankee Stadium crowd to serenade him with chants of his name in the top of the ninth inning of Game 5. With tears in his eyes, O'Neill emerged from the dugout for a curtain call after the inning was over, soaking in the moment.

"Two of my kids were born in New York, all of them were raised in New York, so I felt like I was a New Yorker at that point," O'Neill said. "I don't have a bad thing to say about anything that happened while I played in New York. Looking back, the trade was obviously the greatest thing that ever happened to me."

O'Neill finished his Yankees career with a .303 average, 185 home runs, 858 RBI, and an .869 OPS in 1,254 regular season games, adding 10 more home runs in 76 postseason contests. He won four rings with the Yankees, giving him five for his remarkable career, leaving an indelible mark in the Bronx, where he hit .310 for his career. The Yankees announced they planned to retire his No. 21 in 2022.

For all the talk about Yankee Stadium being the biggest pressure cooker in baseball, O'Neill was far more relaxed in the Bronx than he had ever been in Cincinnati.

"When you play at home and you're close to home, you put pressure on yourself because your family, and your brothers, your sisters, your mom and dad, they hear every pitch," O'Neill said. "For some reason, when I got to New York, I felt like I was away from everything. People were still listening and watching games, but because I wasn't at home, it was different. I think the intensity and the attitude of New York, I enjoyed that. The importance of every game, I liked that. It wasn't a social event to go to a baseball game; it was, 'Did the Yankees win or lose?' That was all that mattered."

27

Orlando Magic

By now, you've surely heard the legend of Orlando "El Duque" Hernandez, who escaped from Cuba and found his way to New York, becoming a star pitcher for the best team in baseball.

Hernandez's tale has been told so many times, the details have become as murky as the water he and seven others braved to find their way to a better life.

Some have said Hernandez escaped on a 20-foot fishing boat, while others have described the vessel as a rickety raft. The truth probably falls somewhere in between, but those particulars are mostly inconsequential.

Hernandez *did* find his way out of Cuba on December 26, 1997, sailing—floating?—to an island in the Bahamas called Anguilla Cay, where the U.S. Coast Guard found him and the others a few days later.

An agent named Joe Cubas was able to secure humanitarian visas for Hernandez, his wife, and one of the other defectors, who made their way to Costa Rica, where Hernandez would train in advance of a February showcase for major league teams.

Hernandez had been banned from baseball in August 1996 by the Cuban government, which believed he had helped his half-brother, Livan, defect nearly a year earlier. He had pitched for the Cuban national team since 1988, helping his country win the gold medal in the 1992 Olympics. Following Livan's defection, Orlando was not part of the Cuban team that won its second consecutive Olympic gold, this one in Atlanta in 1996.

Without the ability to play baseball, Hernandez found part-time work at a psychiatric facility, where he earned less than $10 a month. This was no way to live, he thought, prompting him to find a way out—even though leaving Cuba would mean leaving his mother and his two young daughters behind.

Now Hernandez was in Costa Rica, waiting to sign a multi-million-dollar contract to play baseball in the best league in the world. The New York Mets, Seattle Mariners, Detroit Tigers, Cincinnati Reds, and Anaheim Angels all expressed some level of interest, but the Yankees and Cleveland were emerging as the favorites to sign the right-hander.

For Hernandez, the decision was relatively easy. As long as the terms were roughly the same, he wanted to pitch for the Yankees. He had been given a blue Yankees T-shirt several years earlier, which he would wear beneath his Cuban national jersey when he pitched. He began to learn whatever he could about the Yankees' history, gobbling up any information he could find about these mythical legends with names like Babe, Whitey, and Mickey.

Cubas was asking for $8 million over four years, while the Yankees had offered $5 million. The two sides settled on a $6.6 million deal, and before too long, Hernandez—who said he was 28 years old despite some evidence that he was actually 32—was headed to Tampa to join his new team.

"When I thought back on how much I had respected the organization, I knew that if I had the chance to pitch for the Yankees, it would be an incredible experience," Hernandez told *Yankees Magazine* in 2018. "When the opportunity actually presented itself, I didn't want to pass it up."

Upon arriving at George M. Steinbrenner Field for his first spring training, Hernandez was in awe of his surroundings: the names on the lockers around him, many of whom he had read about or watched on television, and the sheer volume of equipment—gloves, spikes, balls, etc.—available, something that was sorely lacking back home.

"From the gloves and shoes piled up in the lockers, to the food spread, to the trainer's room," David Cone told *Sports Illustrated*. "You could see he was amazed."

Bernie Williams was one of the first players to welcome Hernandez, who had no idea that Williams—a native of Puerto Rico—spoke Spanish.

"Without that much access to coverage of sports outside of Cuba, I didn't know that he was Hispanic—when you think about the name Bernie Williams, it doesn't sound Latino," Hernandez told *Yankees Magazine*. "But it was a nice surprise to know that I could communicate with him, especially considering what a great teammate he was."

"I was one of the few people that was able to communicate with him at the beginning of his tenure as a Yankee," Williams said. "He felt lot of pride in his background as a Cuban baseball player, so he was always kind of comparing things to the way he did things in Cuba. It was an interesting coming of age for him to come into this different level of baseball."

Just as Dorothy knew she and Toto weren't in Kansas anymore, Hernandez was most definitely no longer in Cuba. Only he wasn't wearing ruby slippers, nor was he longing for a return home.

"What greater freedom is there than to be a member of the New York Yankees?" Hernandez said through a translator at his first Yankees press conference.

Hernandez hadn't pitched competitively in a year and a half, so the Yankees assigned him to Class A Tampa to begin the season. It became evident rather quickly that he was ready for more, so he moved to Triple A Columbus, where he continued to have success. Still, the Yankees were being deliberate with their plan for Hernandez, not wanting to repeat the same mistakes they had made a year earlier with Japanese import Hideki Irabu.

Uncertain whether David Wells' shoulder would be healthy enough to make his start against the Tampa Bay Devil Rays, the Yankees brought Hernandez to the Bronx on June 2 as a backup plan. Wells made the start, but Cone showed up that day with an issue: he had been bitten on his right index finger by his mother's Jack Russell terrier. Cone was lined up to pitch the next day, so the Yankees scheduled Hernandez to start in his place.

"El Duque" made his big-league debut on June 3, 1998, limiting the Devil Rays to one run over seven innings, striking out seven.

Wearing No. 26—his number when he pitched in Cuba— in honor of his father, Hernandez's high leg kick and varying arm angles kept Tampa Bay's hitters off balance, delighting the

Yankee Stadium crowd of 27,291 as they witnessed the birth of a new pinstriped star.

"I was really emotional during the national anthem, and I wanted to just take it all in and enjoy the atmosphere in the Stadium," Hernandez told *Yankees Magazine*. "But I was especially touched by the people in the seats who were waving Cuban flags. I had to tell myself at that point, 'Hey kid, you always wanted to make it to the big leagues and to pitch for the Yankees. Now you're here, and you've got to do what you've got to do. This is your chance.'"

Hernandez was once again doing what he loved, playing the game that had been taken away from him nearly two years earlier.

"After the game, he burst out in tears," catcher Jorge Posada said that day. "It was an emotional game for him. He dedicated it to his mother and daughters, to his people in Cuba and the Hispanic community in New York. On the mound, he wasn't nervous at all. He could throw any pitch in any count for strikes."

Baseball in the United States was the same game he had played all his life, though one thing confused him: why hadn't he been allowed to pitch the entire game? Reliever Mike Stanton took over and pitched the final two innings, closing out the 7–1 win.

"In Cuba, you pitch until you die," the pitcher told *Sports Illustrated*. "When you can't pitch with your arm, you go with your heart."

Hernandez pitched a complete game against the Montreal Expos in his second start, then worked into the eighth inning against Cleveland nine days later. Torre emerged from the dugout with two outs to remove "El Duque" for a reliever, but Hernandez didn't want to depart.

"When I went out to get him, he didn't know what the hell I was doing out there," Torre said. "I had to pry the ball out of his hand, because I guess he had never come out of a game."

Hernandez remained in the rotation for the rest of the 1998 season, going 12–4 with a 3.13 ERA. The Yankees—who won an AL-record 114 games—were 16–5 in his 21 starts, helping Hernandez finish fourth in AL Rookie of the Year voting.

"We get this guy from Cuba who was highly touted, but most guys that come from the other countries don't do so great right away," Tino Martinez said. "We didn't know what to expect from him. He was coming here to face some really good major league hitters that he had never faced before, but his tenacity and work ethic, the guts he had on the mound, he wasn't afraid of anybody and he knew how to mix things up. When he pitched, we knew we had a great chance to win."

"He could spin up a gem as good as anyone," catcher Joe Girardi said. "I think we trusted him as much as anyone because of his competitiveness."

As successful as Hernandez had been, he had to take his place in line when the postseason arrived. Wells, Cone, and Andy Pettitte were lined up to start the first three games of the AL Division Series against the Texas Rangers, leaving Hernandez slotted to pitch Game 4. The Yankees swept the series, postponing Hernandez's postseason debut.

New York would face Cleveland in the AL Championship Series. Unaware of the customs of major league teams, Hernandez assumed he would get the ball in the series-opener; after all, he was next in line, right?

"El Duque thought he was starting Game 1, because he was the fourth starter and the other three had pitched," Girardi said. "He was not happy when he found out that wasn't the case."

Hernandez returned to the back of the line as Wells, Cone, and Pettitte started the first three games against Cleveland. The Yankees won Game 1, but Cleveland rebounded with victories in Games 2 and 3; New York's regular season had been historic, but now the Yankees were counting on a rookie—albeit an experienced one—in the most important game of their season.

"I was a little nervous because he hadn't pitched in more than two weeks," Torre said. "We were down two games to one, I was in the hotel coffee shop in Cleveland and George wanted to see me. I went upstairs to his suite, and he asked me about Duque. I said, 'I'll tell you one thing: he's not nervous. He's down there in the coffee shop, and it was so busy, he was helping the waiters serve tables.' He just did what he did."

Paul O'Neill gave Hernandez a quick lead with a solo home run against Dwight Gooden in the first inning, then the Yankees scored two more runs in the fourth. The first run was more than enough for Hernandez, who blanked Cleveland over seven innings, then watched Stanton and Mariano Rivera throw a scoreless inning apiece, evening the series.

"The things he had gone through in his life, a big moment wasn't going to scare him," longtime Yankees broadcaster Michael Kay said. "He embraced it. He headed toward the light rather than moving away. There are a lot of players that move away from the light, but the light didn't bother him at all. He was all about the light. He had such a flair for the dramatic, he was almost theatrical in the way he went about it."

The Yankees won the next two games, advancing to the World Series, where they swept the San Diego Padres to complete their extraordinary season. Hernandez started Game 2, allowing one run over seven innings.

"I had pitched in a lot of big games in international tournaments with the Cuban national team, so it wasn't the first time my team was really counting on me," Hernandez told *Yankees Magazine*. "But I was always able to keep baseball in perspective. At the end of the night, it's still a game, and there will always be more games for both teams. Regardless of whether it was the regular season or the postseason, I took the mound with the same mindset."

The Yankees were World Series champions, but as the team returned to New York to prepare for a ticker-tape parade down the Canyon of Heroes, Hernandez received a gift far more valuable than a diamond-encrusted ring.

The night before the parade, Hernandez was reunited with his mother, Maria; his two young daughters, Yahumara and Steffi; and his ex-wife, Norma. They had been granted permission by Cuba to fly to the United States to see Hernandez.

Cardinal John O'Connor of New York helped make the visit happen, sending a message to Cuban President Fidel Castro on behalf of Hernandez. Within hours, Castro sent word through the Cuban Ambassador to the United Nations that he would allow Hernandez's family to travel to New York. Steinbrenner sent a plane to fly them from Miami to New York, where they reunited with Hernandez and joined him at the parade. The U.S. State Department said the family would return home after the visit, though they were ultimately allowed to remain in the U.S. permanently.

Hernandez won 17 games in 1999, his first full season with the Yankees. New York won the AL East again, then steamrolled its way through the postseason to capture a second straight World Series title.

"He fed off the crowd, especially in New York," Martinez said. "He just loved when he would get to two strikes and the fans would stand and go crazy, he fed off that. He also fed off getting booed on the road; nothing fazed him. It seemed to make him better."

Hernandez went 3–0 with a 1.20 ERA in four starts that October, winning the ALCS Most Valuable Player award. "El Duque" started Game 1 in all three rounds ahead of more accomplished teammates Cone, Pettitte, and Roger Clemens, the five-time AL Cy Young Award winner who had been traded to the Yankees prior to the season.

"I asked Roger, 'Who do you think should pitch Game 1?' and he said Duque," Torre said. "I said, 'OK, I just wanted to get your take on that.' That's what's tough for a manager, to make sure when you get to the postseason that you don't ignore someone with the ability of Roger Clemens, who was always used to being No. 1. I always wanted to go right to the guy and ask him what his decision would be. It worked out."

Hernandez had mixed results in 2000, going 12–13 with a 4.51 ERA in 29 starts. Come October, he stepped up his game as he had in his first two years, winning all three of his starts in the first two rounds of the postseason. He lost his lone World Series start against the Mets—his first defeat in 10 postseason starts—but the Yankees wrapped up the series in five games, winning a third consecutive championship.

Injuries limited Hernandez to 17 games (16 starts) in 2001, and although he delivered a couple of vintage starts in the postseason, the Yankees lost to the Arizona Diamondbacks in the World Series, missing out on a fourth straight title. He pitched 24 games (22 starts) in 2002, and late in the season, he and Posada—who would often jaw at each other on the mound during games—had a physical confrontation in the clubhouse prior to a game.

"They were both competitors out there; they brought the best out of each other," Martinez said. "Jorge knew when to get on him and Duque didn't like it at times, but he knew that it was the right thing to do."

Hernandez was moved to the bullpen for the ALDS, which the Yankees lost to the Anaheim Angels in four games. The Yankees traded him to the Expos as part of a three-team deal in January 2003, though he never pitched a game for Montreal after injuring his shoulder. He returned to the Yankees as a free agent in 2004, going 8–2 with a 3.30 ERA in 15 starts after coming back from shoulder surgery.

"He reminded me a lot of David Cone in that you would hate facing him as a right-handed hitter," said John Flaherty, who faced Hernandez while playing for the Devil Rays before catching him with the Yankees in 2004. "He would drop down, he would be really creative out on the mound. I'm a guy who hated the breaking ball, but he could throw three different types of drop-down and have all this deception. It was a nightmare to try to hit him, but what a pleasure it was to catch him."

The Chicago White Sox signed Hernandez in 2005, and while he pitched only 128⅓ innings during the regular season and four innings in the postseason, he earned a fourth World Series ring. Chicago traded him to the Diamondbacks after the season, then Arizona dealt him to the Mets in May 2006.

Hernandez won nine games for the Mets that season and was tabbed to start Game 1 of the NLDS, but he suffered a calf injury that knocked him out of action for the postseason. He re-signed with the Mets for 2007, winning nine more games for the club, but foot surgery forced him to miss all of 2008. He tried comebacks with the Texas Rangers and Washington Nationals over the next two years, but he never made it back to the big leagues.

On August 18, 2011, Hernandez announced his retirement from baseball. He finished his career with a 90–65 record and

4.13 ERA, compiling a postseason record of 9–3 with a 2.55 ERA. In 2013, Hernandez returned to Yankee Stadium to take part in his first Old Timers' Day, receiving a huge ovation from the fan base he thrilled during the team's late-nineties dynasty years.

"It almost seemed like he was built to play on Broadway; he was just that good," Kay said. "It was almost like he was an artist; he had the high leg kick which fans loved, because he was so different. Yankees fans embrace winners, and this guy was a big-time winner. And to think that it all started because a dog bit the tip of David Cone's finger."

28

Open Mike

As October 2000 drew to a close, Mike Mussina's offseason was just getting started.

A five-time All-Star with the Orioles, Mussina was the premier free-agent pitcher, sure to draw interest from pitching-starved teams around the majors. The free-agent process doesn't typically begin in earnest until mid-November, so the 31-year-old was in no hurry to begin dissecting his baseball future.

Then his phone rang. It was Joe Torre.

"I remember my wife picking up the phone and saying, 'Hey, it's Joe Torre,'" Mussina said. "I said, 'Joe, why are you calling me? You just won the World Series.'"

The Yankees had just finished off their five-game World Series triumph over the Mets a few days earlier, celebrating with their third consecutive ticker-tape parade down the Canyon of Heroes. Torre was heading on vacation that week, but before he left the hustle and bustle of New York behind him for some rest and relaxation, he wanted to speak with the pitcher who had frustrated his Yankees time and time again.

"We had to make a decision because he was a free agent and Manny Ramirez was a free agent," Torre said. "I always thought our strength was pitching; I called Moose because I felt in Baltimore, he was the one guy that they counted on to win that day. That's a lot of pressure to put on somebody. I thought he could really fit in great with our club because we didn't rely on any one guy."

Torre and Mussina didn't speak long, but those few minutes laid a foundation for the weeks ahead.

"To think that I was worth calling three days into the offseason," Mussina said, "that was a big deal to me."

In the days and weeks following his conversation with Torre, Mussina fielded calls from a number of Yankees players. Despite five All-Star appearances and five top-five finishes in the American League Cy Young Award vote, Mussina felt like a high school athlete being recruited by college programs.

"He was smart and he had good stuff," longtime Yankees right fielder Paul O'Neill said. "A lot of pitchers have good stuff and don't know how to pitch, and others know how to pitch and don't have great stuff. Moose had everything."

The Yankees were far from the only team calling, though the Montoursville, Pennsylvania, native had made it clear he didn't want to stray far from the East Coast. The Mets, the Red Sox, the Blue Jays, the Braves and Cleveland had all expressed interest, while the Orioles were still holding out hope that their ace would return. Mussina might not have known where he would wind up, but it was not going to be Baltimore.

"I didn't want to stay in a place that you could tell they weren't going to make the same push to be successful as other teams were going to," Mussina said.

By the third week of November, Mussina had seemingly narrowed down his list to the Yankees, Mets, and Red Sox. He was going to be a wealthy man no matter which team he chose, but money wasn't what drove him. Having tasted postseason success with trips to the American League Championship Series in 1996 and '97, Mussina had suffered through three consecutive losing seasons in Baltimore. This was his opportunity to join a contender, one that would afford him the chance to win on an annual basis.

From a baseball perspective, the idea of joining the Yankees seemed like a no-brainer for Mussina, who had watched his division rivals win four World Series titles during the previous five seasons. From a lifestyle standpoint, however, the prospect of living in New York was a bit daunting for the small-town boy.

"When I would come to New York as a visitor, we would stay at the Grand Hyatt right above Grand Central," Mussina said. "There's a fire truck passing by every five minutes. That just wasn't me."

Those concerns were quieted during a November dinner with Torre and general manager Brian Cashman, who assured Mussina that playing for New York didn't necessarily mean living in the heart of the city. A number of players resided in the suburbs of Connecticut, New Jersey, and Westchester County, giving Mussina and his family a variety of options.

"As you mature and get older, you figure out what situations you really want to be in and can you deal with the other stuff that goes that goes with those situations," Mussina said. "After 10 years in Baltimore with only two trips to the playoffs, I wanted to be on a team that I felt had a chance to go to the playoffs all the time. New York had the best opportunity. When you look at the broader spectrum of possibilities and I can live 30 miles the other direction, then let's go do that."

Cashman and Arn Tellem, Mussina's agent, negotiated a six-year, $88.5 million deal that would make the right-hander one of the highest-paid pitchers in the game. It was official: the rich had gotten richer, both literally and figuratively.

The baseball world shook its collective head at the signing. The Yankees had won three consecutive World Series titles and four in five years; did they really need Mussina? What may have seemed like overkill to outsiders was just standard operating procedure in the Bronx.

"When you win a World Series, to win another one, you have to be better," O'Neill said. "Everybody's out there to get you, so it didn't surprise me."

Mussina was joining a starting rotation that already included five-time AL Cy Young Award winner Roger Clemens, Andy Pettitte, and Orlando "El Duque" Hernandez, making the Yankees the odds-on favorites to win a fourth straight championship. And instead of having to face the Yankees' deep lineup five or six times per season, he would be the recipient of its production 30-plus times each year.

"I was getting an opportunity to be in a situation that any player would love to come to; a team that's been that successful with that core of players, guys with that mentality of winning like O'Neill, Tino, Bernie, and Jeter," Mussina said. "I'm not going to say winning was the only option, but that's kind of how it was. It's rare for guys who have had that kind of success to still want to have that kind of success. Sometimes once you reach that level, you just kind of ride it out and say, 'OK, we won; that's great. Now I'm just going to play for me.' That's not how anybody there was; they always played for the uniform."

Signing a multimillion-dollar contract is the fun part. Now came the real challenge: living up to the expectations that accompany a deal of that nature.

"I'm coming into a team that just won the World Series and I basically took David Cone's place on the team, so people kind of reminded me of that at the beginning," Mussina said. "I really just tried to remember that I had pitched in New York before, I was just coming out of this dugout and not the other dugout. Once you step on the grass, it's the same here as every other place."

Mussina fit seamlessly into the Yankees clubhouse during his first season in pinstripes, familiarizing himself quickly with a group of players he previously knew only from a distance of 60 feet, six inches.

"He was relaxed; he had a dry sense of humor, which I enjoyed," Torre said. "We had conversations, he had questions and he wasn't hesitant to ask them. He was a great teammate for everybody. I think everybody really enjoyed having Moose around."

Baseball players are cut from the same cloth whether they're in New York, Baltimore, or any other big-league city, but from the moment Mussina put on his cap with the interlocking NY at his introductory press conference, he knew this experience would be different from anything he had been through during his decade with the Orioles.

Where there were typically six members of the press in the Orioles clubhouse on a typical day, the Yankees clubhouse would regularly have 50 or 60 reporters on hand. Even on the road, the Yankees beat consisted of a dozen traveling reporters, an almost unheard-of number for most teams.

Mussina was the Yankees' shiny new toy. From his first bullpen session in spring training to his final pitch of the season, every move he made during that first year was certain to be dissected in the newspapers and on television, not to mention on *Mike and the Mad Dog*, WFAN's popular drive-time radio show that helped shape the sports conversation in New York. Mussina was not blind to this. The pressure of signing a big deal was hardly a new phenomenon, but for every Ed Whitson who wilted under the bright lights, there was a Reggie Jackson who thrived in the Bronx.

"They're going to write about you whether you did good or bad, so why worry about it?" Mussina said. "I was young enough that I could still do what I had been doing for the 10 years before that. That's how I approached it. I wasn't going to try to do more because I can't, so let's just do what I've done and hopefully it'll be good enough."

Mussina dazzled in his debut. He threw 7⅔ scoreless innings in a win over the Royals, giving the rest of the league a feeling of dread. The Yankees had won three straight World Series titles, and now they had Mussina pitching behind Clemens and Pettitte? It just didn't seem fair.

The rest of April didn't go as well. Mussina didn't record a win in his next four starts—two of them against the rival Red Sox—while posting a 6.29 ERA. Was he destined to become the next Whitson? Despite his uneven opening month, Mussina trusted his talent and mindset, confident that April had been a blip on the radar.

"Everybody puts on the pinstripes and tries to be more than they already were, which earned them the right to put on the pinstripes," Mussina said. "You don't have to be more; just try to be the same."

Mussina quelled any fears that may have developed among the fan base, kicking off a strong stretch with a three-hit shutout of the Minnesota Twins at the Metrodome on May 1. He went on to deliver quality starts (defined as six or more innings with three or fewer earned runs) in 18 of his next 23 outings, providing consistent excellence on the mound every fifth day.

"Every time you add a star, it doesn't mean everything is going to work out perfectly," O'Neill said. "It did with Moose."

On September 2 at Fenway Park, Mussina came one strike away from throwing a perfect game, surrendering a two-out, two-strike single to Carl Everett after retiring the first 26 Red Sox hitters. Mussina had flirted with no-hitters on multiple occasions and even taken a perfect game into the ninth inning four years earlier, but this was as close as a pitcher could get to perfection without actually achieving it.

"The thing with a no-hitter is that anybody can do it," Mussina said. "Clemens never threw a no-hitter and was probably the best pitcher in my era. The guy struck out 20 guys twice but never threw a no-hitter. There are guys we can't even remember and win 40 games in their whole lifetime that throw a no-hitter. It would have been cool to been able to say that, but I got to go to the Hall of Fame, so I'll take whatever happened."

Mussina finished his first year in New York with a 17–11 record and a 3.15 ERA. His 7.1 WAR topped all pitchers in the AL, though he finished fifth in Cy Young voting; his numbers bettered Clemens from virtually every angle, but the Rocket's impressive 20–3 record earned him a sixth Cy Young Award.

Of course, nothing matters in New York until October. Mussina had proved his value during the six-month grind of the regular season, but without postseason success, he would have been considered just another pitcher.

The 2001 postseason was unlike any other, as the Yankees began their pursuit of a fourth straight championship against the backdrop of the 9/11 terrorist attacks that had rocked New York just weeks earlier. The city rallied behind the Yankees; baseball provided an escape from the life-or-death reality that had encapsulated New Yorkers—and all Americans—since the Twin Towers fell on that horrific Tuesday morning just one month earlier.

It looked like the postseason would be a short one for the Yankees, who dropped the first two games of the American League Division Series at home to the Oakland Athletics. They headed for the West Coast on the brink of elimination, handing the ball to Mussina for Game 3.

Facing a stacked lineup that included Johnny Damon, Miguel Tejada, Eric Chavez, Jermaine Dye, and future teammate Jason Giambi, Mussina matched zeroes with Oakland ace Barry Zito through the first four innings. Jorge Posada gave the Yankees a lead with a solo home run in the fifth, handing Mussina the only run he would see all night.

Derek Jeter's infamous "flip play" in the seventh inning will rightfully be the forever snapshot from this game, as the shortstop's heads-up shovel pass from the first-base line nabbed Jeremy Giambi at the plate to preserve the one-run lead. That was the 21st and final out recorded by Mussina that night, as Mariano Rivera was called upon to get the final six outs. Jeter's play may have been the highlight, but if not for Mussina's seven shutout innings, it wouldn't have had the same impact.

"That was an unbelievable game," Tino Martinez said. "That Oakland A's offense was incredible, and in that game and that situation we were in, we needed a great outing to beat those guys. For him to go out there and pitch the way he pitched, it was an outstanding effort by Moose that saved our season."

The Yankees went on to beat the Athletics in five games, advancing to the ALCS, where they breezed past the 116-win Seattle Mariners in a five-game series. The Yankees were back in the World Series for the fourth straight year, and while a number of players were seeking their fourth ring, Mussina was trying to chase down his first.

It wasn't meant to be. Despite a pair of dramatic comeback wins against the Arizona Diamondbacks in Games 4 and 5 at Yankee Stadium, the Yankees lost the final two games of the series in the desert, falling in the decisive Game 7 when Arizona mounted a stunning ninth-inning comeback against Rivera.

Although Mussina remained in pinstripes for the next seven seasons, 2001 proved to be the closest he would get to that elusive ring. The Yankees reached the World Series again in 2003, surviving a grueling seven-game series against the Red Sox that ended with one of the greatest games in franchise history. Mussina played an integral role in the Game 7 victory, coming in from the bullpen to relieve Clemens with runners at the corners and nobody out. A strikeout and a double play later, Boston's lead remained at three runs, but the Yankees mounted a memorable comeback to win the pennant.

Mussina was a model of consistency during the six-year contract, going 92–53 with a 3.80 ERA while averaging 200 innings per season. He signed a two-year contract to return in 2007, though he struggled through the worst year of his career, going 11–10 with a 5.15 ERA while being temporarily demoted to the bullpen.

As he prepared for the 2008 season, Mussina made a decision that can haunt professional athletes late in their careers. Whether he won two games or 20, this would be his final season.

"I had one year on my contract, and I had just come off this cruddy year," Mussina said. "I was sitting on a bench, and I remember saying myself, 'This is it. If I have another bad year, it's obviously time to quit; if I have a good year, I'm almost 40 years old and I want to get out of here on a good year.' Because of that, the anxiety of the next contract or any of that didn't exist at all the whole season."

That lack of anxiety helped Mussina navigate his way through a poor start to the season; he was 1–3 with a 5.75 ERA after four starts, making his decision—one he kept within his inner circle, not wanting the world to know he was hanging up his spikes at the end of the year—look justified.

Mussina, no longer able to produce the mid-90s fastball that had helped him to so much success throughout his twenties and early thirties, had changed his pitching style as he moved into his mid-thirties. A crafty veteran considered to be one of the smartest pitchers in the game, Mussina willed his way through the rest of the first half, going 10-3 with a 3.10 ERA over his next 15 starts.

He had 11 wins at the All-Star break, creating some buzz that a 20-win season—something he had never accomplished—was within reach.

"He was very cerebral when he took the mound," Bernie Williams said. "That took him further into his career even beyond the years when he was not at his best physically with his arm speed and his velocity. He was still a very good pitcher because he knew how to pitch."

Mussina won five of his first seven starts after the break, giving him a 16–7 record in mid-August. He won just one of his next five outings, however, leaving him with 17 victories and three starts left in the season—and, as he had privately decided, his career.

Victories against the White Sox and Blue Jays gave Mussina 19 wins, the third time in his career he had reached that mark. He had one start left to achieve the 20-win season that had eluded him during the first 17 years of his career, and with the Yankees eliminated from postseason contention for the first time in 15 years and the old Yankee Stadium having hosted its final game the previous week, his pursuit of that 20th win was the most intriguing storyline of the season's final days.

He almost didn't have a chance to make that final start after taking a line drive off his elbow in the start against Toronto, but Mussina wasn't going to be denied this one final shot. A Saturday rainout also meant a doubleheader against the Red Sox on the final day of the season; manager Joe Girardi allowed Mussina to choose which game he wanted to pitch, and with rain in the forecast, he decided on the day game, giving him a better chance of the contest being played.

"I'm in my hotel room and the weather doesn't look that good," Mussina said. "I'm like, 'Whatever. This is the last day. If we don't play, we don't play.'"

The weather held up, allowing Mussina to do his part with six scoreless innings. He handed a 3–0 lead to the bullpen, then paced around Fenway's small visiting clubhouse for two innings before returning to the dugout to watch Rivera close out the ninth, securing win No. 20.

"When I was 1–3 in April or when I got hot into the summer, it was, 'Whatever happens, happens,'" Mussina said. "I was glad I stayed healthy and made all my starts, but it was time to go."

Mussina announced his retirement seven weeks later, holding firm to the decision he had made 10 months and 20 wins earlier. With 270 career victories, Mussina would have had to commit to pitching three more seasons to give himself a realistic chance at 300, and with his 40th birthday just weeks away, he decided 270 was enough.

In his eight seasons with the Yankees, Mussina went 123–72 with a 3.88 ERA, winning another five games in the postseason. His first contract is widely considered to be one of the best free-agent signings in club history, though the Yankees never won a World Series during his tenure.

"We were this close to winning twice in the first three years I played there," Mussina said. "It's not like it really changed; we went to the playoffs the first seven years I was there. We had opportunities. We won 100 games three or four times. That's a lot of wins. We won 100 games with teams that I didn't know how we won 100 games. We found a way to win."

Eleven years after he retired and six years after he first appeared on the ballot, Mussina was elected to the National Baseball Hall of Fame. He chose not to have either the Yankees or Orioles logo on his plaque, believing that his work with both franchises contributed to his place in history.

"There's no way to differentiate between which one got me there; one gave me the opportunity, the other team put me on the world stage for eight years," Mussina said. "You win 100 games for two teams, that's a lot of games. To win 100 games for the Yankees, that's pretty cool. There aren't a lot of guys who can do that. Not a lot of guys win double digits for 17 years in a row. There are some quirky little things that I was able to do. I didn't win five Cy Youngs or all that crap, but I did some other stuff along the way. Just enough."

29

King of Swing

GEORGE STEINBRENNER WAS NOT A MAN KNOWN FOR PATIENCE.

The Boss had just watched his Yankees fall to the Diamondbacks in a classic World Series, taking Arizona the distance despite scoring a total of 14 runs over seven games.

"I'm not a good loser," Steinbrenner said. "I believe in what Ernest Hemingway said: 'The way you get to be a good loser is to practice losing.' I don't want to practice."

They may have won four consecutive American League pennants and four World Series championships in six years, but the Yankees had failed to extend their title run to four in a row, something that hadn't been accomplished since the 1949–53 Yankees won five straight.

One of the first moves was to fire hitting coach Gary Denbo, the apparent scapegoat for the team's woeful hitting in the Fall Classic. But Denbo's departure wouldn't fix the lineup's problems, especially with the retirement of Paul O'Neill and the impending free-agent departures of Tino Martinez, Chuck Knoblauch, and Scott Brosius.

Steinbrenner quickly set his sights on the biggest free-agent bat available: Jason Giambi.

Giambi, the American League's Most Valuable Player in 2000 and runner-up in 2001, was the perfect combination of power and patience, the ideal tonic for what Steinbrenner considered to be an underachieving Yankees lineup.

The Athletics—an up-and-coming team that had taken the Yankees to Game 5 in back-to-back AL Division Series in 2000 and '01—had tried to sign Giambi to an extension in spring training, offering him a six-year, $91 million contract. But Oakland refused to include a no-trade clause, killing the chance of a deal.

"We had an amazing team, but I didn't know where the A's were going to stand," Giambi said. "We didn't get something done in spring training; there was a point where they tried, but then they didn't make any other offers and just kind of shut it down because it didn't work out."

The talks with Oakland were at an impasse, so Giambi's agent, Arn Tellem, sat him down prior to the 2001 season and explained how the next eight or nine months would play out.

"There was a good feeling that the Yankees were going to come after me, for sure," Giambi said.

Giambi played out his final year prior to free agency, confident that his performance would help him land a contract he felt was worthy of his immense offensive talent.

The decision paid off, as Giambi hit .342, leading the league with a .477 on-base percentage, a .660 slugging percentage, 47 doubles, and 129 walks. He hit 38 home runs with 120 RBI, finishing second to Ichiro Suzuki of the Seattle Mariners in a tight MVP vote. Giambi was more than a home run hitter; he was one of the most dangerous, well-balanced offensive threats in the entire league.

"He was one of my favorite guys to compete against when he was with Oakland," said John Flaherty, who faced Giambi while playing for the Tampa Bay Devil Rays. "As a catcher, trying to figure out how to get him out was an incredible challenge. He seemed like such a good dude; he enjoyed competing and really treated everybody with respect."

During the 2001 ALDS, Giambi sat by his locker in the visiting clubhouse at Yankee Stadium and entertained a scrum of New York reporters. Dressed in a green Dri-FIT shirt with matching spandex leggings, Giambi appeared to be comfortable with the attention, cracking jokes and showing the type of fun-loving personality that was seemingly missing from the Yankees roster. He may have looked like the Incredible Hulk, but Giambi was the antithesis of angry.

"Man, I hope that guy signs with the Yankees," one Gotham scribe said as the crowd departed the clubhouse. "He would absolutely own this city."

As the offseason commenced, the Yankees went into full-court press mode in their attempt to woo Giambi to New York. Joe Torre reached out to him, much the same as he had a year earlier while recruiting Mike Mussina. Hall of Famer Yogi Berra and New York City Mayor Rudy Giuliani also called Giambi, making their pitch to bring the slugger to New York.

Giambi was the prize of the offseason, and with the Yankees on the warpath to add his thunderous bat, the rest of the league seemed resigned to the idea that the rich would be getting richer for a second consecutive offseason.

"The Yankees were the only ones that came after me, to be honest with you," Giambi said. "The A's didn't make an offer and other teams had kind of thrown it out there, but they wanted me to sign for less years. The Yankees came out and made me a big offer early, which may have taken a lot of teams out of the bidding right away. The Yankees and Mr. Steinbrenner came for me with full force."

On December 13, the Yankees made it official, introducing Giambi at a packed Yankee Stadium press conference. The deal was for seven years and $120 million, which at the time marked the fourth-largest contract in the game's history.

Dressed in a gray three-piece suit with a yellow shirt and yellow-and-blue tie, Giambi walked into the Stadium Club with an unfamiliar look. The player who had appeared on the cover of *Sports Illustrated* in 2000 with tattooed arms, his trademark goatee, and long hair had been replaced by one with a clean, Yankee-like haircut and a fully shaven face. Baseball's ultimate frat guy had graduated, taking a job at a Fortune 500 company.

"That's the type of respect Mr. Steinbrenner deserves," Giambi said. "When you have a man that is committed to winning like that and is bringing you in there to try to win a World Series, that was the last thing on my mind. I wasn't worried about cutting my hair or shaving my face; it was a respect thing for me. I never looked at it as something bad."

With the No. 16 he wore in Oakland unavailable (it was retired for Whitey Ford), Giambi chose No. 25 because the digits added up to 7, the number of his father's all-time favorite, Mickey Mantle.

"Well, pop," Giambi said at the press conference. "It's not 7, but it's pinstripes."

Giambi wasn't the only newcomer in 2002; Robin Ventura was imported to replace Brosius at third base, while Rondell White signed a free-agent deal to take over for O'Neill in right field. David Wells rejoined the Yankees rotation for the first time since 1998, and reliever Steve Karsay was signed to help get the ball to Mariano Rivera.

The core of Torre's championship clubs remained intact, but there was plenty of new blood on the roster, which general manager Brian Cashman hoped would translate into a new hunger, fighting off the complacency that can set in following such a successful run.

"That's why you go to New York, to have an opportunity to win," Giambi said. "You know the owner is going to do everything he can to win a World Series. He was amazing as an owner, but he was a huge baseball fan. He loved the fans, he loved everything about what the Yankees brought, so when you have an owner like that, it wasn't about what it was going to cost. It was about, 'What is it going to take to win another World Series?'"

When Giambi arrived in Tampa for his first spring training as a Yankee, it was eminently clear that complacency was not going to be an issue.

The clubhouse was filled with homegrown Yankees, players such as Rivera, Derek Jeter, Jorge Posada, Bernie Williams, and Andy Pettitte, all of whom had a singular focus from the day they arrived at camp.

"As players, I don't think you can really get a taste of what it's like until you're actually there," Giambi said. "It's kind of a different mindset when you go there, because it's all about winning a world championship. That was the atmosphere they built with Mr. Steinbrenner and Joe and Derek. It's like, 'Hey, we've got a chance to win a World Series every year.' I don't think any other ballclub in Major League Baseball has that attitude. There are some that say they do, but most teams believe, 'Here's our window to win, so we better win.' And whether they do or not, at some point, they change over with some young guys and kind of start over. The Yankees don't rebuild; they just reload."

Winning was nothing new for Giambi, who had played an integral role in the Athletics' early 2000s resurgence. Dealing with the spotlight that came with being the Yankees' shiny new toy was a different story altogether.

Reporters would log every swing Giambi took in batting practice during spring training, counting the number of home runs he hit. The media requests flooded the team's public relations department, as every outlet wanted a piece of the newest Yankees slugger. In Oakland, Giambi dealt with a small handful of beat writers and an occasional television or radio reporter. Only he wasn't in the Bay Area anymore; he was playing in the media capital of the world for the city's biggest team.

"New York is like a different planet than Oakland," Giambi said. "You have so many TV stations, so many newspapers, and it's like the Mecca of show business. When you walk in, you're like a deer in the headlights with everything that's going on. There's so much stuff that goes on there that you don't even realize. When you're a visiting player, you get to touch it because people want to interview you, but when you become a Yankee, that's a whole different universe, for sure."

Even with the massive amount of attention being thrust in his direction, Giambi stayed true to himself. Upon his arrival in Tampa, Steinbrenner greeted his new star with a big hug, then offered him two words of advice: "Be yourself."

Giambi might have looked different than he did in Oakland, but his personality remained remarkably consistent. Few sentences were completed without an F-bomb, while anybody that walked up to his locker was welcomed with a warm "Hey, buddy" or "What's up, bro?" The contract hadn't changed who Giambi was, nor had the pressure of performing in pinstripes.

After all, the games didn't count yet. If the pressure was going to get to Giambi in March, it was going to be a very long seven years.

"He was a great clubhouse guy," Williams said. "He brought a certain level of relaxation to the team; with him, things weren't as tense. He relied on his great natural ability to play the game and to have this sort of loose attitude. Don't get me wrong, he was a hard worker and he did everything that he needed to do to be the player that he was, but he also knew how to have fun playing the game, which was something that we weren't always very good at."

Giambi would often walk around the clubhouse in a T-shirt that read PARTY LIKE A ROCK STAR, HAMMER LIKE A PORN STAR, RAKE LIKE AN ALL-STAR. That was the way he led his life, and whether he was making $120 million or $120,000, that was unlikely to change.

"You knew how dangerous he was as a hitter, but you didn't know him as a person," Mussina said. "The entertainment factor that you got with him was something else. When you do the same thing every day for more than six months, you need some personalities. He definitely had a personality, which was great. The same 25 guys in a clubhouse, on the bus, on the plane, it can all become monotonous."

He even brought his lucky gold thong with him from Oakland, lending it to slumping teammates to help them break out of a funk at the plate. Even Derek Jeter gave the undergarment a try during a career-worst 0-for-32 slump; he hit a home run in his first at-bat that day.

"The golden thong is legendary" Giambi told ESPN Radio's Dan Le Batard in 2019. "It's never not gotten a hit."

Giambi had made a seamless transition with his new club, but as the season began, it was time to justify the Yankees' decision to sign him in place of Tino Martinez, a fan favorite during the late-nineties championship run.

The first couple weeks didn't go well. The Yankees jumped out to a 7–1 start, but Giambi didn't look like himself at the plate. He had no extra-base hits in those eight games, causing the typical quick-trigger reactions from fans, some of whom called local sports radio station WFAN to pronounce him a bust after just 29 at-bats.

"When you're visiting player and you play well in front of Yankee fans, they're thinking, 'This guy hits a home run every at-bat'—but they're only seeing you six times a year," Giambi said. "There's an energy about New Yorkers. When you play there as a visitor—and even more as a home player—that energy makes you want to succeed. You really want to do well there, which puts that pressure on you."

Giambi picked it up over the next month, and on May 17, in the Yankees' 42nd game of the season, he finally had *that moment* he had been waiting for.

It was a Friday night in the Bronx, and the Yankees were hosting the Minnesota Twins in the first game of a three-game weekend set. The offenses came out swinging; the Twins scored three times against Mussina in the second inning, then the Yankees banged out seven runs between the fourth and fifth, seizing an 8–3 lead.

Minnesota answered with a six-spot in the sixth to take a one-run lead, but Williams hit a game-tying homer in the bottom of the ninth. Rain began to fall during extra innings, and when the Twins scored three times against lefty Sterling Hitchcock in the top of the 14th, the Yankees looked like they would come up on the short end of this marathon.

The Yankees wouldn't go down quietly, loading the bases with one out against right-hander Mike Trombley. With the rain falling harder by the minute, Giambi stepped to the plate and crushed the first pitch he saw—the 494th pitch of the game—into the right-center field bleachers. The fans that had remained for the duration of the soggy, five-hour, 45-minute game had been rewarded with the biggest swing of Giambi's brief Yankees career.

"The thing I love that you will never get anywhere else is that moment when they tell you, 'Now you're a Yankee,'" Giambi said. "I'm not kidding you, everywhere I've gone, different countries, one of the first things any Yankee fan says to me is, 'I remember when you hit the grand slam walk-off against the Twins.' It's etched in stone; that's the day I became a Yankee. It's the coolest thing on the planet. When you sign, those are the moments you're envisioning. I wanted to do that every night."

Giambi didn't hit walk-off homers every night, but he had a phenomenal debut season with the Yankees, hitting .314 with 41 home runs, 122 RBI, and a 1.034 OPS. He finished fifth in AL MVP voting, though his stellar season went for naught as the Yankees were eliminated by the Anaheim Angels in a four-game AL Division Series.

Giambi also produced 41 homers in his second season, though his pull-happy approach—a common issue for left-handed hitters trying to take advantage of Yankee Stadium's short right-field porch—caused his average to fall to .250, while he led the league with 140 strikeouts. Giambi also led the league with 129 walks, resulting in a superb .412 on-base percentage.

The Yankees reached the World Series in 2003, outlasting the Red Sox in a classic seven-game AL Championship Series. Giambi's two solo home runs against Boston ace Pedro Martinez helped spark the memorable comeback, which was capped by Aaron Boone's walk-off home run in the 11th inning.

There was no fairy tale ending for Giambi and the Yankees, however, as the Florida Marlins defeated them in the World Series. Giambi had hit 82 homers in his first two seasons in New York, and as he headed into his age-33 season, there was no reason to think he would slow down any time soon.

Little did Giambi know that his world would be turned upside down before the 2004 season ever started.

Giambi had been subpoenaed to testify to a federal grand jury in December 2003, part of the Bay Area Laboratory Co-Operative (BALCO) federal investigation. During his testimony, Giambi admitted that he had injected himself with human growth hormone and used other steroids including undetectable drugs known as "the clear" and "the cream," a key part of the investigation.

Giambi's testimony was supposed to remain sealed, but in March 2004, a *San Francisco Chronicle* report detailed his leaked admissions, sparking a firestorm. Other players, including Barry Bonds and Gary Sheffield—the latter of whom was in his first spring with the Yankees—were also named in the report.

Although Giambi had been granted immunity in exchange for his testimony, the *Chronicle* report essentially convicted him in the court of public opinion. He initially denied ever using performance-enhancing drugs, following advice from his attorneys.

That was just the start of Giambi's nightmare 2004 season. He battled fatigue, weakness, and nausea throughout the first half, though doctors struggled to identify the root of his problems. He was diagnosed with an intestinal parasite in late June; a month later, it was revealed he also had a benign tumor on his pituitary gland. Giambi returned in mid-September, but it was a lost season for him. After hitting .208 with 12 home runs and 40 RBI in just 80 games, Giambi was left off of the Yankees' postseason roster.

Looking to rebound in 2005, Giambi decided to meet the media 10 days before he was scheduled to report to Tampa for spring training. He wanted to apologize for the distractions he caused the previous season, though with four years and $82 million remaining on his contract, Giambi was very careful not to specify exactly what he was apologizing for.

"I feel I let down the fans, I feel I let down the media, I feel I let down the Yankees, and not only the Yankees, but my teammates," a somber Giambi said. "I accept full responsibility for that, and I'm sorry."

He never uttered the word "steroids," though anybody paying attention knew what he was talking about. Giambi had stepped up and held himself accountable; well, as accountable as he could be without actually saying the S-word. Now he had to start producing on the field if he had any hope of putting his off-field controversy behind him.

Five weeks into the season, Giambi was hitting below .200 with just three home runs, prompting the Yankees to ask his permission to send him to the minors. Giambi refused, choosing to work out his issues with Don Mattingly, the Yankees' hitting coach, rather than disappearing to the team's complex in Tampa.

Slowly but surely, Giambi's bat found new life. In 70 games after the All-Star break, he hit 22 home runs while posting a 1.057 OPS, earning him AL Comeback Player of the Year honors. He belted 37 homers with 113 RBI in 2006, but the Yankees experienced another short October, losing in the ALDS for the second straight season.

In May 2007, more than three years after his BALCO grand jury testimony had been leaked and two-plus years after his non-specific apology, Giambi came clean in an interview with *USA Today*.

"I was wrong for doing that stuff," Giambi told the paper. "What we should have done a long time ago was stand up— players, ownership, everybody—and said, 'We made a mistake.'

"We should have apologized back then and made sure we had a rule in place and gone forward.... Steroids and all of that was a part of history. But it was a topic that everybody wanted to avoid. Nobody wanted to talk about it."

Injuries limited Giambi to just 83 games in 2007, but his admission that season had earned him a new respect from teammates and fans alike. Just as Andy Dufresne had traveled through a river of shit and come out clean on the other side in *The Shawshank Redemption*, Giambi had undergone a similar restoration of his own.

"To go through that, then come back and be productive was rewarding," Giambi said. "The way that people viewed me after that, never having to look over my shoulder wondering if the other shoe was going to drop was a relief. To still come out of it and be the person I am, the way people treated me, it was a gift."

Giambi hit 32 home runs with 96 RBI in 2008, the final guaranteed year of his contract. The Yankees missed the postseason for the first time in 15 years, though the closing of Yankee Stadium created a playoff-type atmosphere during the season's final month. In the final game played at the old ballpark, Giambi's seventh-inning single proved to be the last hit ever recorded there.

When all was said and done, Giambi hit 209 home runs with 604 RBI in 897 games as a Yankee, leaving him ahead of legendary names including Dave Winfield, Roger Maris,

Reggie Jackson, and Paul O'Neill on the franchise's all-time home run list.

Giambi played in one World Series, though he never won a ring during his seven years in pinstripes. Rather than lament his timing—New York won it all the year after he left—he looks at the hole on his résumé with admiration for the teams that have reached the game's highest height.

"Would I have loved to have won a World Series? For sure," Giambi said. "But it's not as easy as everybody thinks. It was part of my journey. I loved being a part of the Yankees; I still love being a part of the Yankees. All the things I went through helped make me the person I am today. I will never look back at being a Yankee and not enjoy every moment."

30

Great Godzilla

THE HYPE WAS REAL. AS IT TURNED OUT, SO WAS THE TALENT.

Hideki Matsui came to the major leagues from Japan with as much fanfare as any player in years. He was the Japanese baseball equivalent of Michael Jordan, yet in signing a three-year, $21 million contract to join the Yankees in December 2002, Matsui joined a team with as much star power as any in the league.

"He was a superstar, but he didn't know it," manager Joe Torre said. "He didn't act like it. That team concept coming from Japan, his unselfishness and respect for the game was evident right away."

A few weeks after he agreed to a contract, the Yankees rented out a ballroom at the Marriott Marquis in Times Square for Matsui's introduction to New York. Unlike a typical free-agent press conference, Matsui's drew roughly 500 international media members, more than five times the number that had welcomed Jason Giambi to the Bronx the previous offseason.

New York City Mayor Michael Bloomberg attended the press conference, joined by Yankees pitcher Roger Clemens and Torre, who interrupted his annual Hawaiian vacation to welcome Matsui to New York.

Known as "Godzilla" for his immense power, some wondered whether the Yomiuri Giants slugger's game would translate to the big leagues. Of the hitters that had made the jump, none had possessed the power stroke that made Matsui famous.

A little more than a month after the press conference, all eyes were on Matsui as he reported to spring training in Tampa. Reporters and fans alike watched each batting practice session to see how Matsui's powerful swing compared to other sluggers, but Yankees bench coach Don Zimmer was interested in something else.

"His batting practice was impressive, but Zim said to me, 'Find out if he'll hit-and-run,'" Torre said. "You learn a lot about somebody when they're hitting 50 home runs a year and then the manager is going to ask about hit-and-runs. When I asked him that, through his interpreter, he said, 'Any time you want.' There was no hesitation. That really told me something."

Matsui—a three-time Central League Most Valuable Player—had averaged nearly 40 home runs per year for Yomiuri between 1996–2002, belting 50 homers in his final season in Japan. It didn't take long for the 28-year-old rookie to endear himself to his new home crowd, crushing a grand slam in his first game at Yankee Stadium.

"Talk about feeling pressure?" Giambi said. "You're not only going to the Yankees, but you're basically bringing a whole country with you. He did everything with such grace and honor and presence."

Matsui hit just 16 home runs in his rookie season, but he drove in 106 runs, made his first All-Star team, and finished second in American League Rookie of the Year voting, though he would have won the award if not for a pair of voters who held his professional experience in Japan against his "rookie" status, leaving him off their ballots entirely.

He had also delivered a pair of signature postseason moments in his rookie year, hitting a big home run in Game 3 of the AL Division Series against the Minnesota Twins at the Metrodome, then rapping a key double in the eighth inning of Game 7 in the AL Championship Series, part of the Yankees' memorable rally against Red Sox ace Pedro Martinez.

"If I had a top-five list of people that I would want at the plate when the game is on the line, he is certainly one of them," Bernie Williams said. "He had a knack for doing great things in pressure situations."

The Yankees opened the 2004 season with a pair of games against the Tampa Bay Devil Rays in Tokyo, giving Matsui's team a firsthand look at his popularity back home.

"We got to see what the reality of his life is, the hysteria," John Flaherty said. "We knew he was a big deal, but it wasn't until then that you realized how big he was. Hideki did such a great job of not carrying himself like an international star; he carried himself just like he was just another teammate."

Broadcaster Michael Kay had always compared traveling with the Yankees to what it must have been like to tour with The Beatles.

"This put it all to shame; this was The Beatles, but the Rolling Stones were also there and maybe Bruce Springsteen, as well," Kay said. "It was just unbelievable the way he was treated;

it was past the level of idealization. He was almost like a God. He handled it with equanimity and he never flinched."

That star power was never apparent inside the Yankees clubhouse, where Matsui was just one of the guys. Derek Jeter always counted Matsui among his favorite all-time teammates, though players on the back end of the roster left their time with him feeling the same way.

"When you have big-name players like that, big superstars, sometimes they treat guys on the team—the lower guys on the team—a little different," pitcher Tanyon Sturtze said. "Matsui was never that guy. He treated everybody in the clubhouse the same no matter who they were; it didn't matter to him whether you had been around for 10 years or 10 days."

Despite the initial language barrier—he learned English rather quickly, but always preferred to do his media interviews with trusted interpreter Roger Kahlon by his side—Matsui's sense of humor was always on display.

"He was one of the few guys on that level who let you in and really let you see who he was," Giambi said. "He's funny, he has a great time, he cracks jokes. That's what makes him so beloved. He just opens himself up to you as a teammate and you get to see this amazing human being."

Matsui's power improved after his rookie year; he had 31 home runs and 108 RBI in 2004, then belted 23 home runs with 116 RBI in 2005, playing in every one of the team's games for the third consecutive season. His reward? A four-year, $52 million deal to keep him in pinstripes.

"He was the ultimate teammate; if Joe Torre had to draw up a perfect player to manage, it would Hideki Matsui," Flaherty said. "He stayed under the radar, didn't need attention, you could pencil him in the lineup every day and you knew you were going to get 25–30 home runs and 100 RBI every year.

For a star player to come to New York and fit in the way he did, what a pleasure it was to play with him."

Matsui's second contract didn't start out on a high note, as he suffered a broken wrist while attempting a sliding catch in left field on May 11. His consecutive-game streak—he had played in all 519 contests since joining the Yankees and 1,768 overall dating back to his days with Yomiuri—was over, but Matsui's concern wasn't for himself. After undergoing surgery that would sideline him for four months, Matsui issued a statement apologizing to his teammates for letting them down.

"A very humble, respectful human being," Torre said. "I can't say enough about him."

Matsui returned at full strength in 2007, delivering the types of numbers to which the Yankees had grown accustomed. He hit his 100th major league home run in August, becoming the first Japanese player to reach that milestone.

Beginning in 2008, Matsui's knees began to ail him, limiting him to 93 games. The pain led to reduced time in the outfield as Matsui became the Yankees' primary designated hitter.

Matsui was entering the final year of his contract as the Yankees opened their new ballpark in 2009. Now exclusively a DH, Matsui hit 28 homers and drove in 90 runs, playing most of the season with constant swelling in his knees.

By the time October rolled around, Matsui's knees were shot, particularly the left one, which had been drained at least twice during the season. He homered in the Yankees' first postseason game but struggled during the rest of the ALDS and the entire ALCS, hitting .222 with one extra-base hit in eight games.

"Any time he would have a couple of bad games, you'd go put your arm around him because we try to pick each other up," Mark Teixeira said. "There was a little bit of a language barrier, but Matsui would just look at you and say, 'I suck.' We would all have a really good laugh."

The Yankees advanced to the World Series on the strength of ace CC Sabathia's left arm and the thunderous bat of Alex Rodriguez, who had five home runs and 12 RBI in the first two rounds.

Matsui started just three games during the World Series against the Phillies, as the Yankees were forced to play by National League rules in Philadelphia, eliminating the DH.

After the Phillies won the opener in the Bronx, the pressure was on the Yankees to even the series before it shifted to Citizens Bank Park for three games. Pedro Martinez and A.J. Burnett were locked in a 1–1 duel in the sixth when Matsui went deep, giving the Yankees a lead they would never relinquish.

"Every time he was called upon to do whatever he needed to do, he was ready," Nick Swisher said. "He looked like he was ready for that moment."

Matsui hit another home run in Game 3, a pinch-hit blast in the eighth inning that gave the Yankees an insurance run. He wasn't much of a factor in the next two games, but Godzilla roared in Game 6; Matsui homered off Martinez once again, finishing the game 3-for-4 while tying a World Series single-game record with six RBI.

The Yankees were world champions for the first time since 2000, and Matsui was World Series Most Valuable Player, the first Japanese player ever to earn that honor. He hit .615 (8-for-13) with three homers and eight RBI, joining Babe Ruth and Lou Gehrig as the only players in history to post a batting average of .500 or higher with three home runs in a World Series.

"My first and foremost goal when I joined the Yankees was to win the world championship," Matsui said. "Certainly, it's been a long road and very difficult journey. I'm just happy that after all these years we were able to win and reach the goal that I had come here for.... I guess you could say this is the best moment of my life."

Matsui signed a one-year deal with the Los Angeles Angels during the offseason, ending his Yankees career after seven seasons. Thanks to a bit of fortunate scheduling, the Angels were the Yankees' opponent for the home opener, allowing Matsui to receive his World Series ring along with the rest of the 2009 team.

"He was a real stud," Kay said. "That was an amazing acquisition; the Yankees got a World Series out of it, and he won the MVP, so he's forever in Yankee lore. He lived up to every bit of hype."

PART 6

THE RIVALRIES

31

Boston Massacres

From the moment Red Sox owner Harry Frazee sold Babe Ruth to the Yankees in 1920, the two teams have been intertwined throughout baseball history.

But while Yankees versus Red Sox has long been considered the best rivalry in baseball—and arguably all of sports—it wasn't always so intense.

Among the early highlights:

- Ruth's move from Boston to New York turned the tide for both teams, as the Great Bambino sparked the Yankees' first dynasty and began a Red Sox curse that lasted more than eight decades.
- Red Ruffing was traded by the Red Sox to the Yankees in 1930, morphing from one of the losingest pitchers in the game to one of its most successful.
- Joe DiMaggio and Ted Williams were legendary adversaries, but the Yankee Clipper's teams won nine

World Series titles while Williams retired with no championships in 19 seasons in Boston. Legend has it that the two players were nearly traded for each other, but the deal fell apart when Boston insisted that a rookie outfielder by the name of Larry "Yogi" Berra also be included.

- The 1949 Yankees beat the Red Sox in the final two games of the season, swiping the American League pennant away from Boston in the process.
- Prior to a game at Fenway Park in 1952, Boston center fielder Jimmy Piersall and Yankees second baseman Billy Martin engaged in a war of words, then exchanged blows in a tunnel underneath the stands.
- Roger Maris hit his 61st home run in 1961 against Tracy Stallard of the Red Sox, breaking Ruth's single-season record.

For those notable moments and many more, it wasn't until the late 1960s that things really heated up between the American League rivals.

"Both teams have to be good for it to be a really good rivalry, and the Red Sox didn't get good until 1967," said Marty Appel, author of *Pinstripe Empire* and a former Yankees public relations director. "For most of those years before then, it wasn't much of a rivalry. You could walk up and buy seats on the day of the game."

On June 21, 1967, the teams engaged in a beanball war that ignited a bench-clearing brawl in the Bronx. Yankees pitcher Thad Tillotson hit Red Sox third baseman Joe Foy in the head in the second inning, while Boston ace Jim Lonborg retaliated in the bottom of the frame, drilling Tillotson on the back of his shoulder.

The two pitchers exchanged words as Tillotson walked toward first base, causing the benches to clear as players spilled onto the field. Within moments, players on both sides were going at it, leaving umpires to try sorting out the mess.

Two years later, the Yankees would welcome a rookie catcher named Thurman Munson to the team, though he didn't assume full-time duties until 1970. Boston's young catcher, Carlton Fisk, also debuted in 1969, though he didn't become the starter behind the plate until 1971.

From that point on, the rivalry was real.

"Prior to that, there was no talk of a rivalry and there was no talk of the intensity that was to fall into place," Appel said. "It was Munson and Fisk's arrivals and the Red Sox finally being good every year that heated up that rivalry."

The Munson-Fisk dynamic really took off on August 1, 1973, when Munson—heading home from third base on a missed suicide squeeze attempt by Gene Michael—barreled into Fisk at the plate, after which the Red Sox catcher kicked Munson away from him. The two men exchanged blows as a full-scale brawl ensued—a sight that would become commonplace whenever the Yankees and Red Sox met throughout the rest of the decade.

"We said a few things and I hit him," Munson told the *Boston Globe* after the game. "He kicked me off him with his foot pretty good. I don't know what he was doing. Is he scratched up? What a (bleeping) shame."

"It was definitely personal," said longtime *New York Daily News* baseball writer Bill Madden. "Munson really hated Fisk. Munson was really sensitive when people would talk about the All-Star Game and who was the better catcher. There was definitely bad blood between those two teams; it was real."

There were other such incidents in subsequent years, but none as ugly as the melee that broke out on May 20, 1976.

It began with Lou Piniella sliding spikes-up into Fisk at home plate while trying unsuccessfully to score from second base. The two got tangled up, causing Fisk to shove Piniella away from him; within seconds, punches were being thrown and both benches cleared.

Pandemonium ensued as the teams found themselves in a rugby-like scrum around home plate. Just as things started to calm down, Red Sox left-hander Bill "Spaceman" Lee—who was holding his left arm against his body after suffering an apparent shoulder injury during the brawl—began yelling at Yankees third baseman Graig Nettles. As Lee has told the story, he tried to throw a punch at Nettles, but his left arm didn't cooperate, leaving him exposed to take a shot from Nettles.

Lee was helped off the field after the fight was broken up, his left arm dangling limply at his side thanks to a torn ligament. A former All-Star who won 17 games in each season between 1973–75, Lee stayed with the Red Sox through the 1978 season before being traded to the Montreal Expos.

"Munson didn't like Fisk, Piniella didn't like Bill Lee, and Nettles hated everybody," said Bucky Dent, who was traded to the Yankees prior to the 1977 season and would make his mark on the rivalry in a major way the following year. "They did not like each other, and you could feel the tension every time we played. It was really intense."

The rivalry was also catnip for the New York tabloids, which would slap images of the two teams on their back pages with regularity. Players read the papers every day, contributing to the hype every time the two clubs faced off.

The intensity wasn't limited to the players on the field. Fans in the stands would occasionally join in, leaving Yankees players on high alert every time they took the field at Fenway Park.

"Mickey Rivers used to wear a helmet in center field because they used to throw things at him like batteries," Dent said. "Chris Chambliss was once standing on third base at Fenway when all of a sudden he felt something in his arm; somebody had shot him with a dart. They threw things all the time. It was crazy."

"Can you imagine?" Appel said. "He just pulled the dart out and it was like nothing happened."

When players weren't fighting each other, they were usually scanning the stands at Fenway Park or Yankee Stadium, looking for the brawls in the seats. The players on both sides didn't care for each other, but when you mixed fans of both teams in such close quarters—many of whom had enjoyed an adult beverage or five—chaos would often reign supreme.

"When you have the combination of the fans hating each other and the players hating each other, that can be really combustible," said Willie Randolph, who was a rookie with the Yankees in 1976. "That's what a real rivalry is; two teams trying to knock each other off their perch and two fan bases in close proximity to each other that have rabid fans."

Only 225 miles separated the two teams, but they routinely found themselves navigating the same territory in the AL East in the late '70s. The stakes were high, which only heightened the intensity every time they shared a field.

"Those teams were tough because they had players that were tough-minded and old school; take no prisoners, don't take any shit, no fraternizing like there is today," Randolph said. "I don't talk to you and you don't talk to me; there was no hugging or patting each other on the back during BP, talking about our families. We didn't recognize each other; we would roll our eyes at each other and snarl at each other before a game."

"I felt it that first year that I went over there," Dent said. "Those two teams, they respected each other but they just really didn't like each other. You did not want to lose to the Red Sox."

The Yankees edged the Red Sox by 2½ games in 1977, ultimately winning their first World Series title in 15 years. Boston held a massive 14-game advantage in mid-July 1978, and although it had dwindled down to 6½ games by the end of August, the Red Sox were in good position to win the division.

The Yankees won nine of their first 11 games in September, moving into a first-place tie with the Red Sox after sweeping a four-game series at Fenway Park in which the Yankees outscored the Sox 42–9. That series would come to be known as the "Boston Massacre," as the Yankees went on to take a 3½-game lead less than a week later. Boston showed its resiliency by storming back during the final two weeks, winning 12 of 14 to pull even with New York on the final day of the regular season.

That set up the famous one-game playoff at Fenway Park, which the Yankees won on the strength of Dent's celebrated home run over the Green Monster.

"You look at all the guys on that team and their makeup— Munson, Nettles, Chambliss, Bucky—that was a special team," Madden said. "Looking back, I'm not surprised that they beat the Red Sox those two years, because even though the Red Sox team had great makeup too, I don't think they had those intangibles that the Yankees did."

The wars continued in the subsequent years, but the Red Sox never finished higher than third in any of the next seven seasons, dulling the stakes between the two rivals.

Still, when a new player joined the Yankees, there was something about the atmosphere of a New York-Boston game that felt different than anything they had experienced in their prior big-league stops.

"I felt it right away," said Don Mattingly, whose first trip to Fenway came as a rookie in 1983. "You could feel it in the crowds; the anger, the passion, the emotion. There were fights all over the place; people just slugging in the stands. You would see a Yankee fan in Boston and think, 'Oh my gosh. I'd hate to be that guy; how can you wear that jersey?' He was just asking for it. And it was the same in our place."

32

Royal Pains

THERE IS NO MORE FAMOUS MOMENT IN THE HISTORY OF Yankees versus Royals than the Pine Tar Game, but the deep feelings between the two clubs go back much further than 1983.

New York and Kansas City had a unique relationship dating back to the 1950s with the Athletics; the Royals did not join the major leagues as an expansion team until 1969.

The Athletics were known by many as the Yankees' farm system, routinely making trades to help supplement New York's roster. The two clubs made 15 trades with each other between 1955 and '59, including the deal that brought Roger Maris to the Bronx.

The Royals endured a couple of dreadful seasons upon entering the league, their lone early highlight coming in their maiden season when Lou Piniella won the AL Rookie of the Year award. Things turned around soon enough; Kansas City posted a winning record three times between 1971 and '75, building a contender with young players including Amos Otis, George Brett, Frank White, Hal McRae, John Mayberry, and Dennis Leonard.

In 1976, the Yankees were also turning a corner, having posted winning records in six of the previous seven years after enduring some brutal years in the mid-1960s. The Yankees won 97 games in 1976, capturing their first American League East title since divisional play had been introduced in 1969. The Royals—who had hired Whitey Herzog as manager in 1975— also reached the postseason that year, capturing the first AL West title in their eight-year history.

The Yankees outlasted the Royals in a classic five-game AL Championship Series—the ALCS didn't become best-of-seven until 1985—to win their first AL pennant since 1964. Brett had tied Game 5 with a three-run home run in the eighth against Grant Jackson, but Chris Chambliss returned the favor in the ninth, belting a pennant-clinching, walk-off home run against Mark Littell to lead off the home half of the ninth.

"Unbelievable! What a finish!" Yankees broadcaster Phil Rizzuto declared. "As dramatic a finish as you'd ever want to see!"

The Yankees lost the World Series to the Cincinnati Reds, but after signing Reggie Jackson as a free agent that winter, New York repeated as division champs in 1977, winning 100 games for the first time since 1963.

Kansas City also repeated in its division with 102 wins, setting up a second straight ALCS showdown between the two clubs. Unlike their first postseason encounter, however, this one got heated.

In the top of the sixth inning of Game 2, the Yankees held a 2–1 lead. The Royals had runners at first and second with one out when Brett hit a ground ball to third base, where Graig Nettles fielded it and threw to second. Willie Randolph received the throw and stepped on second base, but McRae charged past the base and threw himself into Randolph, preventing him from completing an inning-ending double play. Randolph and McRae were entangled on the infield dirt, allowing Freddie Patek to score the tying run from second base on the play.

An incensed Randolph tried to plead his case to second-base umpire Marty Springstead, while Piniella—who had been traded to the Yankees by the Royals in 1973—ran in from left field to protest, as well. Yankees manager Billy Martin stormed out of the dugout to argue with Springstead, but the play stood. Piniella held Randolph back before the young second baseman got himself in trouble, but the Yankees were displeased by the chain of events even after winning Game 2 to salvage a split in the Bronx.

"That was no slide, that was a clip," Martin said. "I didn't play as a gentleman all the time. But I didn't think it was very professional. I told Randolph later: The next time he comes down there, if he's out by five feet even, don't tag him—hit him right in the mouth with the ball.

"Will it be forgotten in time? It'll be forgotten about 1,500 games from now. There's spring training, there's next year, and you will never know when that ball will slip."

Randolph, only 23 years old, was still hot about the play after the game.

"I'm young," Randolph told the *Times*. "He could have hurt me. I've got my career, I've got a family. But he comes in high. Look, everybody slides into everybody, and I like to slide hard, too. But he made it a high rolling block, and it just wasn't called for.

"He got me that way early last season too, and I came down on my wrist and sprained it. Next time, if he's coming into the bag, if he's not down and if I'm throwing for a double play—he'll get hit with the ball."

McRae fired back with some words of his own.

"Maybe I'm playing in the wrong era," McRae told the *Times*. "But that's the way I play ball, and I have for eight years. Maybe high-priced ball players are afraid to get hurt these days."

Munson called McRae's slide "a cheap shot," while Reggie Jackson predicted potential retribution.

"Randolph's a little fellow with bad knees," Jackson told the *Times* after Game 2. "But now your Cliff Johnsons, Thurman Munsons, and Reggie Jacksons and your other guys with good size will go down to second base a little harder. This can charge you up."

The hard feelings lingered as the series shifted to Kansas City. Prior to Game 4, the two teams nearly fought during batting practice.

"We came out early and were stretching on our side of the field while the Royals took batting practice," Randolph said. "Hal McRae was coming out of the cage and Cliff Johnson called him over. Cliff got off the ground and said, 'I don't appreciate you trying to hurt my boy, Willie. Why don't you pick on somebody your own size?'

"I think Hal thought he was kidding, because Cliff was a big teddy bear, always joking around. He wasn't kidding, though. Hal kind of sheepishly laughed, and Cliff said, 'I'm not kidding.' They had to be separated and security ran out on the field or there was going to be a brawl. We really hated each other."

It was reported that Johnson—who was a bench player for the Yankees—challenged McRae to a fight under the stands, but McRae answered by saying, "I don't fight extra men."

The Royals won Game 3 in Kansas City but the Yankees rode 5⅓ scoreless innings of relief from closer Sparky Lyle—the eventual AL Cy Young Award winner that season—to force a decisive Game 5 at Royals Stadium.

Nettles had exacted a touch of revenge in Game 4 with a hard shoulder check into White at second base on a potential double play in the fourth inning, but tempers flared again early in Game 5.

Brett launched a triple over the head of center fielder Mickey Rivers in the first inning, sliding hard into Nettles at third base before pushing him with his arm at the end of the play. Nettles, perturbed by the hard slide, kicked Brett in the chest, nipping his chin in the process. Brett popped up and threw a punch at the third baseman's head, causing both dugouts to empty immediately.

"He kicked me and I slugged him," Brett told reporters. "But I didn't come into him dirty or anything."

Ron Guidry was the first player on the scene, grabbing Brett and throwing him to the ground. Thurman Munson joined in the action, though Guidry—who was starting on two days' rest—was quickly extracted by a teammate or two, not wanting to see the ace ejected from the game. In the end, neither Brett nor Nettles was thrown out by Springstead, the third-base umpire, as the game continued.

"Nettles thought he was pushed, and Brett came up swinging," Martin said after the game. "Springstead told me he wasn't going to throw Brett out. This is a championship game and not the time to be throwing players out. If this game would have been played in July, Brett would have been gone."

The Royals led 3–1 after seven innings, but Jackson—who had been benched by Martin to start the game—cut the lead in half with a pinch-hit RBI single in the eighth. Herzog brought in 20-game winner Dennis Leonard—who had earned a complete-game victory in Game 3—to pitch the ninth, but Paul Blair led off with a single and Roy White drew a walk, prompting the Kansas City manager to call on Larry Gura, who had been hit hard for four runs over two innings in his Game 4 start the previous day.

Rivers singled in a run to tie the game, ending Gura's night after one batter. Mark Littell—the same pitcher who had served up Chambliss' pennant-winning homer the year prior—was the next man up from the bullpen carousel, entering the 3–3 game with runners at the corners and nobody out.

Randolph lined a sacrifice fly to center field, scoring White to give the Yankees the lead. One out later, Piniella reached on a throwing error by Brett, adding another run to give the Yankees a 5–3 advantage. Lyle, who had entered the game to record the final out in the eighth, pitched a scoreless ninth to send the Yankees back to the World Series for a second year in a row. New York beat the Los Angeles Dodgers for the title thanks to Jackson's epic three-homer effort in the Game 6 clincher.

"People talk about the Red Sox rivalry, but the Kansas City–Yankees rivalry was classic," Randolph said. "As much as we hated the Red Sox, the brawls, Bill Lee, Fisk and Thurman, all that stuff, those games with Kansas City were just as intense.

"McRae knocked me into left field, we had collisions at home plate; we hated them. To this day, if I'm sitting in a room and George Brett walked into the room, he won't even speak to me. Maybe he'd give me a little 'How you doing?' or something, but to this day, we can't stand each other. That's how heated that rivalry was."

Kansas City's road to the postseason in 1978 was relatively easy, as the Royals led the AL West for the majority of the second half. The Yankees' path wasn't quite as clear, as New York had to overcome a 14-game deficit to catch the Boston

Red Sox, winning a one-game playoff at Fenway Park on the strength of Bucky Dent's improbable home run.

Yet come October, the Yankees and Royals met again in the 1978 ALCS, the third year in a row the teams squared off for the AL pennant.

New York won the series in four games, overcoming a three-homer game by Brett in the pivotal Game 3. Guidry—the most dominant pitcher in the game that season—hadn't been able to start in the series until Game 4 after pitching the one-game playoff in Boston, but the left-hander was on the mound with an opportunity to clinch the pennant.

Guidry gave up a run in the first inning of Game 4, but the Yankees came back to tie the game in the second on a solo home run by Nettles. White homered in the sixth to give the Yankees a 2–1 lead, which Guidry held through the eighth before Rich "Goose" Gossage recorded the final three outs to wrap up another pennant.

The Yankees beat the Dodgers in the World Series for a second straight year, completing their first back-to-back championship seasons since 1961–62.

Neither the Yankess nor Royals reached the postseason in 1979, but they both returned in 1980, meeting in the ALCS for the fourth time in five years.

Kansas City won decisively in the opener at home, but a questionable send by third-base coach Mike Ferraro cost the Yankees a chance to even the series in Game 2. Trailing by a run in the eighth, Randolph hit a one-out single, putting the tying run on base. Bobby Murcer followed with a strikeout, but when Bob Watson hit a double to left, Ferraro waved Randolph—who had hesitated initially as he broke for second base—around third in an attempt to tie the game.

Left fielder Willie Wilson retrieved the ball and overthrew the first cutoff man, but Brett was there to receive the throw, firing a strike to the plate. Catcher Darrell Porter caught the relay throw and tagged out Randolph for the third out, ending the Yankees' rally. Television cameras immediately focused on a livid Steinbrenner, who was pointing at Ferraro and appeared to be yelling in his direction from his seat.

The Yankees tried to mount another rally in the ninth, but closer Dan Quisenberry got Nettles to ground into a double play with runners at first and second with one out, ending the game.

As Steinbrenner walked to the locker room after the loss, he looked at reporters and said, "My players didn't lose this one."

"George went ballistic," Madden said. "He went past the players' wives section after the game and screamed at Mary Ferraro, 'Your fucking husband cost us this game!'"

The Royals finally got the better of the Yankees, completing the three-game sweep with a Game 3 victory in the Bronx. New York led the game 2–1 in the seventh, but Brett hit a three-run home run off Gossage to give the Royals a two-run lead. Quisenberry pitched 3⅔ scoreless innings to wrap up the first AL pennant in Royals history.

"Sooner or later, a blind squirrel is going to find an acorn," Madden said. "Brett was the centerpiece of that rivalry because he was always right in the middle of everything. He killed the Yankees."

More than 30 years after their last ALCS battle, *New York Daily News* columnist Filip Bondy called Yankees versus Royals "arguably the greatest postseason rivalry in baseball history." The fan bases didn't have the same animosity for each other that existed in New York and Boston, but on the field, it was as fierce as anything baseball had seen.

"For those three straight years, they tended to have the same lineups year after year, so fans from both cities really knew these teams," Appel said. "It was different cultures representing their fan base. We would get off the bus at our hotel in Kansas City and there would be nice little neatly dressed boys with their autograph books; 'Mr. Munson, may I have your autograph?' Then we would go to Boston and it would be the same scene, but we would get off the bus and hear, 'Hey Munson! Fuck you!'"

Baltimore Chops

THE YANKEES AND RED SOX EXPERIENCED SOME EPIC BATTLES during the Joe Torre era, but it wasn't Boston that initially stood in the Bombers' way when they were spawning a dynasty.

In 1995, it was the Seattle Mariners that sent the Yankees home after the American League Division Series, prompting a change in the manager's office. Buck Showalter was out and Torre was in, and while the Red Sox had won the AL East that season, Boston would not prove to be the biggest threat to the Yankees' return to the top.

That was the Baltimore Orioles, a team that hadn't been a major factor within the division since its 1983 championship season, finishing no higher than third place in 10 of the 12 seasons since winning the World Series.

The 1996 Orioles were loaded with talent, sending out a lineup featuring three future Hall of Famers (Cal Ripken Jr., Roberto Alomar, and Eddie Murray), a 50-home-run hitter

(Brady Anderson), a six-time All-Star slugger (Bobby Bonilla), and a future member of both the 500-homer and 3,000-hit club (Rafael Palmeiro).

Baltimore's rotation was led by a pair of pitchers who would become quite familiar to Yankees fans: Mike Mussina and David Wells. A deep bullpen backed up the starters, and with a former World Series–winning manager on the bench in Davey Johnson, the Orioles were a formidable foe for a Yankees team with championship aspirations.

"They had a great team," Yankees first baseman Tino Martinez said. "They had an All-Star team with guys like Palmeiro, Alomar, Ripken, and Brady Anderson, and they had a really good pitching staff. On paper, I think they had the best team in the league."

Even the team's owner, Peter Angelos, had been viewed by many as a Steinbrenner in the making; in 1995, Mike Lupica of *Newsday* referred to Angelos as "Steinbrenner on training wheels." When Baltimore signed Alomar to a three-year, $18 million deal in December 1995, the Yankees responded immediately, inking David Cone—who was being wooed by the Orioles—to a three-year, $19.5 million contract.

"It was probably the biggest offseason card game by two owners I've ever seen," Yankees third baseman Wade Boggs told the *San Francisco Examiner*. "Every time Peter Angelos made a decision, Mr. Steinbrenner was going to counter. I thought we might end up facing each other down the stretch. It was a poker game."

The Yankees and Orioles jockeyed for position atop the AL East for the first two months of the season, though New York began to assert itself in June, finishing the month with a 4½-game lead over Baltimore.

"I don't remember it being bitter," Mussina said of the meetings between the clubs. "Before I was even drafted, the Orioles were at the bottom of the division and not having very good seasons. We finally got a rotation together and made some free agent pickups with guys like Palmeiro and Alomar and we finally were able to play at a competitive level."

The Yankees hit the All-Star break with a six-game lead, but with a four-game series at Camden Yards set to open the second half, things had the potential to change rather quickly.

"One of the writers asked me if I was going to talk to my players," Torre said. "I said, 'When we get off the bus, they're going to know where we are. If I have to motivate them, then there aren't the guys I think they are.'"

Those four games at Camden Yards set the tone for the remainder of the regular season. Derek Jeter's eighth-inning home run off Mussina gave the Yankees the opener, then after a Friday rainout, Wells had stifled New York through eight innings, taking a 2–1 lead to the ninth.

The left-hander returned for the ninth, but 12 pitches later, the Yankees had scored twice on RBI hits by Joe Girardi and Mariano Duncan, earning New York no less than a split of the four-game set. The nightcap started as a slugfest, with each team tagging the opposing starter for five runs over the first four innings.

Darryl Strawberry belted a two-run home run against Arthur Rhodes in the top of the fifth, and after Dwight Gooden found a way to hold the lead in the bottom of the inning, the Yankees bullpen locked it down over the final four innings. Two of those scoreless frames came from Mariano Rivera, who threw multiple scoreless innings out of the bullpen 28 times that year.

"There was always excitement to get those last three outs with [John] Wetteland," Paul O'Neill said. "The seventh and eighth inning were the easy ones."

Andy Pettitte pitched the Yankees to a win in the finale, finishing off the four-game sweep. The lead now stood at 10 games, and while it grew as large as 12 before the end of July, the Orioles weren't going down quietly.

Baltimore picked up eight games in the standings in August, leaving the Orioles well within striking distance. The Yankees led by just three games when the Orioles came to the Bronx on September 17 for their final face-to-face showdown of the regular season.

The opener was washed out by rain before the first inning had been completed, sending George Steinbrenner into a tizzy as he blasted AL president Gene Budig and the umpires for allowing the game to begin.

The Yankees mounted a late comeback on Wednesday thanks to a game-tying hit by Bernie Williams in the ninth and a walk-off single in the 10th by Ruben Rivera. The teams split Thursday's doubleheader, leaving the Yankees with a four-game lead. Both teams finished the season 5–5 over their final 10 games, giving the Yankees their first AL East title since 1980.

"In order to have a really good rivalry, the teams have to play a lot and they have to be battling for the same real estate; that's what it was with the Yankees and the Orioles," said longtime Yankees broadcaster Michael Kay. "There also have to be personalities that don't really like each other, and I think with the Orioles and Yankees, that was certainly the case. They got under each other's skin.

"The Red Sox were almost an afterthought at that point because they weren't fighting for that real estate and the postseason. Those games with the Orioles were great. They were tightly fought. People threw inside, there were a lot of things that rubbed each team the wrong way. I definitely think that supplanted the Yankees and the Red Sox when Joe Torre first got there."

The Yankees had outlasted the Orioles in the AL East, but they weren't finished with Baltimore, which had earned the AL wild card spot with 88 victories. After the Yankees had disposed of the Texas Rangers and the Orioles had upset Cleveland, the defending AL champion, New York and Baltimore were set to meet again, this time in a best-of-seven series with a trip to the World Series at stake.

"It almost felt unfair," Torre said. "We beat them 10 out of 13 times and now we have to face them in the AL Championship Series. You thought, 'How long can this run go?'"

Despite their regular season record against the Yankees, the Orioles entered the series with confidence. New York had gotten a taste of the playoffs in 1995, but the Yankees were hardly viewed as an unbeatable team.

"When we got a situation where we're in the playoffs, there was an attitude of, 'We're the new guy here and we're not going to let anyone push us around,'" Mussina said. "We didn't care who they were."

With the help of a 12-year-old fan named Jeffrey Maier, the Yankees' run against the Orioles continued into October.

Baltimore held a one-run lead with one out in the eighth inning of Game 1 when Jeter lifted a fly ball to right field, where Tony Tarasco backtracked toward the wall, raising his glove as the ball descended. Tarasco didn't even jump, confident he was about to make the catch, but Maier reached his glove over the wall and redirected it into the first row of seats.

Right-field umpire Richie Garcia immediately called it a home run, causing Tarasco to lose his mind. The outfielder began protesting immediately, quickly joined by Anderson and pitcher Armando Benitez, who had given up the home run. Johnson ran out to get his players away from the ump, then began arguing the call, leading to his ejection.

"If he goes down in the clubhouse and sees the replay on this thing, he may be out here again," Bob Uecker said of Johnson on the NBC telecast.

Tarasco insisted he would have made the play if not for Maier, calling Jeter's shot "a routine fly ball."

"Merlin must have been in the house," Tarasco said. "To me, it was like a magic trick, because the ball just disappeared out of the air."

Jeter later said he "couldn't tell" whether the fan interfered on the play.

"I just looked at the umpire and he signaled home run," Jeter said. "I wasn't going to argue."

There was no instant replay in baseball at the time, so the game-tying home run stood. Three innings later, Williams led off with a solo blast into the left-field seats, giving the Yankees a Game 1 victory.

"If there's instant replay back then, that ball might be called out, we don't win that game and it's a whole different series going into the next game," Martinez said. "Those were the breaks we got, and we really took advantage of it."

Mark Teixeira, who would go on to play for the Yankees from 2009 to 2016, was a high school student in a suburb outside of Baltimore at the time. He vividly recalls the aftermath of the Maier incident, which boosted the fan base's level of hatred for the Yankees to an all-time high.

"Anyone who was around in '96 knows that the Yankees were not very well beloved here in Baltimore," Teixeira told the *Baltimore Sun* in 2016. "There was a Jeffrey Maier announcement in our high school that we had to pray for him. I went to an all-boys Catholic school, and you weren't allowed to say bad things about him. You just had to pray for him. So, kind of a good learning experience for us. That was not a fun day for Orioles fans."

There is a misperception that the Maier incident cost the Orioles the series, but Baltimore bounced back the following day and won Game 2, sending the teams back to Camden Yards tied at one game apiece.

The Yankees swept the next three games in Baltimore, claiming their first AL pennant in 15 years.

"We went in there and buzz-sawed them," Torre said. "We were very comfortable playing in their ballpark."

The Maier incident has become part of Yankees lore, while the mere mention of his name in Baltimore brings a scowl to the face of any self-respecting Orioles fan.

Would Tarasco have caught the ball? As adamant as the outfielder and many of his teammates were back in 1996, Mussina isn't so certain.

"The more I watch it, and obviously it's been 25 years or so now, I don't even know if our guy was going to catch it," Mussina said. "Just to have it play out like that, having that kind of meaning, you look 25 years later and video replay might have obviously created a different result. It's one of those things now after all these years that happened; it's unfortunate that it was such a big deal at the time, but it's part of the legend and history of the Yankees and the old Yankee Stadium."

The Yankees went on to win the World Series after eliminating the Orioles in five games, but Baltimore exacted some revenge the following season, winning the AL East and relegating the Yankees to the wild card spot.

"1996 and '97 were pretty good years as far as feeling good about going to the ballpark," Mussina said. "The place was packed, and we were playing really good baseball; we thought we had a chance to do something."

There would be no ALCS rematch, however, as Cleveland sent the Yankees home after a five-game ALDS.

Baltimore opened the season with 10 wins in its first 12 games, but the club was unable to keep pace with the Yankees, who would go on to post one of the best seasons in baseball history.

The two teams opened a series in the Bronx on May 19, 1998, headed in different directions. The Yankees had improved to 28–9 after Wells—now pitching for New York—threw a perfect game against the Minnesota Twins on May 17, holding a 3½-game lead over the second-place Red Sox.

The Orioles limped into Yankee Stadium on a four-game losing streak, their 20–23 record leaving them in a last-place tie with the Toronto Blue Jays. They trailed the first-place Yankees by 11 games.

Hoping a good series in New York would spark their season, the Orioles led the opener 5–3 in the eighth inning when Williams hit a three-run home run off Benitez that gave the Yankees a lead.

With the ballpark still buzzing in the aftermath of Williams' blast, Benitez drilled Martinez in the upper back with his next pitch. Both benches emptied immediately, and as Martinez glared at the pitcher, Benitez looked toward the Yankees dugout, dropped his glove, and raised his hands, practically challenging the opposing team to a fight.

Martinez didn't throw the first punch, however. As the two teams exchanged harsh words near the mound, Yankees relievers Graeme Lloyd and Jeff Nelson darted in from the bullpen and went after Benitez. Pandemonium ensued as players on both sides began throwing punches and wrestling each other to the ground.

"The fight just seemed to have a life of its own," umpire Larry Young told *Referee Magazine* in 2021. "I have never seen anything like that before."

The scrum moved toward the third-base dugout, where an irate Martinez—who had been hit by Benitez in an identical situation a few years earlier while playing for the Seattle Mariners—was being held back by players and coaches from both teams. Just when things appeared to be settling down, Darryl Strawberry fired a punch at Benitez, knocking them both into the Orioles dugout.

Both teams spilled into the dugout, where things got even uglier, as reliever Alan Mills sucker-punched Strawberry, bloodying his face.

"It's scary to begin with, having so many guys throwing punches and running around with people on the ground, people stepping on everybody," Martinez said. "It's part of the game at times, unfortunately. Fortunately, nobody got hurt and we were able to move on, but those are things where you can get a couple guys injured. If you get Derek Jeter or Bernie Williams by accident and they're out for the rest of the year, that can change an entire season."

Order was eventually restored, though Benitez, Mills, Strawberry, Nelson, and Lloyd were later suspended by the league for their roles in the fracas. Benitez received the longest suspension—eight games—but the Yankees didn't think the penalty was harsh enough.

"I thought it should be more," general manager Brian Cashman said. "I'm not happy about that. I thought Benitez, he's the guy who started it. He should've had a lot more."

Calling it "the worst I've seen in 25 years in the game," Steinbrenner was incensed by Benitez's actions, calling on AL president Gene Budig to suspend the Orioles reliever for a month.

"I thought it was a classless act committed by a guy who I understand his done things like this before," Steinbrenner said. "It has no part in the game with players being paid what they're paid. I guess maybe the best way to get rid of it is to do away with the DH.

"Hopefully [Budig] will react. Now, he may react by saying he wants Peter Angelos and I to go three rounds and settle it— and I'm ready. I'm working out three days a week."

Orioles manager Ray Miller equated Strawberry's punch with Benitez's pitch, calling it "as cowardly as throwing a ball at someone," but Miller later issued an apology to Martinez and the Yankees, making it clear that Baltimore did not condone Benitez's actions.

"It was the result of the action of one individual, an immature young man," Miller said. "The feeling of, 'I'll hurt you if I can't beat you' doesn't represent the feelings of the Baltimore Orioles."

As good as the Yankees were that season, the incident seemed to galvanize them. The entire league was taking aim at New York, and the Yankees weren't going to be pushed around.

"It was good to see," Torre said of his players' reaction. "You don't like to see fights breaking out, but as far as a response to what happened, it was good to see.... We're a family, and you can't have somebody pick on somebody in your family."

Three more players were hit by pitches the following night, but the teams remained under control. Hideki Irabu hit two Orioles batters in the game, prompting a standing ovation from the Bronx crowd when he departed. Lloyd relieved him, getting a standing ovation of his own—an oddity for the reliever, who had experienced many ups and downs since joining the club during the 1996 season.

"I looked up to make sure I brought in the right pitcher," Torre quipped after the game.

After the series, Steinbrenner said he hoped the animosity between the two clubs would not spill over into any future meetings.

"Let's get it behind us," Steinbrenner said. "The way to get these guys is by winning the pennant and winning the American League East."

The Yankees did just that, winning nine of 12 games against the Orioles on their way to a 114-win season. New York reclaimed its AL East crown, finishing 35 games ahead of fourth-place Baltimore in the standings.

"Having that situation happen to us, I think it really cemented us as a team and brought us even more together in that game, that fight," Williams told the *New York Post* in 2019. "And it propelled us to have the year that we had, I think in many ways."

Torre's team went on to win its second World Series title in three years, then added two more championships in 1999 and 2000. Games between the two clubs at Camden Yards commonly felt like Yankees home games, as thousands of pinstriped fans would make the three-hour drive, invading enemy territory. The postseason became an annual ritual for the Yankees, while the Orioles didn't return to the playoffs until 2012.

Naturally, that meant another showdown with the Yankees.

Jeter, Rivera, and Andy Pettitte were the lone holdovers from the battles of 1996–97, but Baltimore fans had two new targets of their ire: Alex Rodriguez and Teixeira.

The hatred for A-Rod was easy; everyone from just about every fan base outside of New York had contempt for the three-time AL MVP, who not only made more money than anybody else in the game, but had admitted to the use of performance-enhancing drugs.

The loathing of Teixeira was more personal in Charm City. A native of nearby Severna Park, Maryland, Teixeira had chosen to sign with the Yankees as a free agent in December 2008, spurning his hometown club. Never mind the fact that the Orioles' best offer came in at seven years and about $140–150 million, significantly less than the eight-year, $180 million deal the first baseman signed with the Yankees. Teixeira had grown up as an Orioles fan, though he made no secret of the fact that Don Mattingly had been his favorite player.

Joe Girardi—now the Yankees manager—had vented his frustrations with the Orioles in his early years on the job after Baltimore pitchers—right-hander Jeremy Guthrie, in particular—had made a habit of plunking his hitters. Not all of them were intentional—some of Baltimore's young pitchers struggled badly with their control—but it didn't change the fact that Yankees hitters were commonly leaving games with seam marks on various parts of their bodies.

"Too many, just too many," Girardi said in 2010 after Guthrie hit Derek Jeter, the 10th Yankee he had drilled since 2007. "I don't really understand it. I know he likes to pitch inside. But it's just too many. That doesn't include the ones in spring training. It's too many."

When the teams were set to meet in the 2012 ALDS, the matchup stirred up memories of 1996–1998, when the Orioles were the Yankees' biggest rival.

The Yankees beat the Orioles in the best-of-five series, getting a vintage complete-game performance from ace CC Sabathia in the decisive game at Yankee Stadium.

The moment of the series came in Game 3 in the Bronx, when Girardi sent veteran Raul Ibanez out in the ninth inning to pinch-hit for A-Rod, who was 1-for-12 with seven strikeouts in the series to that point. Ibanez tied the game with a home run, then ended it three innings later with a leadoff homer in the 12th.

"I'm one of the leaders of this team; maybe 10 years ago I react a much different way, but I'm at a place in my career right now where team means everything," A-Rod said after the game. "I don't think there was anybody in the ballpark more excited for Raul than me."

Showalter—who had been hired to manage the Orioles in the middle of the 2010 season—and Girardi had a run-in during the 2013 season when the Yankees manager appeared to accuse Baltimore third-base coach Bobby Dickerson of stealing signs, but cooler heads prevailed before the situation turned ugly.

Under Showalter, Baltimore returned to the postseason again in 2014 and 2016, but they didn't cross paths with the Yankees in either year. The ensuing years didn't feature many fireworks between the two clubs, as the Orioles entered a rebuilding phase, dampening the competitive aspect of the matchups between the two.

Someday, the Yankees and Orioles may reignite their rivalry, and when it happens, the video of Maier's interference and the 1998 brawl will assuredly be splashed across televisions, tablets, and cell phones around the baseball world.

"It was real," Girardi said of the rivalry. "Those were pretty good battles."

New York, New York

FOR YEARS, THE IDEA OF A CROSSTOWN RIVALRY BETWEEN the Yankees and Mets was a fantasy.

The Bronx Bombers had been baseball's most successful franchise for four decades before the Mets ever took the field, winning championships while fielding rosters loaded with future Hall of Famers.

When the Dodgers and Giants abandoned New York in 1958, the Big Apple became a one-team town. The Yankees ruled the city, winning the World Series that season and picking up two more championships in 1961 and '62. They didn't just rule New York; the Yankees reigned supreme throughout all of Major League Baseball.

In 1962, the Mets came into existence, losing 100 or more games in five of their first six seasons. National League baseball fans gravitated toward the newcomers—no Dodgers or Giants fan in their right mind would switch allegiances to support the hated Yankees—but when it came to the all-important act of winning, the boys in the Bronx had no competition in town.

Interleague play would not be introduced to the major leagues until 1997, so the Mets' lone shot at bragging rights came at the annual Mayor's Trophy Game, an exhibition game played between the two teams during the regular season.

Despite the lack of actual stakes, fans would pack the host ballpark for a chance to see the Yankees and Mets square off. The first meeting between the teams came in 1963, and while the game meant very little to the two-time defending champion Yankees, the Mets—who were managed by former Yankees skipper Casey Stengel—took the contest very seriously.

Stengel used his best pitchers in the exhibition, helping the Mets earn a victory. The Yankees had the last laugh, finishing the season with 104 wins while winning another American League pennant. The Mets lost 111 games, which was actually an improvement from their 120-loss debut the prior season.

The annual event continued throughout the 1960s, and while it was often seen as a blip on the Yankees' radar, the game served as one of the Mets' biggest days of the year. The Mets won five of the first seven meetings; their win in September 1969 proved to be a good omen, as they went on to win the World Series a month later.

The Mayor's Trophy Game began to take on added importance in 1973, when George Steinbrenner and a group of investors purchased the Yankees. Steinbrenner did not like losing to any team, but losing to the Mets left a particularly bad taste in the owner's mouth—even if the game didn't mean anything.

"We hated the Mayor's Trophy Game," said Willie Randolph, who debuted with the Yankees in 1976.

"We hated it because we had to win. We always had that extra pressure on us because bragging rights were everything in the city. We exhaled after that game every year. It should have been fun, but it wasn't. George was not going to be happy if we didn't beat the Mets."

The Yankees won the game in four of the first six years of the Steinbrenner regime.

"It was a meaningless game in the standings, but it meant so much to the city and even more to The Boss," Randolph said. "George would walk through the clubhouse before the game making sure that we knew how important this game was."

Attendance had waned in the late 1970s, causing the series to be suspended in 1980 and '81. The Yankees and Mets would also meet in spring training exhibition games, a time when teams are trying to prepare for the regular season rather than emphasizing wins and losses.

But Steinbrenner wasn't built that way. Any time his team took the field, he wanted to win. It didn't matter that the games meant literally nothing in the standings; if there was an opponent in the other dugout, The Boss wasn't going to be satisfied with anything other than victory. The fact that Yankees–Mets spring games would often be televised in New York only added to Steinbrenner's burning desire to win.

"It didn't feel like a big deal to me, but it felt like more of a big deal to Mr. Steinbrenner," Don Mattingly said. "The Boss did not like losing those games. But you're never going to have the same juice in an exhibition game as you would a real game."

That didn't stop Steinbrenner from berating managers Billy Martin and Lou Piniella after meaningless losses to the Mets.

"When games were broadcast from spring training, you knew they were important; when games were broadcast from spring training and it was the Yankees and the Mets, they were mega-important," said longtime Yankees play-by-play broadcaster Michael Kay, who was also a beat writer for the *New York Post* and *New York Daily News.* "I don't know if it's spilled over to the players, but I know that the pressure was put on Billy Martin and Lou Piniella that those were games that had to be won."

Steinbrenner's obsession with the Mets prompted the Yankees to rush 18-year-old pitching prospect Jose Rijo to the big leagues, hoping to find their own version of Dwight Gooden, the Mets' phenom. Kay recalled a spring game that pitted the two pitchers against each other, resulting in an overhyped matchup.

"That place, for an exhibition game in a minor league ballpark, was crackling with electricity," Kay said. "It meant something to the fans, and I know it meant something to George Steinbrenner. That game was just one indication of how big it was; it almost had a quasi-postseason feel to it."

The Mets' memorable 1986 season only heightened Steinbrenner's fixation with his crosstown competitors. The Yankees hadn't won the World Series since 1978, and given the star power in Queens with players such as Gooden, Darryl Strawberry, Gary Carter, and Keith Hernandez, Steinbrenner's Yankees suddenly had to compete for space on the all-important real estate of the local tabloid back pages.

"In those days, the teams thought about perception and battling for the same entertainment dollar in New York," Kay said. "In the '80s, the Mets were the sexy team that had won a championship. Those were big games for George."

The 1983 Mayor's Trophy Game marked the end of that tradition, though the teams continued to play occasionally during spring training.

Brian Cashman, who joined the Yankees' front office as an intern in 1986, saw the strain that Steinbrenner's preoccupation with the Mets caused on the club over the years.

"It was a nuisance; I didn't look at them as rivals, but The Boss obviously did—and he made our lives miserable because of it," Cashman said. "We could never lose to the Mets in an exhibition game; he made it like a mini–World Series. If I had my druthers, I would never have played them. We would spend spring training getting our team ready to play for the regular season; you're not trying to fire on all cylinders to win an exhibition game, but he didn't look at it that way. He looked at it as ticket sales, he looked at it as winning the back pages, ratings on the television, burying your crosstown rivals."

As Joe Torre was nearing the end of his first spring training as Yankees manager in 1996, he received a visit from Steinbrenner. The Yankees were preparing to face the Mets in one of their final exhibition games, and The Boss wanted to make sure Torre knew how important it was to him that his team come out on top.

"You always had to beat the Mets," Torre said. "Kiddingly, George was in my office in spring training, and he said, 'Let's beat these guys.' I said, 'George, let me ask you a question: if you had a choice of winning two out of three here against the Mets, or two out of three in Cleveland, which one would you choose?' He said, 'Don't ask me that question.' He would rather win exhibition games against a crosstown rival than three games that count."

The 1997 season introduced a whole new chapter into the Yankees-Mets rivalry. Major League Baseball created interleague play, pitting American League and National League teams against each other in regular season games for the first time in history. Games between two New York teams would finally have meaning for the first time since the Dodgers and Giants left town in 1958, while the Yankees would play a consequential game against a crosstown opponent for the first time since the mid-1950s, when they faced Brooklyn in the World Series four times in a five-year stretch.

The Yankees were defending World Series champions, so although the Bronx had hosted actual postseason games nine months earlier, the three-game series against the Mets at Yankee Stadium in June 1997 felt like the biggest games the city had seen in years.

"Those games were always sold out, and you'd have a mix of Mets and Yankees jerseys in the stands no matter which stadium you were in," Paul O'Neill said. "There was a different feeling about playing those games; sometimes as a player, you didn't even want to go through that in June or July. There was a playoff atmosphere, but it was just another game on the schedule.

"And Mr. Steinbrenner also made it apparent that we weren't supposed to lose to the Mets."

Some things never change.

Dave Mlicki was the unlikely hero in the first-ever regular season Subway Series game, throwing a complete-game shutout to give the Mets the historic victory.

"The Mets winning the first game really put a lot of pressure on Torre, because George wanted to win those games," Kay said. "Those games now meant something more than just the optic; it was an important part of the season."

David Wells pitched the Yankees to a win in the second game of the series, while Tino Martinez delivered a walk-off RBI single in the 10th inning of the finale, giving the Yankees a series win.

More than 168,000 fans attended the three games, as the city buzzed all week about a weekend series in the middle of

June. Traditionalists might have hated interleague play, but fans in New York loved it.

"When we played the Mets in '97, for those three games, the entire city was electric," Martinez said. "Everywhere you went, every restaurant, people were all fired up whether they were Yankees fans or Mets fans. It was so much fun to play in because that had never happened before in the World Series or anywhere else. The fans really loved it and we enjoyed it, as well."

The annual three-game series had been a highlight of the baseball season in New York in 1997–98, so when MLB expanded the interleague schedule in 1999 to include six games—three in each ballpark—it doubled the fun for fans around the city.

The Yankees and Mets split their six games in 1999, the highlight coming on July 10, when Mariano Rivera suffered a rare meltdown at Shea Stadium. Trailing by a run in the ninth inning, the Mets had runners at second and third when Torre opted to intentionally walk Mike Piazza to load the bases. Unheralded utility infielder Matt Franco was sent to pinch-hit for Melvin Mora, delivering an unlikely game-winning hit against the great Rivera. The winning pitcher for the Mets that day was a right-handed reliever named Pat Mahomes, whose son, Patrick, would become a National Football League Most Valuable Player and Super Bowl champion two decades later.

The Subway Series was officially a hit, but some viewed Yankees versus Mets as more of a novelty than a true rivalry. That all changed in 2000.

That year's edition featured the first two-stadium doubleheader, the result of a June rainout in the Bronx. With the teams slated to play three games at Shea Stadium the following month, the decision was made to play a doubleheader on Saturday, July 8. The first game was to take place at Shea Stadium as planned, then the teams would board buses and head to Yankee Stadium for the nightcap.

"They closed the Triboro Bridge for us to get to Shea Stadium, then they did it again when we went back after the game," Williams said. "We were in a convoy of buses, and they closed the whole thing with a police escort. It was just a spectacle."

The Yankees won the opener in Queens, getting five solid innings from Gooden, the former Mets ace who had played with the Yankees in 1996–97, then returned in 2000.

Roger Clemens started the night game, and while nobody realized it at the time, he was about to become one of the most despised figures in the history of the Mets fan base.

The five-time American League Cy Young Award winner got through a quick first inning, bringing Piazza to the plate to lead off the second for the Mets. Piazza—a five-time All-Star who had come to the Mets in a May 1998 trade—had owned Clemens in the past, going 7-for-12 with three home runs. The three homers had come in their three most recent meetings.

Clemens' second pitch sailed high and inside, beaning Piazza on the bill of his helmet. The catcher hit the deck and stayed down, sprawled out in the batter's box as manager Bobby Valentine and the Mets' training staff rushed out of the dugout to tend to him.

Piazza remained down for a minute or two before being helped to his feet. One Mets trainer held the back of Piazza's belt to stabilize him, eventually helping him walk off the field. Clemens stood near the mound watching the scene, looking distraught over the incident.

"I'm glad to hear he's all right," Clemens said. "It was supposed to be in. I wanted it to be belt high."

Clemens insisted the ball had gotten away from him, and that there was no intent behind the pitch. The pitcher had a team trainer call over to the Mets clubhouse to check on Piazza's condition, but Valentine made it clear that he believed the beaning was intentional.

"My player, who's had pretty good success against their pitcher, got hit in the head," Valentine said after the game. "I've seen him hit guys in the head before."

Piazza suffered a concussion, forcing him to skip the All-Star Game in Atlanta a few days later. When Piazza spoke with reporters the following day, he angrily accused Clemens of throwing at him.

"I don't want to say he intentionally hit me in the head, but I think he intentionally threw at my head," Piazza said. "There's no place for that in baseball."

Informed that Clemens had said the pitch was an accident, Piazza fired back at the Yankees pitcher.

"I have no respect or appreciation for his comments," Piazza said. "Roger Clemens is a great pitcher, but I don't have respect for him now at all.

"I could respect the fact of his throwing inside. Getting hit in the ribs and body are part of the game. But he has very good control; he only walked one guy. If he knew he had to come up and hit the next inning, I think he would have been more careful. I think it was very much an intentional pitch."

With their interleague meetings behind them, the Yankees and Mets would have to wait until the following summer for any fallout from Piazza's beaning. Or would they?

Both teams reached the postseason; the Mets finished the season with wins in nine of their final 11 games to capture the NL wild card spot, while the Yankees held on for the AL East title despite losing 15 of their final 18 games.

Seeking their third straight World Series title, the Yankees woke up once the calendar turned to October. They got past the Oakland Athletics in a five-game ALDS, then beat the Seattle Mariners in a six-game ALCS to capture another pennant.

The Mets breezed through the NLDS with a four-game win over the San Francisco Giants, then beat the St. Louis Cardinals in a five-game NLCS, advancing to their first World Series since 1986.

It had taken 38 years, but the 7 train and 4 train were finally on a collision course. The Yankees and Mets were set to meet in a true "Subway Series," the first in New York City since the Yankees and Dodgers met in the 1956 World Series.

"At that point, we had won three already," Martinez said. "The Mets had a great team, but The Boss basically said if we had lost to the Mets, it would have been like we never won three to begin with."

"It would have felt incomplete to lose to the Mets when we were the favorites to win it, but I was very conscious of the fact that in a short series, anything can happen," Williams said. "For nothing else than bragging rights, winning that series definitely meant the world to us."

The players knew what was at stake, but they weren't the ones who would feel the true brunt of Steinbrenner's anger if the Yankees lost to the Mets on baseball's biggest stage.

"It was one of the least enjoyable World Series I've ever had," Cashman said. "You knew going into it that we better not lose."

"They had everything to lose and nothing to win," Kay said. "They were supposed to win because they had won two championships in a row before that. If they lost, they would have never heard the end of it."

Game 1 was a classic duel between Andy Pettitte and Al Leiter that remained scoreless into the sixth inning. Mets rookie Timo Perez made a baserunning blunder in the top of the sixth, getting thrown out at the plate after misjudging Todd Zeile's double. David Justice gave the Yankees the lead with a two-run double in the bottom of the inning, but the Mets countered with three runs in the seventh, putting them in position to steal the opener in the Bronx.

O'Neill drew a 10-pitch walk against closer Armando Benitez with one out in the ninth to put the tying run on base, then after singles by Luis Polonia and Jose Vizcaino loaded the bases, Chuck Knoblauch hit a sacrifice fly that forced extra innings. Vizcaino delivered a walk-off single against Turk Wendell in the 12th to give the Yankees the series-opening win.

As the teams prepared for Game 2, all talk revolved around Clemens, who was slated to start for the Yankees. It had been more than three months since he had hit Piazza in the head, but the buildup for their next showdown had the baseball world buzzing.

"It was brutal; you'd go out to pick up your laundry or dry cleaning and they're talking about it," Torre said.

"You'd go to another store and it's the same thing. You couldn't hide from it. You couldn't get five minutes off from it because everybody was talking about it."

Clemens made quick work of the first two Mets batters, striking out both. Piazza stepped to the plate, and regardless of which colors fans were wearing, the entire crowd of 56,059 sat on the edge of their seats for this matchup.

Piazza took the first two pitches for called strikes, then watched Clemens miss with his third offering, moving the count to 1-2. Clemens fired an inside fastball—no, not *that* inside— that Piazza hit foul, shattering his bat in the process.

The barrel of the splintered bat landed near Clemens, who picked it up and threw it toward the first-base line, where it whizzed by Piazza, who was running to first base.

"I was like, 'Oh my God, what's he doing?'" said Martinez, the first baseman. "I didn't think he was throwing it at him. I think he was just trying to get rid of the bat, but Piazza was jogging to first for some reason. When he threw it, it looked worse than what it was. Emotions get high. Roger was always fired up. That created quite a stir."

A stunned Piazza turned toward Clemens and took a couple steps in his direction, causing both benches to clear. Following a minute or two of yelling, the Yankees and Mets—who had been separated by umpires—returned to their respective dugouts and continued the game.

"When the inning was over, we went in the locker room and Roger was sitting in the trainer's room just huffing and puffing; he was really juiced up," Martinez said. "It was early in the game, so I told him, 'Rocket, we need you—stay in the game for us.' He pitched a great game for us after that, but it was an intense situation, for sure."

Clemens shut out the Mets for eight innings, turning a 6–0 lead over to the bullpen. Right-hander Jeff Nelson gave up a two-run homer by Piazza, then Jay Payton smacked a three-run blast off Rivera later in the inning, cutting the Yankees' lead to one run. Rivera got the final out to escape, giving the Yankees a 2–0 lead in the best-of-seven series.

"That first game was grueling, then we almost gave it up in Game 2," Torre said. "It was definitely a high-wire act playing the Mets and knowing you had to win whether they were better than you or not."

The Mets won Game 3 at Shea Stadium to get back into the series, but the Yankees bounced back with a victory in Game

4, a game that opened with a leadoff home run by Derek Jeter. The Yankees were clinging to a one-run lead in the fifth when David Cone, who had been demoted to the bullpen following a dreadful season, came in from the bullpen with two out in the fifth to retire Mike Piazza, one of the signature moments of the series.

The Mets led Game 5 by one run in the sixth inning, but Jeter hit a game-tying home run against starter Leiter. The game remained tied into the ninth, when Leiter was still on the mound for the Mets. The left-hander struck out Martinez and O'Neill, then walked Jorge Posada, putting the go-ahead runner on base. Scott Brosius singled, then Luis Sojo poked a single up the middle, scoring Posada to give the Yankees the lead.

Rivera came in for the bottom of the ninth, issuing a one-out walk to Benny Agbayani, who moved to second base on defensive indifference, then to third on an Edgardo Alfonzo fly ball. The Mets' final hope was Piazza, who hit a fly ball to center field.

"It was probably the most scared I've been when Mike hit that ball," Torre said. "I screamed, 'No!' because any time he hits a ball in the air, it's a home run in my mind."

This time, the ball stayed in the yard. Williams squeezed the final out to clinch the Yankees' third consecutive—and, in many ways, most important—championship. Jeter was named World Series MVP.

"We were kings of the city; we were still *the* team in town," Randolph said. "That was probably the biggest exhale I ever had. I needed a vacation when that one was over. I needed to go to an island, have a bunch of piña coladas, and relax."

When the Yankees visited Shea Stadium the following season, Clemens was not lined up to pitch, taking away the possibility that a Mets pitcher would throw at him in retaliation for the Piazza beaning and/or bat throw.

In 2002, Clemens finally started a game at Shea, meaning he would have to step into the batter's box. Mets starter Shawn Estes—who was a member of the Giants when the Clemens–Piazza drama was unfolding two years earlier—fired his first pitch toward Clemens' left thigh, but the ball sailed behind the batter, missing him entirely. Both benches were warned by home-plate umpire Wally Bell, essentially putting an end to the issue.

The Mets wound up getting their revenge on Clemens, anyway. In the fifth inning, Estes—who was hitless on the season—hit a home run against the right-hander, then Piazza took Clemens deep in the sixth, much to the delight of the Queens crowd.

Clemens declined to address the Piazza drama after the game, though Posada told reporters, "I'm glad it's all over. Hopefully, we can go on now."

The two-plus decades since the Subway Series have seen some memorable moments, such as Rivera's 500th save, Luis Castillo's dropped pop-up that gifted a win to the Yankees, Jacob deGrom's major league debut, and more.

"Those were really fun, because it's almost like the city stopped no matter what was going on in New York during that series," Mark Teixeira said. "We understood what it meant to the fans, and at the end of the day, that's why we play. We don't have jobs if fans don't show up, go to the games and watch on TV. It was almost like a little bit of a gift to the fans; we wanted to put on a good show for New York."

But after the crosstown rivals faced each other with the ultimate prize on the line, many believe the regular season interleague matchups don't carry quite the same cachet that they once did.

"I thought interleague watered it down, to be honest," Torre said. "People made more of it than it was when we played the Mets. When you're with the Yankees, it's a one-way street; you had to beat them, only because of your history against their history."

Rekindling the Rivalry

IN THE LATE 1970S, THERE WAS NO BIGGER RIVALRY IN
baseball—or sports, for that matter—than the Yankees and Red
Sox.

Bucky Dent provided the biggest highlight, but it was the
brawls between the two clubs—think Thurman Munson versus
Carlton Fisk or Bill "Spaceman" Lee versus Graig Nettles—that
put the hatred between the two sides on full display for all to see.

As rosters began to turn over in the 1980s, the intensity
between the Yankees and Red Sox began to fizzle. Neither club
won a championship in the '80s, playing second fiddle to the
American League's contenders throughout the decade.

The Yankees fell in the AL Championship Series in 1980,
then lost the World Series in 1981; they would not make
another postseason appearance until 1995.

The Red Sox had slightly more success during that same period, losing the 1986 World Series along with a pair of ALCS in 1988 and '90.

"There wasn't enough juice because they both weren't great at the same time," said longtime Yankees broadcaster Michael Kay, who covered the team for the *New York Post* and *New York Daily News* in the 1980s. "The personalities on those teams were not as hateable. Roger Clemens would push their buttons when he would throw up and in, but in the 1980s, it wasn't much of a thing. It was still a thing for fans, but the players didn't look at it that way. What were they fighting for? It just didn't have any juice to it."

"For a while when I first got there, they were more of a rival from the past," said Paul O'Neill, who was traded to the Yankees before the 1993 season. "The games didn't really live up to that."

Bernie Williams had heard the legendary stories from older teammates; the tales of brawls and beanballs got him amped up to face the Red Sox when he finally got to the major leagues, but by the time he got there, those hard feelings seemed to reside primarily in the stands.

"When I came to the Yankees in 1991, the rivalry was kind of dwindling away," Williams said. "It wasn't really as intense for the players as it was for the fans. I always saw fights erupting whether we were at Fenway Park or Yankee Stadium."

Whereas players such as Fisk, Munson, Nettles, and Carl Yastrzemski played against each other for several years, the advent of free agency had caused significant player movement. The matchups between the Yankees and Red Sox featured different names every year, erasing the lingering animosity that had previously festered from season to season.

"Getting to the big leagues and playing the Yankees when I got up there in '92 as a member of the Red Sox, there was nothing there," said John Flaherty, who went on to play for the Yankees a decade later. "Neither team was any good."

"It still boils back down to both teams fighting for the same thing," said Willie Randolph, who retired after the 1992 season and returned to the Yankees, first as assistant general manager, then as third base coach. "That's what it's all about. Fighting for first place, trying to catch each other, that kind of thing."

How different was the modern-day rivalry than it had been during the late '70s? Wade Boggs, an eight-time All-Star and five-time batting champion during his 11 years with the Red Sox, signed a free-agent deal with the Yankees after the 1992 season. Could you imagine Yastrzemski or Jim Rice trading in their Boston uniforms for pinstripes?

"When Wade Boggs came to us in 1992, people were talking about how selfish he was, that he was a selfish ballplayer and how he was going to ruin our clubhouse," Jim Leyritz said. "By the end of '92, he was the judge in our clubhouse kangaroo court. That's how well he fit into our team."

Boggs' arrival coincided with the Yankees' turnaround; they finished 88–74 in 1993 after slogging through four losing seasons, then had the AL's best record in August 1994 when the players went on strike, ultimately canceling the postseason.

The Red Sox ran away with the AL East in 1995, while the Yankees edged the California Angels for the first-ever AL wild card spot. Both teams lost their respective best-of-five AL Division Series, keeping them from what could have been an epic showdown with a trip to the World Series on the line.

That would come soon enough.

But not before the Yankees ended their 15-year championship drought with a World Series victory in 1996, the first year under manager Joe Torre. The Red Sox missed the playoffs that year and the next, while the Yankees returned to October in 1997, losing to Cleveland in the ALDS.

Both teams were contenders, and while the Yankees were in the midst of a dynastic run, the Red Sox had pulled off a trade after the 1997 season that would change the course of the rivalry—and baseball history—forever.

The Red Sox acquired Pedro Martinez, the reigning National League Cy Young Award winner, adding the frontline starter Boston sorely needed.

The Red Sox fell victim to Cleveland in the 1998 ALDS, while the 114-win Yankees rolled through the postseason en route to their second World Series title in three years.

Martinez faced the Yankees just once during the first five months of the 1999 season, beating New York on May 18 with seven innings of two-run ball at Fenway Park.

"I thought Dodgers–Giants was something when I was growing up, then I was part of the Cubs–Cardinals rivalry," Torre said. "But nothing comes close to Red Sox–Yankees."

Nearly four months later, Martinez took the mound in the Bronx and delivered one of the most memorable starts of his career, limiting the Yankees to just one hit and no walks while striking out 17 in a complete-game victory. The 17 strikeouts were the most ever against the Yankees, who avoided a shutout thanks to Chili Davis' second-inning home run, but didn't manage another hit.

"We didn't get beat by the Red Sox," O'Neill said after the game. "We got beat by Pedro Martinez."

The Yankees would go on to win the AL East that season, while the Red Sox earned the AL's wild card spot. New York breezed by the Texas Rangers in the ALDS, while Boston needed five games to advance against Cleveland, setting up the first-ever ALCS between the two rivals.

"You knew it was a rivalry and you heard names like Bucky Dent, Carlton Fisk, and Reggie Jackson, but the distance between the teams prevented it from being that intense," O'Neill said. "When Boston got good, it became a pins-and-needles rivalry."

The first two games were tightly contested, but the Yankees emerged with a pair of one-run victories. As the series moved to Fenway Park, Martinez was slated to take the mound in Game 3 against Clemens, the former Boston ace who had been traded to the Yankees prior to the season in a deal with the Toronto Blue Jays.

Clemens was hit hard by his former team, allowing five runs while recording only six outs. That was more than enough run support for Martinez, who fired seven shutout innings, striking out 12 to pull the Red Sox back into the series.

"Pedro was just a great competitor; when he's out there, he doesn't like you and you don't like him—and he doesn't care," Yankees first baseman Tino Martinez said. "That mentality is what made him so good. Besides his talent, his gamesmanship and wanting to dominate a game made him so tough. He just really wanted to take it to the Yankees—or anybody else he pitched against."

Fortunately for the Yankees, Martinez never saw the ball again. New York won Games 4 and 5, clinching the pennant with a pair of lopsided victories. The series turned out to be a dud, but Martinez's effort was a preview of what the Yankees would have to deal with in the coming years.

The battles in the ensuing years were fierce, especially when Martinez pitched.

Martinez snapped a personal five-game winless streak against the Yankees on May 30, 2001, striking out 13 over eight innings in another classic performance. After the game, the pitcher expressed his exhaustion regarding the constant talk of the rivalry, invoking the name of the most legendary figure in New York–Boston history.

"I'm starting to hate talking about the Yankees," Martinez said after his gem. "The questions are so stupid. They're wasting my time. It's getting kind of old. I don't believe in damn curses. Wake up the damn Bambino and have me face him. Maybe I'll drill him in the ass, pardon me the word."

On July 7, 2003, Martinez—peeved that Clemens had hit Kevin Millar with a pitch two days earlier—hit Alfonso Soriano in the hand on a checked swing, then drilled Derek Jeter on his hand in the next at-bat, knocking both players out of the game.

"They had some personalities that, from our side, we could not stand," Flaherty said. "It became personal. Pedro is the one that jumps out at you; he was so dominant, but the way he went about things, hitting some of our guys like Derek and Soriano, constantly dusting people and brushing them back, he pitched with an edge and some anger and intimidation. That gets your attention right away."

A dozen years later, in his autobiography *Pedro*, Martinez admitted that those pitches were thrown with a purpose. In fact, Martinez proudly noted that nearly every hitter he drilled throughout his career was done intentionally.

"I told some teammates, 'At least I gave them a discount on an ambulance—they both got to go in the same one,'" Martinez wrote. "That comment surprised Derek Lowe. He told me he figured that when I hit batters, it was an accident 90 percent of the time. He was 100 percent wrong. When I hit a batter, it was 90 percent intentional."

George Steinbrenner suggested that Major League Baseball investigate Martinez for his habit of hitting opponents, a comment that didn't sit well with the Boston ace.

"Georgie Porgie, he might buy the whole league, but he doesn't have enough money to buy fear to put in my heart," Martinez told reporters.

If 1999 had served as the spark to reignite the rivalry, 2003 had become a full-blown explosion.

"If you play for New York or Boston, you're not allowed to like the other side," said Mike Mussina, who joined the Yankees in 2001. "It's like Duke–North Carolina; you're just not allowed. It's almost like when you sign up to play for the Yankees, at the bottom of the contract, it said, 'You can't like the Red Sox.'"

Regular season matchups would be treated like postseason games, often airing on national television for the entire country to witness. Fans couldn't get enough of Yankees–Red Sox, but for the participants themselves, the series took on an intensity that few regular season games ever had.

"Those games almost felt like World Series games," Yankees first baseman Jason Giambi said. "Weeks before we would play them, people were already talking about it. I'm like, 'We're playing Detroit—that's three weeks away.' People were already trying to get that feeling going of playing the Red Sox."

The Yankees edged the Red Sox in the 2003 season series, winning 10 of their 19 meetings. But New York ended the year with 101 wins, finishing the season in first place, six games ahead of Boston. Both teams took care of business in the ALDS, setting up another ALCS showdown.

"It was torture, but at least it's OK to be tortured when it's postseason," Torre said. "They always magnified every game we played them, but at least in the postseason, it makes sense to do that."

The teams split the two games at Yankee Stadium, sending the series back to Fenway Park knotted at a game apiece.

Game 3 was the main event: Pedro versus Clemens. And unlike many modern-day prize fights, this one lived up to the hype.

The fireworks began in the fourth inning when Martinez threw behind Karim Garcia's head, a pitch that was ruled to have hit the outfielder in the back. Yankees bench coach Don Zimmer was among those barking at Martinez from the dugout, though the game continued without incident.

Warnings were issued to both dugouts, but those didn't do much to defuse tempers on either side.

Soriano followed with a double play, during which Garcia slid hard into second baseman Todd Walker. Garcia exchanged words with Walker, Martinez, and pretty much any other Red Sox player in his way, bringing players from both sides out of their respective dugouts.

Martinez and Jorge Posada barked at each other, prompting the pitcher to point at his head, a potential warning that Posada might be his next target. Clemens had to be held back by umpires as he emerged from the dugout, but once again, there was no altercation beyond the shouting.

"They legitimately hated each other," Kay said. "The Pedro years with Posada, I think there was genuine dislike. That's what you need in a rivalry like this."

The Yankees led the game 4–2 in the middle of the fourth. Manny Ramirez led off for Boston, seemingly looking for a reason to go after Clemens. The fourth pitch of the at-bat sailed head-high but appeared to be over the inside part of home plate. Ramirez took exception, immediately taking a step toward the mound, pointing and shouting at Clemens.

"That ball's not even close!" Fox analyst Tim McCarver said on the broadcast.

Both benches emptied, as players met in the middle of the field as if they were the Sharks and the Jets. Tempers ran hot, though no punches were exchanged; most players simply yelled at each other, expressing their distaste for the other side. The lone physical confrontation was an unlikely one. Zimmer, Torre's 72-year-old sidekick, ran toward Martinez, continuing to berate him as he had done in the top of the inning. But as Zimmer reached Martinez, the pitcher grabbed the septuagenarian by his bald head, flinging him to the ground.

"I was more surprised to see Zim get across the field that fast," Giambi said after the game. "You don't spend as many years as he has in the game without getting involved."

Zimmer was taken to a hospital after the game but came away from the skirmish with only a cut on the bridge of his nose.

In his book, Martinez said the Zimmer incident—which resulted in a $50,000 fine for the pitcher—was the "only regret" from his Hall of Fame career.

"Some days I feel more people remember me as the angry young man who pushed down a defenseless old man than as the pitcher who won three Cy Young Awards and a world title and wound up in the Hall of Fame," Martinez wrote. "In my entire baseball career, my reaction to Zimmer's charge is my only regret."

Even New York City Mayor Michael Bloomberg chimed in on the Martinez–Zimmer affair.

"If that happened in New York, we would have arrested the perpetrator," Bloomberg told the Associated Press. "Nobody should throw a 70-year-old man to the ground, period.... You just cannot assault people, even if it's on a baseball field."

As if the fourth-inning scuffles weren't enough, a pair of Yankees—Garcia and reliever Jeff Nelson—got into it with a member of the Red Sox grounds crew who was cheering for the home team while standing in the New York bullpen in the ninth inning. Things had officially spiraled out of control.

"I asked him, 'If you want to cheer for them, why don't you go over in their bullpen?'" Nelson said after the incident. "He jumped up and got in my face and took a swing at me and got tackled."

Assault charges were filed against both Nelson and Garcia two months later, though the two players agreed to a deal the following October that included a six-month probation period and 50 hours of community service each.

Commissioner Bud Selig issued a statement the following day, taking both the Yankees and Red Sox to task.

"I'm very disappointed in the behavior of some of the participants in last night's game between the Boston Red Sox and the New York Yankees," Selig said. "I have instructed the umpires and told the clubs that any future misconduct by either team will not be tolerated and will be dealt with severely."

The rest of the series was played without incident, going the distance to a winner-take-all Game 7 at Yankee Stadium. The Red Sox jumped out to a 4–0 lead against Clemens, and while the Yankees hung around thanks to a pair of Giambi home runs against Martinez, Boston held a 5–2 lead in the eighth.

The Yankees mounted a comeback in the eighth, scoring three times against Martinez, who stayed on the mound even after manager Grady Little appeared ready to lift him. The game moved to the 11th inning, where Aaron Boone launched a pennant-winning walk-off home run, joining Dent on the list of most hated athletes in Boston history.

"It's always intense, but that time was one of those heightened intensities where the teams probably didn't like each other a lot," said Boone, the Yankees' third baseman who became New

York's manager after the 2017 season. "It was absolutely two heavyweights going at it and you knew it. It made for great theater."

It seemed the Red Sox were destined to play second fiddle to their rivals, as the "Curse of the Bambino" now stood at 85 years. Yes, the same curse named for the man Martinez wanted to drill in the rear end.

The rivalry extended beyond the field of play, too. In 2002, the Yankees signed Cuban pitcher Jose Contreras, who was also being wooed by the Red Sox. Boston team president Larry Lucchino was not pleased, telling the *New York Times*, "The evil empire extends its tentacles even into Latin America." An urban myth claimed that Red Sox general manager Theo Epstein kicked over chairs in his hotel room when he learned that Contreras had signed with the Yankees, though that was later proved to be untrue.

Still licking their wounds in the wake of Boone's home run, the Red Sox spent Thanksgiving weekend in 2003 completing a trade for Diamondbacks starting pitcher Curt Schilling, who had helped lead Arizona past the Yankees in the 2001 World Series.

The Red Sox were in talks to make an even bigger trade later in the winter, a deal that would have brought reigning AL MVP Alex Rodriguez to Boston. Ramirez would have been shipped to the Texas Rangers for A-Rod, while the Red Sox would have also sent shortstop Nomar Garciaparra and pitching prospect Jon Lester to the Chicago White Sox in exchange for outfielder Magglio Ordonez and pitching prospect Brandon McCarthy.

But the MLB Players Association refused to sign off on the trade, which would have required A-Rod to take a pay cut, nixing the deal before it could be completed. One month later,

Boone blew out his knee playing pickup basketball, prompting the Yankees to swoop in and trade for A-Rod.

"You're always locking heads with those guys because they have the same ability you do to sign a player or acquire a player—and they gravitate to the same type of players that we do," longtime Yankees general manager Brian Cashman said. "The rivalry isn't just with the game on the field; it's also with the ownership groups, the front offices, fighting for players in the draft, international, the trade front. The war is constant and it's nonstop."

The Yankees had lost the 2003 World Series to the Florida Marlins, unable to complete their championship quest after Boone's memorable home run. The 2004 season was expected to be another slugfest between New York and Boston in the AL East, and while the Red Sox resided in first place for most of the first two months, the Yankees seized control of the division in early June.

For Torre and his counterpart, Red Sox manager Terry Francona, the Yankees–Red Sox series were more of a hassle than anything. The games counted the same as any others, yet the spotlight thrust upon them made them feel so much bigger.

"During the season where every game is like a world war, I thought it was too much," Torre said. "I understood it, because they're trying to create excitement, but it was tiring. Terry or I would call each other after the series was over and say, 'I'm glad this crap is over for another six weeks.'"

When they took the field at Fenway Park on July 24, the Yankees held a commanding 9½-game lead over their rivals in the division. New York had won the series opener the night before, and like virtually other game between these two teams at that time, Saturday's game was a nationally televised affair.

The Yankees held a 3–0 lead with two out in the third inning when Boston starter Bronson Arroyo brushed A-Rod off the plate, then plunked him on his left elbow with his next pitch. Rodriguez stared down Arroyo as he began a slow walk up the first-base line, shouting, "Throw that shit over the fucking plate!"

Red Sox catcher Jason Varitek stepped in front of A-Rod as the two began exchanging pleasantries. Home plate umpire Bruce Froemming tried to get in between them, but it was a fruitless act. As the two continued to jaw at each other, Varitek—still in his full catching gear—shoved Rodriguez in the face with his catcher's mitt and his bare hand, causing the benches to clear.

"Varitek was genius in how he baited him into that," Randolph said. "I kept telling A-Rod, 'Don't take the bait. Don't do it. Let sleeping dogs lie.' Varitek knew exactly what he was doing. A-Rod wanted to be a real Yankee, wanted to be a tough guy."

Unlike the incident in the prior year's ALCS, this one got ugly.

Varitek and A-Rod wound up in the middle of a scrum, but Tanyon Sturtze—the Yankees' starting pitcher that day—came flying out of the dugout and grabbed Gabe Kapler by the neck, peeling him off the pile. Seconds later, Sturtze was battling Kapler and Trot Nixon, taking a punch from Kapler that caused him to bleed near his left ear.

"You get in there as fast as you can and you try to help out," Sturtze said. "Alex was in a really bad spot; once you get in the bottom of those piles, really bad things happen. Gabe happened to be the first person I got to, then I just started taking people off the pile as best as I could. Things happen, but it's just protect-mode time and you just go into the fight to help your teammates. We were all professionals, but we didn't like many of the guys over there. They felt the same way."

The Yankees held a 9–4 lead after scoring six runs in the sixth inning, but the Red Sox rallied for an 11–10 win as third baseman Bill Mueller hit a two-run, walk-off home run against Mariano Rivera.

The win—or was it the brawl?—seemed to breathe new life into the Red Sox, who would make a huge move the following week, trading Garciaparra to the Chicago Cubs in a four-team deal that landed first baseman Doug Mientkiewicz and shortstop Orlando Cabrera in Boston.

Boston went 42–18 over its final 60 games, though that wasn't enough to overtake New York, which went a respectable 36–23 after August 1. The Yankees won the AL East by three games, extending their streak of division titles to seven consecutive seasons. And for the seventh straight year, the Red Sox finished second.

"Varitek shoving a glove in A-Rod's face, Pedro tumbling Don Zimmer because Zimmer went at him; you couldn't write a better script," Williams said. "It was as entertaining as anything in baseball in those years. That era revived the personal animosity in the rivalry on the players' side. We had a little beef with them."

Both teams breezed through their ALDS matchups; for the second straight year, Torre's Yankees and the Red Sox—now managed by Francona—were headed on a collision course in the ALCS.

The Yankees won the first two games at home, beating Schilling and Martinez. The series moved to Fenway Park, where the Yankees' bats throttled the Sox in Game 3, a 19–8 pounding that had New York one win away from a seventh trip to the World Series in nine years. No MLB team had ever come back from an 0–3 deficit in a best-of-seven series, and given the nature of the beating the Yankees had handed out in Game 3, few expected the series to even make it back to the Bronx.

"In the beginning of that series, it came so easily for a couple games," Mussina said. "We won Game 3 so big, it felt like every inning we came up, we hit a home run. It was so easy to get to that point."

The Red Sox stunned the Yankees in Game 4, coming back against Rivera in the ninth inning with the help of Dave Roberts' infamous stolen base. David Ortiz—who would become one of the greatest antagonists in the history of the rivalry—hit a walk-off home run against Paul Quantrill to keep Boston's season alive.

Game 5 saw another late-inning comeback and another Ortiz walk-off hit; the Red Sox had forced the series back to New York for Game 6. Suddenly, the pressure had shifted to the Yankees, who just 48 hours earlier appeared to be steamrolling their way toward another championship.

"Walking from the bullpen to the dugout at Fenway Park after Game 5, it felt to me like we were down in the series instead of being up," Flaherty said. "That's how quickly things change when you lose a couple of late, dramatic games at Fenway. You almost forget that you're still in the driver's seat."

"When we went back to New York, just knowing how it felt, how the atmosphere was, you could kind of sense it wasn't going to go well," Mussina said. "And that's how it went; it didn't go well."

Dealing with a dislocated tendon in his right ankle that he suffered earlier in the postseason, Schilling and the team doctor had decided to try an unorthodox procedure to temporarily secure the tendon in place, giving the right-hander a chance to pitch in Game 6. Television cameras zeroed in on the ankle early in the game, catching a glimpse of blood seeping through his sock from the point of the incision.

The "Bloody Sock Game" made Schilling—who held the Yankees to one run on four hits over seven innings—an instant Boston legend. The game also featured the bizarre sight of A-Rod slapping the ball out of Arroyo's glove in an attempt to keep a Yankees rally alive, another sign of the Yankees' desperation.

"That team over on the other side, they responded well," Derek Jeter said. "They had three games that were do-or-die. Now we're going to have to respond."

Dent threw out the ceremonial first pitch to Yogi Berra prior to Game 7, but that turned out to be the highlight of the Yankees' night.

Ortiz hit a two-run homer in the first inning, then Johnny Damon belted a grand slam in the second. Boston led 6–0, stunning the Yankees and silencing the stadium that bears their name. Boston cruised to a 10–3 win, completing the greatest comeback in baseball history.

"Devastating; it still hurts," Sturtze said. "That was my best shot at getting a ring, so it hurts more for me than it probably does for a lot of other guys on that team that ended up getting another one in '09 or had a bunch before that. I can still see Johnny Damon hit that grand slam."

The Curse had been broken. As Tyler Kepner of the *New York Times* wrote after Game 7, "The nerd kissed the homecoming queen. Paper beat scissors; scissors beat rock. Charlie Brown kicked the football. The Red Sox beat the Yankees for the American League pennant."

The Red Sox went on to sweep the St. Louis Cardinals in the World Series, bringing their 86-year championship drought to an official end. Although the rivals split their two epic ALCS showdowns, the historic nature of Boston's comeback felt so much bigger—especially since the Red Sox finished the job with a World Series title, something the Yankees had been unable to do in 2003.

"Losing to the Red Sox and helping Boston start this run where they've won four championships, that's something that will never be forgotten," Kay said. "The pain of 2004 is much, much bigger than the joy of 2003. If there's still a world in 3024 and Joe Buck VIII is doing the games on Fox 9, there's going to be a graphic about MLB teams that have blown 3–0 leads and the first one is going to be the 2004 Yankees losing to the Red Sox—the one team you wouldn't want to blow it to."

36

New Kids in Town

WHEN THE TAMPA BAY DEVIL RAYS BEGAN PLAY IN 1998, they were a typically bad expansion team, finishing their debut season with a 63–99 record.

The Yankees set an American League record with 114 wins that season, eventually rolling through the postseason for their second World Series title in three years.

Yet every time the Yankees and Devil Rays faced off, the pressure on New York to win was immense. Tampa Bay wasn't a threat within the American League East, but for George Steinbrenner—a resident of Tampa—the Devil Rays were the pesky little team in his own backyard.

"He did not want to get embarrassed in his hometown, especially losing to a bad team," said Bill Madden, longtime *New York Daily News* columnist and author of *Steinbrenner: The Last Lion of Baseball*. "He definitely put more emphasis on those games in Tampa."

From the first time the teams matched up in a meaningless Grapefruit League game, Steinbrenner's investment in these games was evident. Joe Torre was instructed to play his stars against Tampa Bay, even if the game was on the road, where rosters typically consist of two or three regulars and a host of minor league players. Players began to jokingly refer to these exhibition games as the "World Series," though to The Boss, there was nothing funny about it.

"You always had to beat Tampa, but it wasn't good enough to beat them 2–1," Torre said. "You had to beat them 10–1."

The Yankees won 11 of their 12 meetings with the Devil Rays in 1998, outscoring them 60–22. Tampa Bay finished 51 games behind New York, and yet that one Devil Rays win probably irked The Boss as much as any of his team's 48 losses all season.

"It was his backyard and he wanted to dominate his opponent," said Brian Cashman, who was in his first season as the Yankees' general manager. "How dare we lose to these guys?"

The Yankees might have dreaded their games against the mostly overmatched Devil Rays, but for the Tampa Bay players, they looked forward to these games above all others. It wasn't because they thought they were going to beat the big, bad Yankees, but rather because the presence of the Bronx Bombers at Tropicana Field meant the seats would actually be filled.

"That was our chance to play in front of a lot of fans," said Tanyon Sturtze, who pitched for the Devil Rays from 2000 to '02, then for the Yankees from 2004 to '06. "There was really no rivalry; we lost 100 games a year and the Yankees were on top all the time. We were still trying to find our way as an organization."

John Flaherty, who played for Tampa Bay from 1998 to 2002 before joining the Yankees in 2003, said the games against the

Yankees had "a lot more juice" because of the attendance, which would increase dramatically when New York was in town.

"They felt like bigger games," Flaherty said. "They were so good that it was tough for us to compete; when we did beat them, we felt like it was a big game for us. One year, we beat them in three straight games at the end of the year, which was a big deal for us."

It was a big deal for Steinbrenner, too. The year was 2000, and the Yankees were stumbling down the stretch in their efforts to win a third consecutive World Series title.

Torre's club lost 15 of its final 18 games, including an ignominious three-game sweep at the hands of the Devil Rays in St. Petersburg during the final week of the regular season.

The Boss was so incensed by the sweep that he ordered the team's charter plane to sit on the tarmac for two hours before taking off for Baltimore, where the Yankees were finishing the season. (They were swept there, too.)

Steinbrenner took it personally any time his Yankees lost to the Devil Rays, especially after he had pushed for Major League Baseball to award an expansion franchise to the Tampa Bay area. Steinbrenner had lived in Tampa since the mid-1970s, getting involved with myriad local charities and establishing himself as a pillar of the community.

And with the Yankees' spring training and minor league facilities resting in the middle of the city, Steinbrenner would often say—and rightfully so—that there were more Yankees fans in Tampa than Devil Rays fans.

Ushers at Tropicana Field would see regulars at Devil Rays games dressed in Tampa Bay garb, but when the Yankees came to town, those same fans were donning pinstripes and rooting for the visiting team.

Five years into their existence, the Devil Rays tried to import some of that Yankees mystique, hiring Lou Piniella to manage the club. Piniella—a member of the Yankees' 1977–78 World Series champions—brought some of that Bronx attitude to Tampa Bay, but the Devil Rays were simply outmatched against Torre's team, which was in the midst of a run of nine consecutive AL East titles.

The Yankees went 14–5 against Piniella's Devil Rays in his first season as manager, then took 15 of the 19 meetings in his second year.

"Lou had a relationship with George; he ran in some of those same Tampa circles," said Marc Topkin, who has covered the Rays for the *Tampa Bay Times* since the club's inception in 1998. "I think beating the Yankees meant more to Lou than it did to any of the other managers because of his personal history. Unfortunately, he was in a position where it didn't happen very often."

The Yankees' hostility toward the Devil Rays was evident in 2004, when Hurricane Frances caused a delay in Tampa Bay's travel schedule for a Labor Day doubleheader at Yankee Stadium. As the Yankees waited all day for the visitors to arrive, the front office asked the commissioner's office to award a forfeit victory—something that hadn't happened in a situation such as this since 1918.

Commissioner Bud Selig declined the request. The Devil Rays' weekend home games had already been canceled, but Tampa Bay's players chose to stay home as the storm approached, making sure their families were safe and sound before the team left town. Yankees officials insisted that Tampa Bay could have departed Tampa two days earlier—before the storm hit the area—privately accusing Tampa Bay owner Vince

Naimoli of ordering the team to stay home to avoid paying two extra days of travel expenses.

The Devil Rays pulled up to Yankee Stadium shortly after 6:00 PM, roughly one hour before the first pitch was thrown. The Yankees won the game.

Piniella finally got the better of his former club in 2005, leading the Devil Rays to an 11–8 record against the Yankees, and while the team finished the season 67–95, it was a step in the right direction for a club that had only reached the 70-win mark for the first time the previous season.

"During their first decade, the Rays had to find little victories," Topkin said. "Winning one game or winning a game that meant something to the Yankees meant a lot to the Rays, because they were not on anything resembling equal footing in any other way."

The annual standings reflected the lopsided nature of the matchup. By the end of its first decade, Tampa Bay had recorded only one 70-win season, taking up permanent residence in the AL East's basement. Under Joe Maddon, who had succeeded Piniella in 2006, the Devil Rays lost 101 and 96 games, continuing their decade-long run as a major league team in name only.

All the losing had its rewards, however. The Devil Rays—who dropped "Devil" from their name after the 2007 season—had earned a number of high draft picks thanks to their woeful record. Tampa Bay selected in the top three in the MLB draft six times between 1999 and 2007, owning the No. 1 overall pick three times during that stretch.

"The way the new game, the new chess board, is designed, losing is rewarded, which eventually takes the losers into the winner's bracket," Cashman said. "All the rules of the game are to penalize winning, which drags down winners into the losers' category as well. It's a way to allow every franchise's fan base to have an opportunity to taste success. At some point, the Rays were going to become a legitimate contender."

Having drafted players such as B.J. Upton, Evan Longoria, and David Price, the future was looking brighter for the Rays. Tampa Bay was at the forefront of the analytic revolution, enabling the Rays to identify affordable talent that fit their payroll structure. More importantly, the team also appeared to be undergoing an attitude adjustment on Maddon's watch.

During a Grapefruit League game at George M. Steinbrenner Field in March 2008, Rays infielder Elliot Johnson barreled into Francisco Cervelli in a home-plate collision, breaking the minor league catcher's wrist. Joe Girardi—who had taken over for Torre after the 2007 season—was incensed, saying the play was "uncalled for" in an exhibition game.

Maddon chirped back, telling reporters, "I never read that rule," characterizing it a "good, hard baseball play."

Several Yankees were dismayed by the Rays' aggressive style. Shelley Duncan, a part-time first baseman/outfielder, sent a not-so-subtle message that the book had not been closed on this incident.

"What it does is it opens another chapter of intensity in the spring training ballgames," Duncan said at the time. "They showed what is acceptable to them and how they're going to play the game, so we're going to go out there to match their intensity—or even exceed it."

Duncan added that there would be "no malicious intent in terms of carryover," but the Rays' mindset and approach to the game would add "a different type of fire to your gut" the next time they played.

That came just four days later, this time at the Progress Energy Park in St. Petersburg. With the Johnson–Cervelli incident still fresh in everybody's mind, umpires issued warnings prior to first pitch, a rarity for an exhibition game.

Heath Phillips, a young non-roster left-hander for the Yankees, hit Longoria with a pitch in the first inning, resulting in an immediate ejection. That was merely an appetizer; an inning later, Duncan slid hard into second baseman Akinori Iwamura with his spikes raised, displaying that fire he had spoken of days earlier.

Rays right fielder Jonny Gomes took exception to the slide, darting in from the outfield and shoving Duncan. Both benches cleared, and while no punches appeared to be thrown, the lines had been drawn between the teams.

"That was really the first sign of the Rays punching back," Topkin said.

Maddon called Duncan's slide a blatant, premeditated attempt to injure Iwamura, differentiating it from the collision that injured Cervelli.

"In Tampa, that play you saw at home plate was a good, hard baseball play. What you saw today was the definition of a dirty play," Maddon said. "There's no room for that in our game. It's contemptible. It's wrong. It's borderline criminal, and I could not believe they did that…. I don't know what the difference is between that and a high stick in hockey. But it was that bad."

Even after watching replays of the slide, Duncan didn't understand why the Rays were so upset by his actions.

"I believe both instances are definitions of players playing the game hard," Duncan said.

The Rays had made it clear that they were not going to be pushed around by anybody, not even the Yankees. Whether the incident served as a rallying cry for Tampa Bay remains unclear, but Maddon's team won 97 games that season, capturing its first AL East title. The Rays made it all the way to the World

Series, while the Yankees watched from home, having missed the postseason for the first time in 15 years.

The Yankees flexed their financial muscle prior to the 2009 season, signing CC Sabathia, A.J. Burnett, and Mark Teixeira. New York went on to win the World Series that year, but the Rays weren't going away any time soon.

Derek Jeter recorded his 3,000th hit with a home run against Price in July 2011, and while that highlight has been replayed hundreds of times in the Bronx, the Rays countered later that season with one of the greatest moments in their brief history— and not just because it came against the Yankees.

It was Game 162 of the 2011 season, and Tampa Bay needed a win—as well as a Red Sox loss to the Orioles—to reach the postseason. The Yankees, who had already locked up the AL East title, jumped out to a 7–0 lead, putting the Rays' playoff hopes in serious jeopardy.

Girardi had decided to rest his primary late-inning relievers, giving them an extra day off before the AL Division Series. The Yankees patched together the first seven innings with a hodgepodge of pitchers, and given their lead, relievers Boone Logan, Luis Ayala, and Cory Wade should have been able to record the final nine outs.

The Rays scored six times against Logan and Ayala in the eighth inning, then tied the game in the ninth on Dan Johnson's pinch-hit home run against Wade, storming all the way back to keep their season alive. Tampa Bay walked off with a win in the 12th as Longoria belted a game-winning home run against Scott Proctor, sending them to the playoffs after the Red Sox had blown a lead of their own in Baltimore in similarly stunning fashion.

"That was one of the craziest days in baseball," said Nick Swisher, the Yankees' right fielder that season. "That was an amazing moment in Rays history, and the fact that it was against us made it even better for them."

Tampa Bay had become a difficult place for the Yankees to play, replacing Anaheim as the Bombers' personal house of horrors. Tensions always seemed to run high when the two teams met at the Trop, and over the next decade, there would be many heated moments that nearly escalated into something far uglier.

Despite the vast disparity in payroll, the two teams were now jockeying for position in the AL East on an annual basis, though the Red Sox and Orioles were doing their part to make it a deep division. Still, the fact that the Yankees trained in Tampa and housed their minor league complex in the city seemed to keep them at the top of the Rays' hit list.

"I think the Rays have had a bit of a chip on their shoulder," Topkin said. "Beating the Yankees does seem to mean a little more to them for various reasons. The Red Sox and the Yankees are the teams the Rays are always going to be fighting in the AL East, and then when you factor in the number of Yankees fans in the Tampa area, the Rays can feel like they're playing second fiddle in their own city at times."

The rivalry reached new heights in 2017, when Rays reliever Matt Andreise drilled Aaron Judge with a pitch, a clear retaliation after Yankees pitcher Tommy Layne plunked Corey Dickerson, the outfielder who had swatted a pair of home runs earlier in the game.

The teams soon began to throw inside to each other with great frequency. Sabathia was often in the middle of the action, most notably in a September 2018 game when he drilled catcher Jesus Sucre to retaliate after Rays reliever Andrew Kittredge had thrown behind Yankees catcher Austin Romine in the top of the inning.

"That's for you, bitch!" Sabathia shouted toward the Rays dugout, seemingly indifferent to the $500,000 innings bonus he had forfeited due to his ejection. (The Yankees wound up paying Sabathia the bonus, anyway.)

Sabathia was back at it again the following season, this time throwing at Rays outfielder Austin Meadows in response to Luke Voit and Gary Sanchez getting hit in the previous series. "I was definitely trying to hit his ass," Sabathia was seen yelling as he walked off the mound.

The 2020 season—played in front of empty ballparks due to the COVID-19 pandemic—didn't do much to ease the tension. The Yankees continued to accuse the Rays of pitching inside, but when New York closer Aroldis Chapman fired a 101-mph fastball near the head of Rays infielder Mike Brosseau, the anger reached a boiling point for Tampa Bay manager Kevin Cash, who excoriated the Yankees after the game.

"It's poor judgement, poor coaching, it's just poor teaching what they're doing and what they're allowing them to do," Cash said, referring to Yankees manager Aaron Boone and his staff. "The chirping from the dugout. Somebody needs to tell me, go pull up the numbers, who has hit who more, but I can assure you that other than three years ago, there hasn't been one pitch thrown with intent from any of our guys. Period. Somebody has to be held accountable."

Then Cash delivered the line that inspired a very popular Tampa-area T-shirt.

"The last thing I'll say on it, is that I have a whole damn stable full of guys that throw 98 mph," Cash said. "Period."

* * *

The on-field acrimony between the two teams has all the makings of a bitter rivalry. The atmosphere? Well, that leaves something to be desired. Even as the Rays have become an annual contender, seats at the Trop remain relatively empty— except when the Yankees or Red Sox are in town, bringing out New York and Boston fans in droves.

"If they were geographically closer, it would probably be crackling more," Kay said of the budding rivalry. "There's some dislike between these two teams, for sure; but it's hard when you go to the ballpark in St. Pete and the upper deck is covered by a tarp. As long as the place isn't jammed, I don't know if you can still bring that electricity."

Hal Steinbrenner, who assumed control of the Yankees in November 2008, resides in Tampa just as his father did. The Rays have become a bigger thorn in the Yankees' side than they ever were during The Boss' time, but the younger Steinbrenner doesn't hold the same hostility toward his hometown team. That's not to say that he doesn't enjoy a win over the Rays; given his locale, he might even like that more than a victory against the hated Red Sox.

"There's no doubt it's a good rivalry," Steinbrenner said. "At times, the players haven't liked each other much, which seems to be one of the components of a great rivalry. We play a lot of games against them just like with the Red Sox. It can definitely be more painful for me walking around Tampa, so it's even more of a rivalry for me."

Acknowledgments

Writing a book is a great personal accomplishment, but it wouldn't be possible without the help of a number of people.

Thank you to those who lent their time and insight to make this project successful: Marty Appel, Aaron Boone, Brian Cashman, Tony Clark, Bucky Dent, John Flaherty, Jason Giambi, Joe Girardi, Ron Guidry, Derek Jeter, Michael Kay, Jim Leyritz, Bill Madden, Tino Martinez, Don Mattingly, Mike Mussina, Paul O'Neill, Willie Randolph, Hal Steinbrenner, Tanyon Sturtze, Nick Swisher, Mark Teixeira, Marc Topkin, Bernie Williams, and Dave Winfield.

Special thanks to Joe Torre for writing the foreword. What a privilege to have a Hall of Famer involved with this project.

This marks my third collaboration with the wonderful folks at Triumph Books. Thanks to Bill Ames for bringing me in on this project, Publisher Noah Amstadter, and of course Michelle Bruton, who helped guide me through the process and was a terrific sounding board on many fronts.

A big thank-you to Stacey Glick, who has been an incredible confidant for several years. You're the best.

Some of my best friends in the business have always been there for me, whether it's offering ideas or simply letting me vent. I can't possibly name them all, but Jeff Passan, Evan Drellich, Marc Carig, Bryan Hoch, Peter Abraham, and Tyler Kepner deserve a special shout-out. Ditto to Gregg Klayman, Matt Meyers, and Alyson Footer at MLB.com, who allowed me to pursue this opportunity and are three of the best in the business.

This book is also written in memory of Todd Levine, a great, supportive friend who is missed more than he could ever know.

Mom, Dad, and Ellen, thanks for always being there for me, encouraging me to be my best.

Naturally, the biggest thank-you goes to Dena, Ryan, and Zack, who make me smile and inspire me every day.

Sources

Books

Mantle, Mickey, and Herb Gluck. *The Mick*. Jove Publications, 1986.

Martinez, Pedro, and Michael Silverman. *Pedro*. Mariner Books, 2015.

Williams, Ted, and John Underwood. *My Turn at Bat: The Story of My Life*. Simon and Schuster, 1969.

Newspapers and Periodicals

Associated Press

Baltimore Sun

Boston Globe

Chicago Tribune

Hartford Courant

Newsday

New York Daily News

New York Post

New York Times

Referee Magazine

San Francisco Examiner

Saturday Evening Post

Sports Illustrated
The Village Voice
Washington Post
Yankees Magazine

Television
YES Network

Websites
baseballhall.org
espn.com
medium.com
mlb.com
sabr.org
yankees.com/yankeesondemand
YouTube